SENSING WORLD, SENSING WISDOM

ANCIENT ISRAEL AND ITS LITERATURE

Thomas C. Römer, General Editor

Editorial Board:
Mark G. Brett
Marc Brettler
Corrine L. Carvalho
Tom Dozeman
Cynthia Edenburg
Konrad Schmid

Number 31

SENSING WORLD, SENSING WISDOM
The Cognitive Foundation of Biblical Metaphors

Nicole L. Tilford

SBL PRESS

Atlanta

Copyright © 2017 by Nicole L. Tilford

All rights reserved. No part of this work may be reproduced or transmitted in any form or by any means, electronic or mechanical, including photocopying and recording, or by means of any information storage or retrieval system, except as may be expressly permitted by the 1976 Copyright Act or in writing from the publisher. Requests for permission should be addressed in writing to the Rights and Permissions Office, SBL Press, 825 Houston Mill Road, Atlanta, GA 30329 USA.

Library of Congress Cataloging-in-Publication Data

Names: Tilford, Nicole L., author.
Title: Sensing world, sensing wisdom : the cognitive foundation of biblical metaphors / by Nicole L. Tilford.
Description: Atlanta : SBL Press, [2017] | Series: Ancient Israel and its literature ; number 31 | Includes bibliographical references and index.
Identifiers: LCCN 2017001216 (print) | LCCN 2017002611 (ebook) | ISBN 9781628371758 (pbk. : alk. paper) | ISBN 9780884142201 (hardcover : alk. paper) | ISBN 9780884142195 (ebook)
Subjects: LCSH: Metaphor in the Bible. | Metaphor.
Classification: LCC BS1199.M45 T55 2017 (print) | LCC BS1199.M45 (ebook) | DDC 220.6/6—dc23
LC record available at https://lccn.loc.gov/2017001216

Printed on acid-free paper.

Contents

Abbreviations vii

1. Introduction 1
   1.1. Mind-Body Dualism   4
   1.2. Meaning before Language   10
   1.3. Conceptual Metaphors   13
   1.4. Linguistic Extensions   17
   1.5. Summary   21

2. Historical Context 25

3. Perception 35
   3.1. A Universal and Cultural Paradigm   35
   3.2. A Biblical Paradigm   46

4. Seeing 51
   4.1. Typology of Sight   51
   4.2. COGNITION IS SEEING   58
   4.3. Summary   66

5. Hearing/Speaking 69
   5.1. Typology of Hearing and Speaking   70
   5.2. COGNITION IS HEARING/SPEAKING   74
   5.3. Summary   89

6. Touching 91
   6.1. Typology of Touch   92
   6.2. COGNITION IS TOUCHING   99
   6.3. Summary   114

CONTENTS

7. Ingesting 117
   - 7.1. Typology of Ingestion — 117
   - 7.2. COGNITION IS INGESTING — 123
   - 7.3. Summary — 134

8. Breathing 137
   - 8.1. Typology of Breath — 137
   - 8.2. COGNITION IS BREATHING — 141
   - 8.3. Summary — 146

9. Moving 149
   - 9.1. Typology of Movement — 150
   - 9.2. COGNITION IS MOVING — 156
   - 9.3. Summary — 170

10. Complex Metaphors 173
    - 10.1. Metaphorical Extensions — 173
    - 10.2. Metaphorical Blends — 178
    - 10.3. Metaphorical Clusters — 191
    - 10.4. Summary — 198

Conclusions 199

Bibliography 213
Ancient Sources Index 225
Modern Authors Index 245

Abbreviations

Primary Resources

Abr.	Philo, *De Abrahamo*
Agr.	Philo, *De agricultura*
Plac.	Galen, *De placitis Hippocratis et Platonis* (*On the Doctrines of Hippocrates and Plato*)
De an.	Aristotle, *De anima*
Eth. nic.	Aristotle, *Ethica nicomachea*
Hist. an.	Aristotle, *Historia animalium*
Leg.	Philo, *Legum allegoriae*
Metaph.	Aristotle, *Metaphysica* (*Metaphysics*)
P.Anastasi	Papyrus Anastasi
Phaed.	Plato, *Phaedo*
Phaedr.	Plato, *Phaedrus*
Resp.	Plato, *Respublica* (*Republic*)
Sacr.	Philo, *De sacrificiis Abelis et Caini*
Tim.	Plato, *Timeaus*

Secondary Resources

AB	Anchor Bible
AJSL	*American Journal of Semitic Languages and Literature*
ANET	*Ancient Near Eastern Texts Relating to the Old Testament.* Edited by James B. Pritchard. 3rd ed. Princeton: Princeton University Press, 1969.
AMT	R. C. Thompson, *Assyrian Medical Texts.* London: Oxford University Press, 1923.
Atlantis	*Atlantis: Journal of the Spanish Association of Anglo-American Studies*
AYB	Anchor Yale Bible

AzTh	Arbeiten zur Theologie
BETL	Bibliotheca Ephemeridum Theologicarum Lovaniensium
BibInt	*Biblical Interpretation*
BibInt	Biblical Interpretation Series
BSac	*Bibliotheca Sacra*
BRLJ	The Brill Reference Library of Ancient Judaism
BZAW	Beihefte zur Zeitschrift für die alttestamentliche Wissenschaft
CAD	*The Assyrian Dictionary of the Oriental Institute of the University of Chicago.* Edited by Ignace J. Gelb et al. Chicago: The Oriental Institute of the University of Chicago, 1956–2006.
CNI	Carsten Niebuhr Institute
COS	*The Context of Scripture.* Edited by William W. Hallo. 3 vols. Leiden: Brill, 1997–2002.
CurBR	*Currents in Biblical Research*
CurBS	*Currents in Research: Biblical Studies*
CT	Coffin Texts
CT	*Cuneiform Texts from Babylonian Tablets in the British Museum*
ECL	Early Christianity and Its Literature
FRLANT	Forschungen zur Religion und Literatur des Alten und Neuen Testaments
HKAT	Handkommentar zum Alten Testament
HSM	Harvard Semitic Monographs
HUCA	*Hebrew Union College Annual*
HvTSt	*HTS Teologiese Studies/Theological Studies*
IBC	Interpretation: A Bible Commentary for Teaching and Preaching
ICC	International Critical Commentary
Int	*Interpretation*
JBL	*Journal of Biblical Literature*
JNES	*Journal of Near Eastern Studies*
JQR	*Jewish Quarterly Review*
JSOT	*Journal for the Study of the Old Testament*
JSOTSup	Journal for the Study of the Old Testament Supplement Series
KAR	*Keilschrifttexte aus Assur religiösen Inhalts.* Edited by Erich Ebeling. Lepizig: Hinrichs, 1919–1923.

KTU	*Die keilalphabetischen Texte aus Ugarit*. Edited by Manfried Dietrich, Oswald Loretz, and Joaquín Sanmartín. 2nd ed. Münster: Ugarit-Verlag, 1995.
LHBOTS	The Library of Hebrew Bible/Old Testament Studies
LXX	Septuagint
Miscelánea	*Miscelánea: A Journal of English and American Studies*
MT	Masoretic Text
OBO	Orbis biblicus et orientalis
OTL	Old Testament Library
PHSC	Perspectives on Hebrew Scriptures and Its Contexts
SBLMS	Society of Biblical Literature Monograph Series
SHR	Studies in the History of Religions
StBibLit	Studies in Biblical Literature
STDJ	Studies on the Texts of the Desert of Judah
TDOT	*Theological Dictionary of the Old Testament*. Edited by G. Johannes Botterweck, Helmer Ringgren, and Heinz-Josef Fabry. Translated by John T. Willis et al. 15 vols. Grand Rapids: Eerdmans, 1974–2006.
UF	*Ugarit-Forschungen*
VAT	Vorderasiatische Abteilung Tontafel. Vorderasiatische Museum, Berlin
VT	*Vetus Testamentum*
VTSup	Supplements to Vetus Testamentum
WBC	Word Bible Commentary
WMANT	Wissenschaftliche Monographien zum Alten und Neuen Testament
ZAH	*Zeitschrift für Althebräistik*

1
Introduction

The Bible is full of metaphors. Whether describing God as a jealous husband or detailing the twisted paths of the wicked, biblical authors use metaphors to express their core religious beliefs. But what are metaphors? Are they simply literary flourishes added to a text for artistic effect? Or are they more deeply ingrained cognitive patterns that structure the way that the human brain processes information and conceptualizes its environment?

Until recently, most theorists understood metaphors as literary devices, rhetorical embellishments that make a text more aesthetically pleasing by substituting one term for another. Thus, following the definition provided by Aristotle in the fourth century BCE, such thinkers as Bede, Maimonides, and Thomas Hobbes argued that metaphors were stylistic ornaments that beautified a text by extracting words from their original, literal contexts. Twentieth-century biblical scholars generally held similar notions. Although recognizing that the Bible was full of metaphors, scholars believed that metaphors were merely rhetorical flourishes that enhanced the artistic quality of the biblical text. For instance, in his discussion of metaphors in the Song of Songs, Robert Alter argued that "in a good deal of biblical poetry, imagery serves rather secondary purposes" and that "metaphoric invention would not appear to have been a consciously prized poetic value."[1] Although Alter recognized different degrees of metaphorical creativity—conventional images, intensive images, and innovative images—he criticized those who would look "naively" to the life setting of ancient Israel to understand the rhetorical impact of poetic metaphors in the Bible.[2] Such a belief in the secondary nature of biblical

---

1. Robert Alter, *The Art of Biblical Poetry*, rev. ed. (New York: Basic Books, 2011), 237.
2. Ibid., 232, 237–39.

metaphor has led scholars either to misread biblical metaphors as theological propositions or to treat them as rhetorical embellishments that distract the serious scholar from more important considerations, such as the historical impetus behind the creation of the Bible or the theological positions espoused therein.[3]

This perspective began to change in the 1980s. Drawing upon the insights of early modern philosophers such as Jean-Jacques Rousseau, Friedrich Nietzsche, and Max Black, scholars began to recognize that metaphors were intimately connected to concrete experience and have the capacity to structure human thought. Thus, in *Metaphors We Live By*, George Lakoff and Mark Johnson argued that what we call metaphors are actually linguistic realizations of what they called "conceptual metaphors," that is, basic cognitive structures by which individuals organize their perception of reality. According to their conceptual metaphor theory, metaphors are not simply literary flourishes; they are *the* fundamental cognitive device by which humans think.[4]

Under the influence of such theorists, biblical scholars have begun to argue that the metaphors we find within the Bible existed prior to their literary expression and provided ancient individuals a way of understanding the world around them. The majority of the articles in the 1993 special volume of *Semeia* on *Women, War, and Metaphor in the Bible*, for instance, either adopted or implicitly responded to Lakoff and Johnson's model, and Mary B. Slzos's 2001 dissertation on "Metaphor in Proverbs 31:10–31" was specifically aimed to "shape" this model to suit the needs of biblical scholarship.[5] More recently, Job Jindo has examined the cognitive under-

---

3. See, for instance, studies of the Lady Wisdom metaphor by William Albright ("The Goddess of Life and Wisdom," *AJSL* 36 [1919-1920]: 258–94), Helmer Ringgren (*Word and Wisdom: Studies in the Hypostatization of Divine Qualities and Functions in the Ancient Near East* [Lund: Ohlssons Boktryckeri, 1947], Bernhard Lang (*Wisdom and the Book of Proverbs: A Hebrew Goddess Redefined* [New York: Pilgrim, 1986]), and Burton Mack ("Wisdom Myth and Myth-ology," *Int* 24 [1970]: 46–60), each of whose interest in the literary figure was secondary to the historical, social, or theological reality that it could reveal.

4. George Lakoff and Mark Johnson, *Metaphors We Live By* (Chicago: University of Chicago Press, 1980).

5. Claudia Camp, "Metaphor in Feminist Biblical Interpretation: Theoretical Perspectives," *Semeia* 61 (1993): 24; Mary B. Szlos, "Metaphor in Proverbs 31:10–31: A Cognitive Approach" (Ph.D diss., Union Theological Seminary, 2001). See also Szlos, "Body Parts as Metaphor and the Value of a Cognitive Approach: A Study of the

pinnings of prophetic metaphors in the book of Jeremiah, and various scholars have analyzed conceptual metaphors as they appear in Psalms, Job, Judges, Chronicles, Isaiah, and Hosea.⁶

Of course, such adoption has not been without criticism. For instance, in the aforementioned *Semeia* volume Mieke Bal argued that the model's focus on universal origins "obscures important historical changes and differences," especially those arising from gender.⁷ Similarly, David Aaron argued that the model is too universal, lacks the capacity for strong analysis (its evidence is merely a "long string of examples"), and tends to ignore the semantic ranges of biblical terms.⁸ Although finding value in cognitive linguistics more generally, Ellen van Wolde argued that the theories of Lakoff, Johnson, and others are inconsistent and lack external scholarly support.⁹ These critics raise valid concerns, and I shall address each in the course of this investigation. However, critics notwithstanding, conceptual

---

Female Figures in Proverbs via Metaphor," in *Metaphor in the Hebrew Bible*, ed. Pierre Hecke, BETL 187 (Leuven: Leuven University Press, 2005), 185–95.

6. Job Jindo, *Biblical Metaphor Reconsidered: A Cognitive Approach to Poetic Prophecy in Jeremiah 1–24*, HSM 64 (Winona Lake, IN: Eisenbrauns, 2010). Additional examples include Bonnie Howe, *Because You Bear This Name: Conceptual Metaphor and the Moral Meaning of 1 Peter*, BibInt 81 (Leiden: Brill, 2006); select articles in Ellen van Wolde, ed., *Job 28: Cognition in Context*, BibInt 64 (Leiden: Brill, 2003); the collected essays in Antje Labahn, ed., *Conceptual Metaphors in Poetic Texts*, PHSC 18 (Piscataway, NJ: Gorgias, 2013); Bonnie Howe and Joel B. Green, eds., *Cognitive Linguistic Explorations in Biblical Studies* (Berlin: de Gruyter, 2014); Frederick S. Tappenden, *Resurrection in Paul: Cognition, Metaphor, and Transformation*, ECL 19 (Atlanta: SBL Press, 2016); William E. W. Robinson, *Metaphor, Morality, and the Spirit in Romans 8:1–17*, ECL 20 (Atlanta: SBL Press, 2016).

7. Mieke Bal, "Metaphors He Lives By," *Semeia* 61 (1993): 191. See also the article by Francis Landy in the same volume: "On Metaphor, Play, and Nonsense," *Semeia* 61 (1993): 219–37.

8. David Aaron, *Biblical Ambiguities: Metaphor, Semantics, and Divine Imagery*, BRLJ 4 (Leiden: Brill, 2001). Aaron notes, for example, that it is impossible to know if "understand" is a derivative meaning of a word such as שמע and not part of the original semantic field of the root (106–8).

9. Ellen van Wolde, *Reframing Biblical Studies: When Language and Text Meet Culture, Cognition, and Context* (Winona Lake, IN: Eisenbrauns, 2009).Van Wolde's critique is striking, since her earlier work drew upon Gilles Fauconnier and Mark Turner's model of conceptual blending and her newer book began with the intention of combining conceptual blending with Ronald Langacker's model (for more on these alternative cognitive models, see §1.3 below). Yet in the final evaluation, van Wolde decided that conceptual metaphor theory was ultimately an unhelpful strand of cogni-

metaphor is fast becoming a standard model by which scholars describe and analyze biblical metaphors.

So far, conceptual metaphor studies have been helpful in interpreting select passages within a single pericope or biblical book. The task now is to expand conceptual metaphor theory into a workable model that explains not only how select metaphors developed within a single passage but also how those same metaphors operated and interacted across texts. As I discuss in the following pages, biblical metaphors are shaped by various universal and cultural experiences that transcend individual literary expressions and defy linear explanations. This study explores those underlying impulses and evaluates the cognitive tendencies that shape biblical metaphors. As a case study, I focus specifically on how common sensory activities such as hearing, seeing, eating, and walking developed into the abstract metaphors for knowledge and wisdom that one finds in Proverbs, Job, and Qoheleth. In doing so, I suggest that the development of biblical metaphors was an ongoing, preconscious process by which ancient scribes ascribed meaning to their experiences and organized their cultural worldview. I thus postulate a deep connection between biblical metaphors and the embodied experiences of their authors and audiences.

Before turning to the biblical data, it is necessary to look more closely at conceptual metaphor theory and how it explains the cognitive dimensions of metaphors.

1.1. Mind-Body Dualism

Since the early Greek Platonists, philosophers have speculated about a dichotomy between the mind (or soul[10]) and the body. In the *Phaedo*, for instance, Plato argued for a radical separation between the σῶμα ("body")

---

tive linguistics and that only Langacker's grammatical approach provided the means necessary to study ancient texts.

10. While not every culture or individual conceives of the human intellect as residing in the soul, it is appropriate to speak of the mind and soul synonymously here. Although there were different terms for each, ancient thinkers often assigned those functions that popular Western society associates with the mind (e.g., cognition, reasoning, rationality) to the soul. In the writings of Plato, for instance, rational thought was performed by the ψυχή. Similarly, the Stoics viewed the soul as the mechanism that governed the perceptual and cognitive functions of the body (see, for instance, the discussion of Chrysippus below). Moreover, in popular Western culture, the mind is often considered that which is unique to a person and defines his or her identity of

1. INTRODUCTION

and the ψυχή ("soul"), with the σῶμα being that which is mortal and perceived by perception and the ψυχή being that which is invisible, divine, and immortal:

> Are we not also on the one hand body [σῶμα], on the other hand soul [ψυχή]?... The soul [ψυχή] is most like that which is divine and undying and of the mind [νοητός] and of one form and indissoluble and always in the same manner, but the body is most like that which is human and mortal and of many forms and not of the mind [ἀνόητος] and dissoluble and always changing. (*Phaed.* 79c, 80b)[11]

Since the "soul" (ψυχή) resembles the "mind" (the νόος) and is the only part of the individual capable of accessing the intangible realm of ideas, it is deemed permanent and good, while the body is disparaged as transient and corruptible.[12] This dualistic attitude, with its moral connotations, gradually became a dominant stream in Western thought.

Particularly under the influence of René Descartes, who distinguished ontologically between the purely intellectual (nonmaterial) realm of the mind and the material physical realm of the body, modernity has largely continued to perceive a sharp distinction between mind and body.[13] It is not uncommon for the modern Western individual to operate with a paradigm in which a person consists of two parts, the so-called higher rational inner portion (mind/soul) and the seemingly lower physical emotional portion (body). Under this paradigm, reason is seen as a faculty distinct from the seemingly base realms of bodily movement.[14] It is commonly believed in popular culture, for instance, that the mind can force the body to perform or abstain from certain base activities such as eating, drinking, or sexual intercourse. Similarly, common conceptions of life after death envision the separation of an immaterial, pure soul from the corrupt body.

---

self. It is this self, at least for religiously oriented individuals, that is thought to survive a person after death in the concept of the soul.

11. Unless otherwise noted, all translations of ancient texts are my own.

12. See Hendrick Lorenz, "Plato on the Soul," in *The Oxford Handbook of Plato*, ed. Gail Fine (New York: Oxford University Press, 2008), 243–66, esp. his discussion of the *Phaedo*, 251–54.

13. For a summary of Descartes and his influence on Western thought, see Mark Johnson, "Mind Incarnate: From Dewey to Damasio," *Daedalus* 135 (2006): 46–54.

14. George Lakoff and Mark Johnson, *Philosophy in the Flesh: The Embodied Mind and Its Challenge to Western Thought* (New York: Basic Books, 1999), 17.

This dualistic perception is seemingly reinforced by the processes of the body itself, since the normal processes of the body (such as those of the internal organs) hide below the surface, while the senses and intellectual perceptions are directed outward beyond the body.[15]

Embedded in this intellectual climate, modern Western scholars of religion easily fall victim to the same assumptions, viewing the mind and body as two distinct entities and believing that meaning resides solely in the cognitive sphere, in the words of individual authors or the discourse of the culture in which the text is situated. In the study of Judaism, for instance, many scholars have focused on the religion's mental achievements—scriptures, exegesis, liturgies, commentaries, and so on—denying that the body played a prominent role in the creation of such texts. Such scholars have often been uncomfortable studying the body, either because they fear it would to lead to the equation of Judaism with "savage" religions or because they feel that it diminishes the unique character of Judaism.[16] For instance, in a rather impassioned critique of the history of the body in Jewish scholarship, Leon Wieseltier insisted that it is Judaism's *texts*, its intellectual view of the world, that makes Judaism unique. According to him, the study of Judaism should be a study of Jewish ideas; to do otherwise would turn Jews into just "another tribe."[17] While this situation is slowly changing under the influence of such scholars as Howard Eilberg-Schwartz and Daniel Boyarin, such a *conscious* interest in the body reflects the pervasiveness of an *unconscious* division between mind and body.[18] Jews are either people of the *book* or people of the *body*.

---

15. Mark Johnson, *The Meaning of the Body: Aesthetics of Human Understanding* (Chicago: University of Chicago Press, 2007), 4; Johnson, "Mind Incarnate," 47.

16. For more on these prejudices, see the extended discussion in Howard Eilberg-Schwartz, *The Savage in Judaism: An Anthropology of Israelite Religion and Ancient Judaism* (Bloomington: Indiana University Press, 1990), 1–87.

17. Leon Wieseltier, "Jewish Bodies, Jewish Minds," *JQR* 95 (2005): 442.

18. See Howard Eilberg-Schwartz, *Savage in Judaism*; Eilberg-Schwartz, "The Problem of the Body for the People of the Book," *Journal of the History of Sexuality* 2 (1991): 1–24; Daniel Boyarin, *Carnal Israel: Reading Sex in Talmudic Culture*, New Historicism 25 (Berkeley: University of California Press, 1993). By focusing on the Jewish body, Eilberg-Schwartz and Boyarin specifically seek to counter the idea that Jews are people of the book (i.e., mind). Yet, as Wieseltier ("Jewish Bodies, Jewish Minds," 436–37) argues, Eilberg-Schwartz's and Boyarin's insistence that Jews are "'people of the body' ... bases its revisionism upon the same coarse dualism of mind and body for which it indicts the scholarship it wishes to revise."

Yet this sharp division between mind and body is problematic. Although modern Western individuals think in terms of a mind-body divide, this division is not naturally predetermined. Since the late nineteenth century/early twentieth century, such philosophers as William James, John Dewey, Maurice Merleau-Ponty, and the cognitive scientists who followed them have increasingly argued that there is no autonomous faculty of reason distinct from normal bodily functions.[19] Rather, the human being's ability to think, derive meaning, and communicate with others stems from his or her daily corporeal experience. As Johnson states, "no body, never mind."[20]

More importantly for this study, the ontological division between mind and body is a cultural construct of the modern West, one that does not seem to have been prevalent among the majority of ancient communities. In Old Babylonian cosmology, for instance, humankind was said to be created out of the body of a god (see Atrahasis 1.192–226). It is through this god's "blood" (*damu*) in particular that humanity's "intelligence" (*ṭēmu*) is derived.[21] Moreover, although surviving the person after death, an individual's "ghost" (*eṭemmu*)—"the power for thought, the ability of the individual to plan and deliberate so that he may act effectively and achieve success"—remained intimately connected to the body, deriving its form from it, being able to be perceived by it, and ceasing to exist without it.[22] Even dead, the body served as the locus for the continued existence of the *eṭemmu*; without it, the *eṭemmu* lost its social and individual identity.[23]

---

19. For an extended discussion of this trajectory, see Johnson, "Mind Incarnate," 46–54; Lakoff and Johnson, *Philosophy in the Flesh*, 16–17.

20. Johnson, "Mind Incarnate," 47.

21. Tzvi Abusch, "Ghost and God: Some Observations on a Babylonian Understanding of Human Nature," in *Self, Soul, and Body in Religious Experience*, ed. Albert Baumgarten, Jan Assman, and Guy Stroumsa, SHR 78 (Leiden: Brill, 1998), 378. Abusch argues that it is no coincidence that *damu* and *ṭēmu* sound alike; it suggests that this connection between blood and intelligence is integrated into the language itself.

22. Ibid., 382. By reading *eṭemmu* as intellect, Abusch is drawing upon Thorkild Jacobsen's reading of *ṭēmu* as the "power for effective thinking, planning, and inspiration." See Thorkild Jacobsen, *The Treasures of Darkness: A History of Mesopotamian Religion* (New Haven: Yale University Press, 1976), 156.

23. Abusch, "Ghost and God," 374–75. As Abusch argues, proper burial was crucial to the survival of the *eṭemmu*; destroying the body deprived the *eṭemmu* of its individual and social identity (475).

In this Mesopotamian cosmology, then, there is an intimate connection between an individual's intellectual capacities, his or her sense of self, and the corporeal experience.

Similarly, as Dale Martin argues, among the ancient Greeks the prevailing view was not a Platonic mind-body dualism but a "one-world" model in which parts of the body fell upon a hierarchal spectrum rather than into sharp oppositions (i.e., the mind was higher and more divine-like than other parts of the body but not distinct from them).[24] The Stoics, for instance, argued that the body was not a container for the soul; rather, the soul was a specific type of πνεῦμα (breath), a natural element that extended through the entire body (σῶμα) and was responsible for governing it (see the theories of Chrysippus recounted in Galen, *Plac.* 287–288). The soul-mind was thus a part of nature that could be studied like any other natural entity.[25] Platonic thought also may not have been as radically dualistic and antimaterialistic as it first appears. As Martin explains, Plato postulated the existence of three different forms of the soul, the highest being associated with the invisible, the lowest being close to and intermingled with the body. All three forms, however, were "mixed together" to form one composite being (*Tim.* 35a, 69c–71a; *Resp.* 434e–444d; *Phaedr.* 246b–249d).[26] Thus, even Plato's model seems closer to the hierarchical spectrum of his contemporaries than a strict contrast between mind and body.

Among the Israelites and early Jews, the same lack of dualism seems to have dominated, with Jews affirming the intimate connection between mind and body well into the medieval ages. Throughout the Hebrew Bible, cognition resides within the body itself, for example, in the לב/לבב ("heart") and the כבד ("liver"). In Deut 29:3, Josh 23:14, and elsewhere, the לב/לבב is the faculty associated with the ability to "know" (לדעת), while elsewhere the לב/לבב is seat of emotions (Neh 2:2; Ps 38:9; etc.).[27] As in Akkadian, the כבד was probably perceived as the seat of human emotions

---

24. Dale Martin, *The Corinthian Body* (New Haven: Yale University Press, 1995), 15. For more on the tripartite nature of the soul, esp. in the *Republic*, see Lorenz, "Plato on the Soul," 254–63.

25. In concluding that the soul was a part of nature that could be studied as such, the Stoics were following Aristotle. For a fuller discussion of these theories, see Julia Annas, *Hellenistic Philosophy of the Mind* (Berkeley: University of California Press, 1992), esp. 5–6, 43–56, 61–70.

26. Martin, *Corinthian Body*, 11–12.

27. Heinz-Joseph Fabry, "לֵב, לֵבָב," *TDOT* 7:414, 419–20; Silvia Schroer and Thomas Stäbli, *Body Symbolism in the Bible*, trans. Linda M. Maloney (Collegeville,

and not a defined soul (e.g., Pss 7:6; 16:9; 30:13; 57:9; 108:2).²⁸ It is unclear if the לב/לבב and the כבד coincides exactly with the organs we call "heart" and "liver" (the לב/לבב, for instance, often connotes "chest" more generally and the כבד "innards"),²⁹ yet they clearly reside in the body. Moreover, there does not seem to have been a sharp bifurcation between these cognitive centers and the rest of the body. The psalmists, for instance, describe a cacophony of "seemingly independent body parts" (tongue, mouth, ear, etc.) of which the cognitive centers are but one example.³⁰ While these parts could operate individually, each could also be controlled and integrated into a composite whole.

There is also no idea that a soul has been placed in the body temporarily and only vague notions that the individual would experience any life divorced from the body hereafter.³¹ Although often translated as "soul" or "spirit," both נפש and רוח were closely tied to the body. The נפש, for instance, was originally associated with the "throat" or "breath" of an individual (see the Akkadian *napištu*). While this meaning is largely absent from the Hebrew Bible, it probably lies behind the most frequent meaning of נפש as the center of a person's physical and emotional appetites.³²

MN: Liturgical Press, 2001), 43–44. When versification differs between the Hebrew and English translations, I follow the Hebrew numbering.

28. P. Stenmans, "כָּבֵד," *TDOT* 7:21–22, based on an emendation of כָּבוֹד to כָּבֵד.
29. Stenmans, *TDOT* 7:21; Fabry, *TDOT* 7:411.
30. Susanne Gillmayr-Bucher, "Body Images in the Psalms," *JSOT* 28 (2004): 312. See, for instance, Ps 22:15–16, where the לב is listed alongside the "bones," "innards," and "tongue" as congruent categories of the body. Gillmayr-Bucher notes how the bones and heart in 22:15 combine to give a "general impression of a total disintegration. The bones and the heart, that is, the support of a physical as well as a mental unity, are lost." As two central parts of the human body, the bones and heart represent the entire individual.
31. See Philip Johnston, *Shades of Sheol: Death and Afterlife in the Old Testament* (Downers Grove, IL: InterVarsity Press, 2002), esp. 218–29; and Ellis Brotzman, "Man and the Meaning of נֶפֶשׁ," *BSac* 145 (1988): 400–409. Brotzman argues, for instance, that such passages as Pss 16:10, 30:4, and 89:49, each of which refers to Sheol, do not refer to a disembodied afterlife but to the "grave" (408–9). Psalm 49:16, on the other hand, may "hint" at life beyond the grave, but that concept is not developed (409). Similarly, Isa 26:19 and Dan 12:2 seem to refer to individual resurrection, but their theme is never fully realized in the rest of the books in which they are found (Johnston, *Shades of Sheol*, 224–27).
32. For the Akkadian etymology of *napištu* and its connection to נפש as "throat" in the Hebrew Bible, see H. Seebass, "נֶפֶשׁ," *TDOT* 9:499–502, 504; Brotzman, "Man

Even when it came to represent the person as a whole, his or her self, or life in general, נפש could still be used synonymously with "blood" (Gen 9:4; Lev 17:11, 14), "breath" (Gen 35:18; 1 Kgs 17:21–22; Job 41:13; Jer 15:9), or "corpse" (Lev 19:28; 21:1, 11; 22:4; Num 5:2; 6:6, 11; 9:6–7, 10; 19:13; Hag 2:13). The most basic meaning of נפש, then, seems to have remained a "creature that breathes," a connotation intimately connected to the corporeal condition.[33] Similarly, רוח, though translated as "spirit," more generally means "breath," "life," seat of "emotions," or center of "cognition." Like the נפש, the רוח resided in the body and does not seem to have survived it after death.[34] As Susanne Gillmayr-Bucher argues, the Israelites "do not so much *have* a body," as if it were something distinct from their true being (i.e., the soul); they "*are* a body."[35]

In antiquity as in modernity, then, mind and body were not two distinct, conflicting entities operating within an individual; rather, they were merely two of many abstract terms that societies used to describe how individuals experienced the world.[36]

1.2. Meaning before Language

Perhaps one of the most important implications of this intimate mind-body connection is the recognition that the development and communication of meaning does not occur on the linguistic level alone. Contra tradi-

---

and the Meaning of נֶפֶשׁ,"405. Brotzman (405 n. 11) identifies five possible occurrences of נפש as throat: Jer 4:10; Jonah 2:6; Pss 69:2; 105:18, Prov 3:22.

33. Brotzman, "Man and the Meaning of נֶפֶשׁ," 403–6. That a person's corpse could be referred to as a נפש supports this connection between the body and the נפש. A person's נפש did not survive him or her after death in an ethereal plane but either evaporated (when the breath expired) or remained tied to the corpse.

34. S. Tengström and Heinz-Joseph Fabry, "רוּחַ," TDOT 13:375–76; the article later notes that "nothing explicit is said of a person's own *rûaḥ*" at death (with the possible exception of Zech 12:1), but since the רוח comes from God, presumably it returns to God at death (386–87). In fact, רוח more frequently refers to a property of God than a human.

35. Gillmayr-Bucher, "Body Images in the Psalms," 325. Gillmayr-Bucher here is speaking specifically about the psalmist perceptive, but the statement could easily apply to the Israelites as a whole.

36. Johnson, *Meaning of the Body*, 2–15 (esp. 11–12). As Johnson states, *mind* and *body* are simply "shorthand ways of identifying aspects of ongoing organism-environment interactions" (117).

tional theories of language and cognition, one cannot assert that abstract meaning is a secondary development that occurs after and apart from concrete experience.[37] Indeed, as Lakoff and Johnson have argued, words are dependent, not on some disembodied mind, but on the immanent nature of the biological and therefore "embodied" human experience. As Johnson states,

> meaning grows from our visceral connections to life and the bodily conditions of life. We are born into the world as creatures of the flesh, and it is through our bodily perceptions, movements, emotions, and feelings that meaning becomes possible and takes the forms it does. From the day we are brought kicking and screaming into the world, what and how anything is meaningful to us is shaped by our specific form of incarnation.[38]

In other words, meanings emerge "from the bottom up," through the biological engagement of individuals with their changing environment.[39] Only after meaning has been acquired through bodily processes is it then extended by principles of analogy into language and abstract thought.

For example, every day individuals engage in simple, physical activities. You walk *out* of the house and sit *in* your car. You reach *into* a bag and take *out* a can of soup. Your very body is a container *into* which you place certain properties (e.g., water, food, air) and *out* of which you expel others (e.g., carbon dioxide, excrement, sweat). Because this physical experience is regular and repetitive, the brain takes note of these activities and organizes its perception of reality based on them. Certain "neurons and neuronal clusters fire in response to certain patterns," and they become fixed "topological features of our neural maps."[40]

These neural clusters, in turn, combine into a complex neural network of what Johnson calls "image schemas," that is, "dynamic, recurrent

---

37. Johnson's view of "embodied meaning," for instance, is specifically aimed at countering representational theories of cognition. Broadly defined, the representational theory states that "cognition (i.e., perceiving, conceptualizing, imagining, reasoning, planning, willing) operates via mental 'representations' (e.g., ideas, concepts, images, propositions) that are capable of being 'about' or 'directed to' other representations and to states of affairs in the external world." Such a position presumes a radical division between "mind" and "body" (ibid., 114).
38. Ibid., ix.
39. Ibid., 10.
40. Ibid., 159, 135.

pattern[s] of organism-environment interactions" by which the human brain shapes and organizes its experience of these ongoing physical activities.[41] For instance, the physical experience of putting objects into and taking them out of certain containers creates a basic impression of CONTAINMENT—a sense of boundaries, of belonging and alienation, of similarity and difference—by which the human brain categorizes a complex environment into a coherent, predictable system, an IN-OUT schema in which some entities are *in* and some are *out*.[42] Thus, prior to the formulation of any words or conscious thought, the human being has created a complex neural network through which it experiences, organizes, and finds meaning in its environment. In this way, "every aspect of our [corporeal] experience [is] defined by recurring patterns and structures (such as up-down, front-back, near-far, in-out, on-under) that constitute the basic contours of our lived world."[43] Even aspects of cognition that seem like highly rational, second-order thought (e.g., categorization) already exist on the most basic level of an individual's interaction with his or her environment.

Image schemas are effective ordering devices because they focus an individual's experience of his or her complex environment on select aspects of that experience. This occurs through a process that Anthony Wallace calls "abstraction." He explains: "Abstraction involves a restriction of attention to selected dimensions both of the environment and of the organism's own response potentialities, and the exclusion of others as irrelevant; it necessarily involves the ignoring of variations within the minimum resolution range permitted by the physiology of the animal."[44]

---

41. Ibid., 136. Johnson uses the label *image schemas*, not because these structures are connected to vision alone (quite the contrary) or specify "mental pictures," but rather to emphasize that schemas are "imagistic." More general than "rich" images (e.g., a mental image of a cat) and more concrete than true abstract concepts (e.g., love), image schemas are the structures by which we organize our perception of reality. See also Mark Johnson, *The Body in the Mind* (Chicago: University of Chicago Press, 1987), 23–30.

42. Johnson, *Body in the Mind*, 30–40. Here I follow the standard practice of Lakoff, Johnson, and their followers by denoting image schemas with small caps.

43. Johnson, *Meaning of the Body*, 135.

44. Anthony Wallace, "Culture and Congition," in *Language, Culture and Cognition: Anthropological Perspectives*, ed. Ronald W. Casson (New York: Macmillan, 1981), 70. Wallace is writing about schemas more generally and without reference to Lakoff and Johnson's image schema theory. His conclusions, however, are consis-

The IN-OUT schema, for instance, focuses the individual's experience of a cup on its ability to act as a container for liquid rather than its ability, say, to be picked up and used as a projectile. By extracting a limited amount of principles out of the variety of information taken in by the perceptual modalities, schemas order our perception of and future engagement with the environment.

Of course, these basic image schemas and the processes by which they develop are taken for granted. When you grasp a cup, you do not think of the neural clusters firing in your brain, the image schemas such clusters create, or the meaning they engender. This all occurs on a subconscious, preverbal level. Such can be seen by studying infants, to whom the world becomes meaningful even before they acquire verbal capabilities. Through their perceptual faculties—by seeing, hearing, moving, tasting, and so on—infants make sense of their environment and are able to communicate with their caretakers. Such communication occurs not only through words (which are a late development) but also through eye contact, nonverbal vocalization, and movement. Although more sophisticated, adults are, in essence, "big babies." Like infants, adults develop meaning by physically seeing, tasting, and moving through their environment without continuously verbalizing (internally or externally) the various processes by which they do so.[45]

1.3. Conceptual Metaphors

On the one hand, image schemas are definite structures; they contain regular features by which we construe order. On the other hand, they are dynamic structures, being flexible enough to be altered in their application.[46] In other words, image schemas construct our experience of the world and are, at the same time, continually transformed by that evolving experience.

In large part, this transformation is possible because the creation of image schemas is multimodal; that is, the perception of and interaction

---

tent with similar statements sprinkled throughout the works of Lakoff and Johnson. For instance, speaking of conceptual metaphors (*Metaphors We Live By*, 141; see also 10–13), Lakoff and Johnson state that "metaphor highlights certain features while suppressing others."

45. Johnson, *Meaning of the Body*, 33.
46. Johnson, *Body in the Mind*, 30.

with any given object activates neurons used for multiple modes of action and perception. The CONTAINMENT schema, for instance, develops from a concurrent operation of the visual, tactile, kinesthetic, and gustatory modalities. When one is having a visual experience of a cup, one is also experiencing the cup as something that can be grasped (tactile), raised (movement), and drunk from (and thus tasted). Even the simplest activities involve complex, integrated multimodal links.

This "neural coactivation" becomes the basis for the extension of schematic meaning, the end product of which Lakoff and Johnson call "conceptual metaphors." The neural parameters of one schema (the "source domain") become "mapped" onto another (the "target domain"), such that the latter is now understood in the terms of the former.[47] For example, in the conceptual metaphor CATEGORIES ARE CONTAINERS, the concepts associated with the source domain (CONTAINMENT) are mapped onto the target domain (CATEGORY).[48]

Table 1.1. Metaphorical Mappings: CATEGORIES ARE CONTAINERS

Source Domain (Containment)		Target Domain (Category)
Items Have a Boundary	→	Categories Have Limits
That Contain Some Entities	→	That Include Some Entities
That Exclude Other Entities	→	That Exclude Other Entities

Just as a cup is perceived as a bounded space with liquid *inside* of it, so also a category such as fruit is perceived as a bounded space that includes items such as pears or apples *inside* of it. Based on the observation that common items tend to be located in the same bounded area, the physical experience of space and containment becomes the basis for conceptualizing categorization. In this way, the sharing of these characteristics establishes a "cross-metaphorical correspondence" that focuses the audience on a spe-

---

47. Lakoff and Johnson, *Metaphors We Live By*, 94. As Joseph Grady notes ("Foundations of Meaning: Primary Metaphors and Primary Scenes" [PhD diss., University of California, Berkeley, 1997], 9), the directionality of this mapping is important; in conceptual mapping, the transference of elements does not flow in both directions.

48. This chart is based on similar charts that Lakoff and Johnson construct throughout their works. The information for the chart comes from their discussions in Lakoff and Johnson, *Philosophy in the Flesh*, 51, 380–81, 544–55; Johnson, *Meaning of the Body*, 141.

cific aspect shared by both schemas while suppressing other elements of the individual schemas, thereby creating a new perception of reality.[49]

Arguably, the existence of conceptual mapping is difficult to prove, leaving many cognitive scientists to suggest alternative models for explaining how meaning develops and extends, such as the idea that schematic extension results from "blending" the elements of different schemas together (so Gilles Fauconnier and Mark Turner) or from cognitively transforming an abstract prototypical "type" (e.g., tree) into more specific "instances" of that type (e.g., oak tree, elm tree, birch) (so Ronald Langacker).[50] Each of these alternatives suggests that preexisting commonalities between source and target domain are necessary for the extension of schematic meaning. Johnson, however, argues that conceptual mapping is not only possible but also highly plausible. For example, based on neuroimaging studies comparing literal and metaphorical sentences about the manipulation of the body to the actual manipulation of the body, Johnson argues that "there must be neural connections between sensorimotor areas of the brain and parts of the brain responsible for higher cognitive functioning."[51] While not definitive, such "existence proofs" suggest that the sensorimotor functions of the brain "do both jobs at once," perceiving external reality and also structuring our conceptions about it.[52]

The conceptual mapping model, then, offers a reasonable explanation for the neurological foundations of schematic extension. Fauconnier, Turner, Langacker, and other such scholars, however, are correct to note that the extension of schematic meaning is not simply the result of concrete source domains being superimposed upon unrelated abstract target

---

49. Lakoff and Johnson, *Philosophy in the Flesh*, 51; Lakoff and Johnson, *Metaphors We Live By*, 96.

50. Gilles Fauconnier and Mark Turner, *The Way We Think: Conceptual Blending and the Mind's Hidden Complexities* (New York: Basic Books, 2002); Ronald Langacker, *Foundations of Cognitive Grammar*, 2 vols. (Stanford, CA: Stanford University Press, 1987).

51. Johnson, *Meaning of the Body*, 167–68. He points, for example, to the studies of Tim Rohrer, who has shown that both literal and metaphorical sentences about the hand (e.g., "she handed me the apple"; "he handed me the theory") "activate primary and secondary hand regions within the primary and secondary sensorimotor maps." Rohrer then compared this mapping to that which occurred when participants actually moved their hands. He found a "high degree of overlap" between the two mappings.

52. Lakoff and Johnson, *Philosophy in the Flesh*, 38.

domains. Although one domain can extend its parameters over another, as in the example of CATEGORIES ARE CONTAINERS above, certain mappings are more likely to occur than others. Domains that correspond in experience are more likely to map onto each other than those that do not. For instance, being angry causes us to feel physically warm, which is subsequently reflected in the conceptual metaphor ANGER IS HEAT.[53] Similarly, since the physiological experience of hunger is associated with the emotional experience of wanting, the conceptual metaphor DESIRE IS HUNGER develops (e.g., "she was *starved* for affection"). Additionally, domains that share structural features are more likely to map: properties map onto other properties (e.g., SHARPNESS to INTELLIGENCE), actions map onto other actions (e.g., BALANCING to CONSIDERING ALTERNATIVES), and so on.[54]

Moreover, the mapping of schematic concepts generally occurs from more physically accessible domains to less accessible ones. Therefore, it is more likely for schemas formed from concrete, sensorimotor domains (e.g., UP-DOWN, CONTAINMENT, IN-OUT) to be mapped onto less concrete domains (e.g., SADNESS, ANGER, KNOWING, SIMILARITY).[55] The conceptual metaphor UNDERSTANDING IS GRASPING, for instance, builds upon the concrete domain of GRASPING in order to provide meaning to the abstract domain of UNDERSTANDING. Just as an object is grasped with greater or lesser intensity, an idea can be "grasped" to varying degrees (being fully understood, somewhat understood, or not understood at all). What we call abstract concepts, then, are actually "systematic mappings from body-based, sensorimotor source domains onto abstract target domains."[56] Thus, modern Western culture understands AFFECTION as WARMTH, IMPORTANT objects as being BIG, TIME as in MOTION, and so forth. The end products of such combinations are not random expressions; rather, they fit into a com-

---

53. Joseph Grady, "Primary Metaphors as Inputs to Conceptual Integration," *Journal of Pragmatics* 37 (2005): 1600.

54. Grady, "Foundations of Meaning," 87–89, 163.

55. Eve Sweetser, *From Etymology to Pragmatics: Metaphorical and Cultural Aspects of Semantic Structure* (Cambridge: Cambridge University Press, 1990), 27; Johnson, *Body in the Mind*, 107. As Grady notes, these latter domains are just as "'real,' psychologically and neurologically," as their corresponding source domains; they just lack the ability to be engaged concretely through the human modalities (Grady, "Foundations of Meaning," 28).

56. Johnson, *Meaning of the Body*, 166, 177.

plex, coherent system of mapping that draws upon our physical experience to communicate meaning.[57]

Joseph Grady has argued, and Lakoff and Johnson have since adopted his line of reasoning, that most metaphors are "molecular"; that is, they are combinations of simpler "atomic" parts called "primary metaphors."[58] A primary metaphor is the most basic form of conceptual metaphor, being derived directly from a "subjective (phenomenological) experience of a basic event" (a "primary scene"). UNDERSTANDING IS GRASPING, for instance, is a primary metaphor for knowledge acquisition, deriving directly from a "correlation between close manipulation of an object and access to information about it."[59] Such primary metaphors as PURPOSES ARE DESTINATIONS and ACTIONS ARE BODILY MOTIONS subsequently combine to form more complex metaphors such as LIFE IS A JOURNEY. Because of this, conceptual metaphors can have varying levels of complexity, ranging from relatively simple primary metaphors to intricately connected complex metaphors.

Whether simple or complex, however, these conceptual metaphors are still preverbal. They order our experience of reality without relying upon a conscious verbal reflection on that process. The concept that UNDERSTANDING IS GRASPING, for instance, not only develops out of a physical engagement with the world; it also helps us understand and structure that engagement even when we do not consciously verbalize the process. While an infant may not know the term *understand*, he or she can figure out that "if you can grasp something and hold it in your hands, you can look it over carefully and get a reasonably good understanding of it."[60] No words or conscious thought need occur for this to happen.

1.4. Linguistic Extensions

This is not to say that there is no development of schemas on the linguistic level. Some of the most creative extensions of meaning occur linguistically, and one can find conceptual metaphors hovering beneath the surface of most, if not all, linguistic expressions. Indeed, it is the ability to extend

---

57. Lakoff and Johnson, *Metaphors We Live By*, 105.
58. Grady, "Foundations of Meaning," 199–244; Lakoff and Johnson, *Philosophy in the Flesh*, 46.
59. Grady, "Foundations of Meaning," 27.
60. Lakoff and Johnson, *Metaphors We Live By*, 20.

meaning linguistically that distinguishes human beings from other types of animals. Yet there is a great degree of continuity between the preverbal extension of schematic meaning and the verbal extension. "More complex levels of [schematic development] are just that—levels, and nothing more."[61]

Take, by way of example, the ideas and terms associated with walking. The physical experience of walking generates a cluster of neural patterns associated with the concept of walking, such as agency, direction, and linear pathways. The subsequent occurrence of the word *walk* in speech or text activates the same neural patterns, the same schemas, as those that would have been activated if one were actually moving through space. Walking remains a linear activity undertaken by an agent in a specific direction. From this perspective, linguistic "concepts are not inner mental entities that represent external realities. Rather, concepts are neural activation patterns that can either be 'turned on' by some actual perceptual or motoric event in our bodies, or else activated when we merely think [or speak] about something, without actually perceiving it or performing a specific action."[62] The linguistic manipulation of a conceptual metaphor activates the same cognitive processes as its nonlinguistic predecessor and in doing so contributes to our conceptualization of the environment.

Because we are imaginative creatures, we can then use language to manipulate these underlying schemas and create new meaning. Take again the experience of walking. It is fairly common to map the kinesthetic expectations of walking onto the experience of living (LIFE IS A JOURNEY):[63]

Table 1.2. Metaphorical Mappings: LIFE IS A JOURNEY

Source Domain (Journey)		Target Domain (Life)
Starting Point	→	Birth
Ending Point	→	Death
Destination	→	Life Goals/Purpose
Motion from Point A to B	→	Process of Achieving Purpose

---

61. Johnson, *Meaning of the Body*, 122.
62. Ibid., 157; see also 160–62.
63. The following chart is based on the discussions found in Lakoff and Johnson, *Philosophy in the Flesh*, 62; and Johnson, *Meaning of the Body*, 177–78.

Path	→	Life Plan/Progress Made toward Goal
Obstacles To Motion	→	Difficulties in Achieving Purpose

Birth is the beginning of our journey. Death is the end. We move through life as one might move through space, following the linear or wandering paths of our experiences. We strive to reach certain goals as if they were physical locations. Many of these associations occur preconsciously based on the common, embodied experience of walking.

Without hesitation, we then manipulate these underlying schemas linguistically to create a variety of scenarios in which daily experience is conceptualized as different forms of movement. We speak of the challenges we face as "obstacles," the people we meet as "companions on the road," people who have come "very far, very fast," and people who are "behind schedule." We speak of college students who have yet to "find direction in life," adults who have "missed the boat," and people who "have a long way to go" to achieve their goals.[64] Such expressions are fairly "conventional" metaphors today; that is, they "structure the ordinary conceptual systems of our culture" without individual language users being consciously aware of their adoption. Yet we are predisposed to accept the validity of these metaphors when we encounter them in language, because they reinforce preexisting, preconscious schemas.[65]

We can also manipulate metaphors creatively. We can extend dominant parts of an image schema, as Robert Frost does when he chooses the road "less traveled by." Since the process of achieving one's goals in life is conventionally viewed as movement through space from point A to point B along a defined path, Frost's poem extends the dominant image of the LIFE IS A JOURNEY metaphor to reflect upon how one makes difficult decisions in life.[66] Similarly, we can extend dormant portions of a metaphor. Because a journey can occur on land, on sea, through the air, or in space, a language user has the option of conceiving of life's journey as one that

---

64. Lakoff and Johnson, *Philosophy in the Flesh*, 61–63; Johnson, *Meaning of the Body*, 177.

65. George Lakoff and Mark Turner, *More Than Cool Reason: A Field Guide to Poetic Metaphor* (Chicago: University of Chicago Press, 1989), 63.

66. See the final stanza of Frost's poem, "The Road Not Taken": "I shall be telling this with a sigh / Somewhere ages and ages hence: / Two roads diverged in a wood, and I— / I took the one less traveled by, / And that has made all the difference."

occurs on foot or by means of any number of vehicles (car, plane, boat, etc.). However, many linguistic expressions that rely upon the LIFE IS A JOURNEY metaphor ignore this aspect of the metaphor; the vehicle element remains dormant. When Tom Cochrane sings that "life is a highway; I want to ride it all night long," he extends this previously dormant element of the LIFE IS A JOURNEY metaphor to create a creative linguistic expression in which the speaker's passage through life is envisioned as enjoyable drive through various destinations.[67] Finally, we can blend different metaphors together, thereby creating novel metaphors that reshape the way we view reality.[68] When Led Zeppelin reflects on "buying a stairway to heaven," for instance, the group is blending together the ideas that LIFE IS A JOURNEY whose final destination is death, that HEAVEN IS A VERTICAL LOCATION in the sky, and that SALVATION IS A PHYSICAL COMMODITY that can be bought and sold.[69] There is, in other words, an imaginative, even playful, aspect to the linguistic expression of metaphors that, as Francis Landy points out, cannot be ignored.[70]

---

67. Tom Cochrane, "Life Is a Highway," *Mad Mad World*, 1991.

68. As noted above, conceptual blending was initially viewed as an alternative to the conceptual mapping process detailed by Lakoff and Johnson. However, as Joseph Grady, Todd Oakley, and Seana Coulson ("Blending and Metaphor," in *Metaphor in Cognitive Linguistics*, ed. Raymond W. Gibbs Jr. and Gerard J. Steen [Amsterdam: Benjamins, 1999], 120) argue, it is best to see the two models as complementary approaches to the same data: conceptual mapping describes the initial formation of primary metaphors, and conceptual blending describes how those primary metaphors can be subsequently manipulated into more complex metaphors.

69. Led Zeppelin, "Stairway to Heaven," *Led Zeppelin IV*, 1971.

70. As noted above, Landy disparaged conceptual metaphor theory. Among other critiques, he faulted the model for its lack of attention to the "playful" aspects of metaphor, that is, the ability of language users to create imaginative worlds that introduce their listeners to new ideas and new possibilities ("On Metaphor, Play, and Nonsense," 220–21, 230–31). If one focuses exclusively on universal primary metaphors, such creativity is certainly easy to lose. If, however, one distinguishes between common primary metaphors and more complex linguistic manipulations of them, one can find room for imagination within conceptual metaphor theory. Indeed, in the complex linguistic manifestations of metaphors that I discuss in chapter 10, the biblical authors creatively use their specific social, cultural, and even gendered contexts to manipulate their inherited metaphors and foster the growth of their students. Conceptual metaphor theory need not be the enemy of creativity. Rather, conceptual metaphors are intimately connected to the creative process.

Still, even in the most novel metaphorical expressions, linguistic expressions draw upon "structure[s] with long-term status in the minds of speakers, which transcend particular linguistic instantiations."[71] Frost's choice between two paths and Led Zeppelin's stairway may be influenced by individual creativity, but the underlying nuances of these metaphors stem from preconscious, cognitive conventions.

1.5. Summary

What we have, then, is a complex yet cohesive model for understanding how metaphors develop. According to this model:

- Abstract meaning is not the purview of language alone; it develops naturally and automatically from our daily corporeal experiences.
- The regular and repeated experience of our environment leads to the development of image schemas, neurological patterns by which we order our perception of the environment. When a concrete image schema maps onto a less concrete concept, it creates a primary conceptual metaphor for understanding our daily interactions. Primary metaphors in turn combine, creating an increasingly expanding network of complex metaphors.
- Much of this schematic development and its extension into conceptual metaphors occurs prior to linguistic expression. It is an automatic process that happens without our conscious knowledge.
- Conceptual metaphors do, however, continue to develop linguistically. We use conceptual metaphors in our everyday speech and elaborate upon them to focus our attention on multiple aspects of human experience.

In the pages that follow I draw upon these insights to examine how biblical authors developed and communicated their core religious values. I focus particularly on how common concrete sensory experiences such as seeing (ch. 4), hearing/speaking (ch. 5), touching (ch. 6), ingesting (ch. 7), breathing (ch. 8), and moving (ch. 9) developed into the most basic metaphors for wisdom. I then conclude by examining how these primary

---

71. Grady, "Foundations of Meaning," 13.

metaphors combined to create the more complex metaphors for wisdom that one finds in biblical wisdom literature (ch. 10). In doing so, I argue that "wisdom" in ancient Israel was a set of deep and abiding cultural metaphors that enabled Israelites and early Jews to comprehend their world, define the proper means of acquiring knowledge, and prescribe appropriate behaviors for their community members to follow. In other words, it was a set of prelinguistic cognitive structures that organized the sage's conception of and interaction with the environment, which biblical authors consciously manipulated to convey specific meanings to their audience.

One of the most important implications that emerges in the course of this study is the realization that the concept of wisdom in ancient Israel was influenced by universal *and* cultural factors. Because of their strong focus on the embodiment of meaning, cognitive scientists often give the impression that a schema's development is exclusively determined by universal, biological factors. Anna Wierzbicka, for instance, compiled extensive lists of universal primitives that lie behind human cognition.[72] Cultural anthropologists and historians, however, argue the opposite extreme: there are no universal frameworks; cultural specifics are the primary factor for determining the formation of meaning. For instance, in their study of human perception, such scholars as Walter Ong, David Howes, and Anthony Synnott have argued that cultures vary greatly with respect to their evaluation of the human perceptual modalities. Since most metaphors are based in some way on perceptual experience, the resulting "conceptual apparatus" of cultures likewise varies.[73] Culture, they imply, determines how a society develops meaning, not biology.

On the one hand, the universalists are correct in drawing attention to the biological dimensions of the development of meaning that is shared across cultures. The "mechanics of metaphor," the process by which

---

72. Anna Wierzbicka, *Semantics, Culture, and Cognition: Universal Human Concepts in Culture-Specific Configurations* (New York: Oxford University Press, 1992), 9–10.

73. Walter Ong, "The Shifting Sensorium," in *The Varieties of Sensory Experience: A Sourcebook in the Anthropology of the Senses*, ed. David Howes (Toronto: University of Toronto Press, 1991), 26–27; David Howes, "Sensory Anthropology," in Howes, *Varieties of Sensory Experience*, 161–91; Anthony Synnott, "Puzzling over the Senses: From Plato to Marx," in Howes, *Varieties of Sensory Experience*, 61–76.

abstract meaning develops, is "fundamentally universal."[74] Since human beings share the same neurological blueprint and cerebral functions, one would expect a certain degree of commonality among schemas across cultures. In fact, our modalities may be prewired in such a way as to make the formation of certain schemas more likely than others. For instance, studies have shown that by five and a half months of age, infants already have developed a basic sense of CONTAINMENT, being "surprised when containers without bottoms appear to hold things."[75] It is hard to believe that such an early development occurs solely as the result of specific cultural influences. Some metaphors, then, are universal in that they are neurologically "wired" into the human being like instincts, are "genetically determined," and are the products of a long process of evolution.[76]

On the other hand, the relativists are correct to note that the meanings cultures *ascribe* to the human corporeal experience and the words by which cultures express those meanings vary greatly, depending upon such variables as social locale, gender, historical context, and language. The ancient Greeks, for instance, ascribed particular value to the visual domain, such that the expressions they used to describe cognitive endeavors often privileged visual language. For instance, Aristotle proclaims sight to be above all other senses, for it "enables us know and [makes] many different things visible" (*Metaph.* 980a; see also *Eth. nic.* 1176 and *De an.* 429a). Some metaphors will thus likely be more prominent in a particular cultural or subcultural unit than others or will be even unique to the individual, based on his or her idiosyncratic experience of the environment.

My analysis argues that biblical metaphors do not develop exclusively from biology *or* culture. Metaphorical meaning develops out of a biological interaction with one's environment, and that environment includes not only the natural world but also the society to which one belongs. In the case of biblical wisdom literature, common perceptual experiences provided the basic cognitive patterns by which Israelite and early Jewish scribes understood the abstract experience of wisdom; the unique cultural

---

74. Aaron, *Biblical Ambiguities*, 3.
75. Jean Mandler, "How to Build a Baby II: Conceptual Primitives," *Psychological Review* 99 (1992): 597.
76. Wallace, "Culture and Congition," 69. Of course, it is unlikely that any one schema will be entirely universal, occurring in every culture; however, many are so widely circulated as to be "nearly universal" and thus can be spoken as such (Grady, "Primary Metaphors as Inputs," 1610).

practices of the scribes determined how they described it. The common experience of hearing, for instance, has led to cognition being understood around the world as a spoken word (e.g., in modern America, in ancient Israel, in aboriginal Australia), while the specific cultural experience of Israelite teachers led to wisdom being described specifically as a public teacher (e.g., in Prov 1:20–33). Ultimately, a full account of a metaphor's development must examine both the "evolutionary and physiological" influences and also the "social and cultural behaviors" by which societies educate "successive generations of children so that they may communicate and perform abstract reasoning."[77] As Chris Sinha states, "we do not have to choose between biological determinism, on the one hand, and cultural arbitrariness and autonomy, on the other hand.... There is simply no contradiction involved in proposing that our cognitive world is constituted by culturally specific variations on universal (or more general) themes."[78] A study of these ancient biblical texts through the conceptual metaphor theory can reveal these dual influences: the universal cognitive processes responsible for the concept of wisdom and the culturally specific experiences that nuance their expression.

Because these complementary impulses not only influenced the initial development of these biblical metaphors but also enabled later communities to adopt these metaphors for their own religious needs, my analysis of this literature suggests that our study of the Hebrew Bible and its reception will benefit from taking into account not only the cultural milieu of the communities that produced and interpreted these texts but also the common corporeal experiences that shaped their literary ventures. In the final analysis, then, conceptual metaphor theory will not only advance our understanding of the cognitive processes by which these specific biblical wisdom metaphors developed but also illuminate the different physical and cultural factors that contributed to the development of biblical traditions more generally throughout history. Only by examining both culture and biology can we understand where wisdom truly comes from, what it meant for ancient biblical communities, and how it was to be engaged. Only by doing so can we understand the formation, development, and interpretation of ancient biblical traditions.

---

77. Johnson, *Meaning of the Body*, 123. See also Lakoff and Johnson, *Metaphors We Live By*, 23.

78. Chris Sinha, "The Cost of Renovating the Property: A Reply to Marina Rakova," *Cognitive Linguistics* 13 (2002): 273, 272.

2

Historical Context

Because metaphors are influenced by the actual embodied experiences of those who utilize them, one must begin by looking at the historical and conceptual context in which they arose. For wisdom metaphors, this means looking at the historical and conceptual context of Israelite and early Jewish sages.[1]

Like any land, ancient Israel was made up of many different social groups: priests who worked in the cultic sites (e.g., Lev 21–22; Num 18), kings who governed the people (e.g., 2 Kgs 3:1–27; 12:1–13:13), shepherds who kept goats or sheep (e.g., Gen 30:27–43; Exod 3:1; 1 Sam 16:11), farmers who tended the fields (e.g., Gen 4:2; Zech 13:5), and craftsmen who built houses or fashioned tools (e.g., 2 Kgs 22:5–6 // 2 Chr 34:10–11; 2 Kgs 24:14, 16).[2] There were also "scribes" (סופרים) and "sages" (חכמים),

---

1. In this volume I use the term *Israelite* to refer collectively to the communities living in Israel before the exile. *Early Jewish* refers to those groups living in and around Israel after the exile that trace their cultural heritage to those preexilic communities. Such nomenclature is not meant to imply that these groups were homogenous, either in their socioeconomic and political composition or in all of their theological or cultural beliefs. Rather, the terms are merely shorthand ways to refer to those groups most directly responsible for the texts that now constitute the Hebrew Bible.

2. The list here is not intended to confirm the historical accuracy of the narratives listed. For instance, to say that Jacob, Moses, and David are examples of shepherds in ancient Israel is not to suggest that Jacob, Moses, and David existed and were actually shepherds. Rather, when a text describes its legendary figures by way of one of these professions, it projects its community's own understanding of human society back onto their ancestors. In other words, these examples are illustrative of the types of professions available in Israel when the text was composed and throughout its history. Jacob, Moses, and David may not have been shepherds, but the people who composed such stories were aware that the profession existed and used it to convey a particular message about their ancestors.

professional classes of educated individuals who kept written records (e.g., 2 Kgs 12:10 // 2 Chr 24:11; 2 Kgs 18:18–19:7 // Isa 36:3–37:7; 1 Chr 24:6), transcribed verbal discourse (e.g., Jer 36:4–18; Ezra 4:8), copied and composed sacred texts (e.g., 2 Kgs 22:3–11; Jer 8:8; Prov 25:1), and even provided advice to the governor or king (e.g., Jer 18:18; 1 Chr 27:32).[3] It is this latter group that was primarily responsible for shaping the wisdom texts into what they are today.

According to the Hebrew Bible, these scribes served in various locales: royal courts (e.g., 2 Kgs 18:18–19:7 // Isa 36:3–37:7), temples (e.g., Jer 36:10, 12, 20–21), the army (e.g., 2 Kgs 25:19 // Jer 52:25), and smaller cities (e.g., 2 Sam 15:12; 20:14–22).[4] In order to copy texts and record dictated speech in these diverse locations, scribes needed to know how to read and write in the various languages of their time, both local Semitic dialects (Hebrew, Aramaic) and international languages (e.g., Egyptian, Akkadian, Greek).[5] Initially these skills were probably taught to

---

3. Leo G. Perdue, *The Sword and the Stylus: An Introduction to Wisdom in the Age of Empires* (Grand Rapids: Eerdmans, 2008), 50. The account in 2 Kgs 22:3–11 does not actually say that Shaphan, the סופר of Josiah, wrote or copied the book of the law but that the priest "found" the book in the temple during remodeling and that Shaphan then delivered it to Josiah. As many scholars point out, however, the narrative about the discovery of the book of the law in the temple is likely a rhetorical device designed to legitimize Josiah's religious reforms by appealing to the antiquity of the prohibitions he enacted. If so, then Shaphan's actions may reflect the participation of scribes in the composition of the book of the law, a legal code that may have served as the *Vorlage* to the current book of Deuteronomy.

4. The locations of these individuals are not always clear, especially whether they served in the royal court or the temple. For instance, in Jer 36 Gemariah and Elishama are both said to have their own chamber (לשכה) that was near to but separate from the king's court. It is not certain that this was in the temple complex, but Perdue (*Sword and the Stylus*, 72–73) argues that the difference between the royal court and the לשכה suggests that "there were two groups of scribes (priestly and royal) located in two similar buildings in the temple complex, adjacent to the palace." For more on the social locale of scribes, see Perdue, *Sword and the Stylus*, 50–57, 66–80.

5. See, for instance, 2 Kgs 18:26 // Isa 36:11, where three court officials (Eliakim son of Hilkiah, the palace master; Shebnah, the סופר; and Joah son of Asaph, the record keeper) ask a foreign messenger to speak in Aramaic rather than the local dialect in order to keep the people from hearing the message of the foreign king. For more information, see Leo G. Perdue, "Scribes, Sages, and Seers in Israel and the Ancient Near East: An Introduction," in *Scribes, Sages, and Seers: The Sage in the Eastern Mediterranean World*, ed. Leo G. Perdue, FRLANT 219 (Göttingen: Vandenhoeck & Ruprecht, 2008), 5.

the scribe by his father, since like priests or farmers, the scribal profession was probably hereditary, with a male child following in the profession of his father.⁶ As the administrative systems of the land developed and more refined skills were needed, specialized schools were created to train young scribes in their craft. As André Lemaire argues, these may have been located in the house of a noted teacher, in the marketplace or other public place, or in a building designated specifically for that purpose.⁷ However, the nomenclature for teacher and student continued to reflect the hereditary origin of the profession. Students were בנים ("sons"), and

---

6. See, for instance, the family of scribes at Jabez listed in 1 Chr 2:55 and the family of Shaphan, the father and sons of which serve as royal scribes in the late monarchy (e.g., 2 Kgs 22:3–20; Jer 36:10–21).

7. André Lemaire, "The Sage in School and Temple," in *The Sage in Israel and the Ancient Near East*, ed. John G. Gammie and Leo G. Perdue (Winona Lake, IN: Eisenbrauns, 1990), 168; see also Perdue, *Sword and the Stylus*, 70. There is considerable scholarly debate about the existence of schools in ancient Israel. The first solid evidence of schools in Israel does not appear until Ben Sira, who refers to a בית מדרש ("house of study," 51:23). Thus, such scholars as R. Norman Whybray and Friedemann W. Golka argue against the presence of schools in preexilic Israel. See, for instance, R. Norman Whybray, *The Intellectual Tradition in Old Testament*, BZAW 135 (Berlin: de Gruyter, 1974), 43; Friedemann W. Golka, *The Leopard's Spots: Biblical and African Wisdom in Proverbs* (Edinburgh: T&T Clark, 1993), 4–15. However, although conclusive evidence is lacking for a formal school in Israel prior to Hellenism, it is plausible that such institutions did exist. Contemporaneous Egyptian and Mesopotamian sources attest to their existence in nearby kingdoms (see Lemaire, "Sage in School and Temple," 168; and the more detailed list in his *Les écoles et la formation de la Bible dans l'ancien Israel*, OBO 39 [Göttingen: Vandenhoeck & Ruprecht, 1981], 94–95; Perdue, "Scribes, Sages, and Seers," 17–31), and schoolboy exercises have been found in eighth- through sixth-century outposts and cities (Lemaire, "Sage in School and Temple," 172). The Hebrew Bible itself refers to "teachers" (2 Chr 17:7–9; Prov 5:13) and hints at the existence of royal, prophetic, and priestly schools (e.g., 1 Kgs 12:8, 10; 2 Kgs 6:1–2; 10:1, 5–6; Isa 8:16; 28:7–13; 2 Chr 17:7–9) (Lemaire, "Sage in School and Temple," 171; Perdue, *Sword and the Stylus*, 70). The increased skill set needed by scribes in late preexilic-period bureaucracies and the spread of literacy necessitated a more formal mode of training. As Michael V. Fox states, "it is likely that there were schools attached to the temple and possibly the court, as in Egypt and Mesopotamia, because there is little reason for *anyone* to write if only a scattered few could read" (*Proverbs 1–9: A New Translation with Introduction and Commentary*, AB 18A [New York: Doubleday, 2000], 8, emphasis original). Consequently, many scholars affirm the existence of Israelite schools, at least in the early exile if not before. See, for instance, Lemaire, "Sage in School and Temple," 165–81; Fox, *Proverbs 1–9*, 7–8; Perdue, *Sword and the Stylus*, 70–80.

teachers were either אמות ("mothers") or אבות ("fathers"), even when there was no direct biological relationship between them.⁸ Those scribes who excelled at their profession and demonstrated mastery of their ancestral traditions were deemed חכמים ("wise ones").⁹ Such "sages" not only were responsible for the administrative duties of the kingdom and likely served in positions of prestige but also taught the next generation of scribes the skills necessary to fulfill their duties and promote the values of their community.¹⁰

According to the ancient sage Yeshua ben Eleazar ben Sira, scribes differed from manual laborers in that they enjoyed the "leisure" (Sir 38:24) to study "the law of the Most High" (38:34) and unravel the mysteries of creation. As Ben Sira states, the scribe

> seeks out the wisdom of all the ancients and busies himself with prophecies; he preserves the sayings of famous men and enters into the circuitous ways of parables; he seeks out the secrets of proverbs and dwells in the riddles of parables. He serves among the great and appears before rulers; he passes through the lands of foreign nations and tests good and evil in people.... If the great Lord desires, he will himself be filled with the spirit of understanding; he will pour forth words of his own wisdom and give thanks in prayer to the Lord.... He will reveal the education of his schooling and will boast in the law of the Lord's covenant. (Sir 39:1–8)

According to Ben Sira, the sage has the freedom to study the law, compile proverbs, and create sayings of his own. Admittedly, Ben Sira's description is an idealized presentation of scribal activities and may reflect the author's attempt to justify his own literary activities. However, this description probably still reflects actual scribal practices. The author of this poem at

---

8. There is some evidence that women served as sages (e.g., 2 Sam 14:1–24; 20:16–22), although men seem to predominate. See Perdue, *Sword and the Stylus*, 71, 104; Claudia Camp, "The Female Sage in Biblical Literature," in Gammie and Perdue, *Sage in Israel*, 185–203.

9. Perdue, "Scribes, Sages, and Seers," 4. As Perdue points out, the adjective חכם could refer to "anyone who possesses a particular skill or specialized knowledge," whether a scribe, craftsman, or priest. However, the nominal form often appears as a title of honor, "reserved for those who were especially acute in their powers of judgment and well known in tradition for their mastery of wisdom as both an epistemology and a body of knowledge."

10. Ibid.; Katharine Dell, "Scribes, Sages, and Seers in the First Temple," in Perdue, *Scribes, Sages, and Seers*, 130, 139–40.

least seems to conceive of his own activities in this fashion, and it is likely that other scribes of his acquaintance did likewise. The poem, after all, does not attempt to defend its position; rather, it presents its description as the natural state of scribes and, if anything, defends the value of nonscribal professions (see Sir 38:31–34).

If this poem does reflect actual scribal practice, then in addition to drafting letters to foreign officials, recording important events for their kings, and educating future generations, scribes gathered the proverbial wisdom of their people, organized them according to their own perception of reality, and added a few of their own. The book of Proverbs, for instance, probably developed in this very manner. As Michael V. Fox observes, the majority of Proverbs (chs. 10–29) reflects the collected wisdom of preexilic Israel. Some sayings grew out of the oral sayings of agrarian villagers and reflect a domestic setting (e.g., Prov 10:5; 12:11; 15:17). Other sayings, however, consider the proper conduct of court officials and thus probably reflect the interests of individuals familiar with that environment (e.g., Prov 23:1–5; 25:6–7).[11] Since court scribes often engaged with foreign emissaries and likely traveled abroad in order to fulfill their duties, many sayings also reflect the international milieu of the time, cast in Israelite terms (see, for instance, the reworking of the Instruction of Amenemope, a twelfth-century Egyptian text, in Prov 22:17–24:22).[12] The scribal class, which spanned multiple locales, gradually collected these diverse sayings and wove them together into a coherent collection. Proverbs 1–9 and 31 were then added at a late, postexilic stage by an elite scribal class who responded

---

11. Some scholars argue that all of Prov 10–29 came from an agrarian context. See, for instance, Claus Westermann, *The Roots of Wisdom: The Oldest Proverbs of Israel and Other People*, trans. J. D. Charles (Louisville: Westminster John Knox, 1995); Golka, *Leopard's Spots*, 4–53. Other scholars suggest that the entire book grew out of schools connected to the royal court and thus reflects the interests of an elite class of professional scribes. See, for example, Hans-Jürgen Hermisson, *Studien zur israelitischen Spruchweisheit*, WMANT 28 (Neukirchen-Vluyn: Neukirchener Verlag, 1968); and Lang, *Wisdom and the Book of Proverbs*. The reality probably is a hybrid between the two, with some sayings originating in the ordinary people of the land and others in the court or school (thus Fox). For a discussion of these scholars and their positions, see Fox, *Proverbs 1–9*, 6–12.

12. Perdue, *Sword and the Stylus*, 49, 93–94, 96–97. See also the Sayings of Agur (Prov 30), which may reflect the Akkadian *apkallu* tradition and the incorporation of the sayings of Lemuel's mother, an Arabic queen, into Prov 31:1–9.

to the older material and recast it according to their own interests.[13] In some sense, then, the book of Proverbs reflects the collected wisdom of the entire people of Israel (common and elite) as it was handed down and preserved. At the same time, Proverbs also reflects the particular interest of the scribal elite, who selected which sayings to include, arranged them in a particular manner, and shaped them to fit their particular conception of the cosmos.[14]

Later scribes reflected on such collected wisdom and reshaped it according to their own perceptions of reality. The books of Job and Qoheleth, for instance, each seem to be an educated response to the type of mentality set forth in Proverbs.[15] Like Proverbs, the book of Job developed in stages. The earliest material (the prose narrative of 1:1–2:13 and 42:7–17) probably originated as a preexilic didactic tale about the origin of suffering and the appropriate responses to it. During the Babylonian exile, various dialogues (3:1–31:40; 38:1–42:17) were composed in response to the earlier tale that challenged the established precepts of Israelite society, most particularly the position set forth in Proverbs and the Deuteronomic History that human righteousness guarantees prosperity while human sin results in punishment and suffering. Finally, sometime before the late Persian period, the speeches of Elihu (32:1–37:24) and a poem on wisdom

---

13. Here, too, scholars differ, with some arguing that Prov 1–9, although later than 10–29, was still preexilic. See, for instance, Perdue, *Sword and the Stylus*, 88; Dell, "Scribes, Sages, and Seers in the First Temple," 127. Perdue argues, however, that, although the collection of Prov 1–9 was preexilic, there was a postexilic redaction of the entire book, at which stage the prologue of Proverbs (1:2–7) and poem on the Woman of Worth (31:10–31) were added (*Sword and Stylus*, 99). However, Fox's argument for a postexilic composition of 1–9 seems more plausible, given the presence of Aramaisms in some of the proverbs, possible allusions to the book of Jeremiah, and the similarity between the intellectual and social concerns of Prov 1–9 and postexilic communities (*Proverbs 1–9*, 6, 48–49, 104). Fox tentatively suggests a Hellenistic date for Prov 1–9 (49), but the evidence is too inconclusive to be certain exactly when the text was composed. It therefore is best to leave the exact dating open to either a Persian or Hellenistic milieu.

14. As Fox states (*Proverbs 1–9*, 11), the authors/redactors of this text "did collect sayings and add some of their own, but most important, they *selected*. They chose what to include and what to ignore, and what they included, they reshaped" (emphasis original).

15. This is not to say that the authors of Job and Qoheleth knew the book that we have today called Proverbs. However, the worldview presented within them responds to the type of worldview preserved in Proverbs.

(28:1–28) were interjected into the book, critiquing the main dialogues and reaffirming the inscrutability of God.[16]

As with Proverbs, the composition of Job thus reflects the activities of scribes who, in the process of gathering and responding to the inherited material, recast their traditions according to their own interests. Yet, these distinct positions on suffering were not harmonized into a single perspective. As Carol Newsom argues, "there is no super-authorial mediation to harmonize the … voices in the service of a single complex truth; there is only their unresolvable, unfinalizable scrutiny of each."[17] The multiple positions on suffering were put into conversation with each other without choosing one as the definitive position. The final book, as Yair Hoffman argues, is thus an "anthology on the subject of recompense," a collection of conflicting scribal voices each responding to and reshaping the preexisting traditions of their society about the nature of human suffering.[18]

The book of Qoheleth reflects a similar process. Although some scholars have suggested a single authorship for Qoheleth, the book seems

---

16. This reconstruction essentially follows that of Perdue (*Sword and Stylus*, 117–18), who argues that the book developed in distinct textual stages, with the narrative being the earliest text to which first the dialogues were added and then the wisdom poem of ch. 28 and the speeches of Elihu in chs. 32–37. It is not clear if the dialogues were composed as an entire unit (as Perdue seems to argue) or as separate debates, in which case they may have been inserted into the prose narrative after their composition. There is, of course, considerable scholarly debate about the relationship between the different parts of Job. Many scholars support, to varying degrees, a gradual composition of the book (thus Perdue). Others scholars argue that the book was composed by one author (see, e.g., Norman C. Habel, *The Book of Job: A Commentary*, OTL [Philadelphia: Westminster, 1985], 35–39) or, at least, was redacted to be read as one continuous debate (see, e.g., Carol Newsom, "The Book of Job as Polyphonic Text," *JSOT* 97 [2002]: 87–108). Given the diversity of form and content within the book of Job, it seems most plausible that the book developed in stages, within different groups reflecting upon and responding to their received traditions. For more information on the debates about the book's development, see Perdue, *Sword and the Stylus*, 123–31. For more on the relationship between Job and previous intellectual traditions of Israel, including the Priestly Code, the Deuteronomic History, and prophetic ideology, see Konrad Schmid, "The Authors of Job and Their Historical and Social Setting," in Perdue, *Scribes, Sages, and Seers*, 151–52.

17. Newsom, "Book of Job as Polyphonic Text," 103. Newsom is speaking particularly of the relationship between the prose narrative and main dialogues, but the observation can just as easily apply to the book as a whole.

18. Yair Hoffman, *A Blemished Perfection: The Book of Job in Context*, JSOTSup 213 (Sheffield: Sheffield Academic, 1996), 113.

to contain at least two different voices, that of the narrator proper (the Teacher, Qoh 1:2–12:8) and that of a later editor (1:1; 7:27; 12:9–14; and perhaps other glosses within the text).[19] The material produced by the Teacher probably stems from the late Persian period (ca. fifth–fourth century BCE) or early Hellenistic period (ca. third century BCE) and presumes an audience already familiar with and committed to the idea that the proper attention to the normative wisdom of Israelite society results in the acquisition of righteousness and prosperity.[20] The Teacher challenges this convention by reflecting at length on the nature and limitations of

---

19. As with Proverbs and Job, there is considerable debate about the composition history of the book of Qoheleth, with some scholars arguing for a single author and others for multiple authors. Fox, for instance, argues that the editorial insertions are part of the rhetoric of the text and that they were composed by the same author who penned the rest of the text. See Michael V. Fox, "Frame-Narrative and Composition in the Book of Qohelet," *HUCA* 48 (1977): 83–106. C. L. Seow, however, argues that this position, while possible, is unlikely and that a later editor was responsible for collecting and arranging the material into the current text. See C. L. Seow, *Ecclesiastes: A New Translation with Introduction and Commentary*, AB 18C (New York: Doubleday, 1997), 38. Still other scholars point to various inconsistencies within the text (e.g., pleasure is affirmed in 2:24–26, 5:17–19 but questioned in 2:2–3, 10–11) to suggest a plethora of authors. For instance, Carl Siegfried suggests the presence of as many as nine editorial hands (Wilhelm Frankenberg and Carl Siegfried, *Die Sprüche, Prediger und Hoheslied*, HKAT 2/3 [Göttingen: Vandenhoeck & Ruprecht, 1898], 2–12). The simplest explanation—that the words of a teacher had been collected by a later editor—seems the most plausible, given the difference in voice and tone between the main text and editorial passages (first person versus third person). As Seow argues, one need not posit the existence of multiple editorial hands to explain the internal inconsistencies. The tensions within the book can easily be explained as a rhetorical device used by the author to "lead his reader to recognize that what one perceives at first glance many not necessarily be reality" (Seow, *Ecclesiastes*, 43). The inconsistencies present within the book thus reflect Qoheleth's main point that life is not as orderly as it first appears. For more on the positions of these scholars and the larger scholarly debate about Qoheleth's composition, see Seow, *Ecclesiastes*, 38–43.

20. Seow suggests a Persian-period dating, based on the presence of Persian loanwords (e.g., פרדסים, "parks," Qoh 2:5; פתגם, "word," 8:11); Late Biblical Hebrew features (e.g., frequent use of ־ש instead of אשר); Persian-era idioms (e.g., חלק, "lot," Qoh 3:22, 5:17–18; כף, with the sense of "small handful," 4:6; בית הסורים, "prison," 4:14); and Persian-era concerns (e.g., focus on economic issues and economic inequalities) (Seow, *Ecclesiastes*, 12–36; Seow, "The Social World of Ecclesiastes," in Perdue, *Scribes, Sages, and Seers*, 189–217). Other scholars, however, suggest a Hellenistic dating due to similarities between Qoheleth and Hellenistic philosophy (see, for instance, Perdue, *Sword and the Stylus*, 198–255).

human knowledge. Although adopting the persona of the "king of Israel" (e.g., Qoh 1:12), the social class of the narrator is unclear. However, the rhetoric of the text suggests that the Teacher belonged to and directed his musings toward an educated elite. The introduction and epilogue specifically cast the book as the "sayings of the wise" (1:1; 12:11) and describes the Teacher as one who "taught the people knowledge, considered carefully and investigated, and arranged many proverbs" (12:9). While this phraseology was added after the fact and may reflect scribal convention, it at least indicates that by the time the book was redacted the Teacher was conceived of as a scribe, performing scribal functions similar to the scribe of Ben Sira.

A later editor collected the material produced by this Teacher, arranged it into its current form, and added an introduction and conclusion. In doing so, the editor reshaped the material, bringing it more in line with conventional scribal conceptions. Thus, where the Teacher encourages the sage to explore the limitations of human knowledge through direct experiments, the editor encourages the audience to attend to the wise words of the Teacher and to be wary of making books of their own (Qoh 12:11–12). Unlike the words of the Teacher, the editor specifically addresses himself to בני ("my son," 12:12), the scribal student. Whatever the social class of the original narrator and his audience may have been, the book of Qoheleth itself reflects the hand of the scribal elite, who collected the sayings of the Teacher and reshaped them according to their perception of life.

In each case, the sages gathered the traditions of their people, reflected upon them, and shaped them according to the concerns and values of their community. While not every scribe would have had the capability or opportunity to engage in such literary activity, the small, elite group of scribes who did were thus able to shape the tradition of their ancestors as they saw fit and produce the distinctive collection of texts that scholars today refer to collectively as "wisdom literature" (Proverbs, Job, Qoheleth, Ben Sira, select psalms, Wisdom of Solomon, 4QInstruction, etc.). Because of their organic development, the so-called wisdom books of ancient Israel do not constitute a self-contained genre. They exhibit a variety of interests, stem from various social locales, and contain within them a range of literary forms (short sayings, poems, dialogue, prose, etc.). To label them a fixed genre would therefore be misleading. Instead, as John Collins rightly states, it is more appropriate to consider these texts "a tradition, held together by certain family resemblances"—for instance, a concern for order, a defined social hierarchy, and a relative absence of Israelite-specific theology—"rather than by a constant essence."[21] Most importantly, these texts share a common worldview originally grounded in the conviction that human beings were capable of understanding the world and thriving by their own innate intellectual capacities. Although this optimism gradually collapsed, the tradition continued to maintain that people's ability to reason—their wisdom—was paramount for understanding how humanity related to the world around them and the divine.

---

21. John J. Collins, *Jewish Wisdom in the Hellenistic Age*, OTL (Louisville: Westminster John Knox, 1997), 1.

3
Perception

As Lakoff and Johnson state, "the metaphor system conceptualizing thought itself does not give us a single, overall, consistent understanding of mental life."[1] As imaginative creatures, we have more than one conceptualization of cognition and often express conflicting conceptualizations in close proximity to each other. Thinking can be a struggle (e.g., I *wrestled* with the idea), an act of digestion (e.g., he *digested* the information), a motion through space (e.g., he *followed* my *train* of thought), and a visual encounter (e.g., I *examined* the argument). Although some conceptualizations of cognition are opaque, seeming to refer exclusively to the cognitive sphere (e.g., we *think*, we *know*, we *believe*), most are intimately connected to human perception; that is, we describe how we think by the things we do. We *see* points, *hear* ourselves think, *grasp* concepts, and *follow* arguments. The phenomenological experience of perception serves as a natural source domain for cognition across the world, such that cognition is frequently conceptualized as a visual, oral, tactile, or kinesthetic experience.

3.1. A Universal and Cultural Paradigm

According to Eve Sweetser, whose 1990 monograph systematically analyzed perceptual metaphors and thrust them into the forefront of cognitive linguistic research, perceptual metaphors for cognition belong to a larger system of conceptual metaphors in which the "internal self is pervasively understood in terms of the bodily external self and is hence described by means of vocabulary drawn (either synchronically or diachronically) from

---

1. Lakoff and Johnson, *Philosophy in the Flesh*, 235.

the physical domain."[2] This MIND AS BODY metaphor, as she calls it, presents cognition as physical processes acting upon physical agents. Ideas, thoughts, and concepts are independent entities that can be seen, heard, moved, or grasped. Since the perceptual apparatuses are primary ways by which humans engage the world, a major subclass of this system conceptualizes COGNITION AS PERCEPTION.[3]

Sweetser's paradigm has fueled scholarly discussion, and many scholars have since identified various metaphors throughout the globe that fit her system (e.g., COGNITION IS SEEING, COGNITION IS HEARING, COGNITION IS TOUCHING). Since human beings around the world have similar perceptual experiences, most scholars have classified these cognitive metaphors as universal metaphors and have taken their existence for granted. For instance, many scholars have identified the metaphor COGNITION IS SEEING as a universal metaphor by which the human intellect is conceived of as a visual process (e.g., I *see* what you mean).[4] However, while the COGNITION IS PERCEPTION paradigm is itself universal, specific aspects of the paradigm vary from culture to culture. For instance, cultures differ over which organ governs cognition. Americans locate cognition in the brain, while the Israelites located it in the לבב/לב ("heart") or כבד ("liver"). Similarly, the properties associated with each modality vary from one culture to the next. Western cultures associate intellection with vision and obedience with hearing, while Australian aboriginal cultures associate intellection with hearing and desire with sight.[5] There are, in other words, varying

---

2. Sweetser, *From Etymology to Pragmatics*, 45.

3. Various terms have been used to describe this subgroup of metaphors. Sweetser (*From Etymology to Pragmatics*, 37) labels them "metaphors of perception." Lakoff and Johnson (*Philosophy in the Flesh*, 236–43) classify this subgroup according to their physical functions: THINKING IS MOVING, THINKING IS PERCEIVING, THINKING IS OBJECT MANIPULATION, and ACQUIRING IDEAS IS EATING. The designation of this class of metaphors as COGNITION IS PERCEIVING here follows that of Rosario Caballero and Iraide Ibarretxe-Antuñano, "Ways of Perceiving, Moving, and Thinking: Re-vindicating Culture in Conceptual Metaphor Research," in "Conceptual Metaphor Theory: Thirty Years After," special issue, *Cognitive Semiotics* 5 (2013): 268–90.

4. See, for example, Grady, "Foundations of Meaning," 3; Lakoff and Johnson, *Philosophy in the Flesh*, 236–43; Fred McVittie, "The Role of Conceptual Metaphor within Knowledge Paradigms" (PhD diss., Manchester Metropolitan University, 2009), 34–36, 47–48; Ning Yu, "Chinese Metaphors of Thinking," *Cognitive Linguistics* 14 (2003): 141–65.

5. Iraide Ibarretxe-Antuñano, "Vision Metaphors for the Intellect: Are They

degrees of specificity to this system of interrelated metaphors, such that a hierarchy of metaphors emerges.[6]

Table 3.1. Hierarchy of Perceptual Metaphors for Cognition

Universal

COGNITION IS PERCEPTION

Relatively Universal

COGNITION IS SEEING	COGNITION IS HEARING	COGNITION IS SMELLING	etc. (e.g., COGNITION IS MOVING, COGNITION IS TOUCHING)

Culturally Specific

KNOWING IS SEEING (e.g., United States, Spain)	KNOWING IS HEARING (e.g., Australia)	KNOWING IS SMELLING (e.g., the Jahai of the Malay Peninsula)	etc. (e.g., KNOWING IS MOVING, UNDERSTANDING IS GRASPING)
DESIRE IS SEEING (e.g., Australia)	AGREEING IS HEARING (e.g., Basque)	GUESSING IS SMELLING (e.g., United States)	
OBEYING IS SEEING (e.g., Basque)	OBEYING IS HEARING (e.g., United States, Spain)	PROPHESYING IS SMELLING (e.g., Basque)	
etc.	etc.	etc.	

Really Cross-Linguistic?," *Atlantis* 30 (2008): 24–25, 28. See also the detailed discussion in Nicholas Evans and David Wilkins, "In the Mind's Ear: The Semantic Extensions of Perception Verbs in Australian Languages," *Language* 76 (2000): 46–92.

6. In establishing this hierarchy, I differ from Sweetser and Ibarretxe-Antuñano. Since Sweetser (*From Etymology to Pragmatics*, 45) argues that perceptual metaphors are universal, she does not allow for a gradation of metaphors. Ibarretxe-Antuñano, on the other hand, argues that there are two levels of metaphors, generic-abstract (COGNITION IS PERCEPTION) and specific-concrete (COGNITION IS SMELLING, COGNITION IS HEARING, etc.). The first is universal, the second culturally dependent. However, since

The fairly abstract metaphor COGNITION IS PERCEPTION is universal and governs how cultures across the globe conceptualize cognition. More specific metaphors such as COGNITION IS SEEING, COGNITION IS HEARING, or COGNITION IS SMELLING do not appear in every culture but are still relatively universal, recurring consistently across the globe. Specific iterations of these metaphors, however, vary across cultures. At times, sight is a source domain for desire (DESIRE IS SEEING; e.g., Australian aboriginals); elsewhere sight is a form of intellect (KNOWING IS SEEING; e.g., modern Americans). A culture can, of course, have more than one conceptualization of cognition. Modern Americans, for instance, frequently conceptualize cognition as seeing, hearing, and smelling, yet each perceptual metaphor reflects a distinct mode of engaging the world. Thus in the modern West seeing is connected to objective knowledge, hearing to subjective knowledge, and smelling to guesswork. These conceptualizations interact, but they are as distinct as their corresponding perceptual apparatuses.[7]

COGNITION IS HEARING, COGNITION IS SEEING, etc. often have similar nuances across congruous cultures, it is reasonable to assume that there is also a degree of universality among these cognitive metaphors. What differs is not the metaphor itself but the specific cultural nuances of it. This observation is consistent with Ibarretxe-Antuñano's research, which hypothesizes a certain degree of continuity among the perceptual metaphors of like-minded cultures (e.g., Western). See, for instance, her comparison of metaphors in English, Spanish, and Basque (a non-Indo-European language) in "Polysemy and Metaphor in Perception Verbs: A Cross-Linguistic Study" (PhD diss., University of Edinburgh, 1999).

Although the chart here is original, the culturally specific examples within it are derived from the various examples listed in Ibarretxe-Antuñano, "Polysemy and Metaphor in Perception Verbs," 53–89; Ibarretxe-Antuñano, "Mind as Body," *Miscelánea* 25 (2002): 93–119; Ibarretxe-Antuñano, "Vision Metaphors for the Intellect," 15–33. The examples listed are intended to be illustrative, not exhaustive.

7. Meir Malul argues that modern Western epistemology differs from ancient: "whereas in the former the interplay looks like being dynamic, holistic, and synthetic, in our contemporary epistemic process we tend to be disjunctive in terms of letting each sense play its own role without being interactively affected by the other senses. We, in short, apply an analytic mode of thinking, whereas the primitive applies a synthetic mode" (*Knowledge, Control, and Sex: Studies in Biblical Thought, Culture, and Worldview* [Tel Aviv: Archaeological Center Publications, 2002], 31). In arguing this, however, Malul overstates the contrast between modern and ancient cognition. Although modern Western individuals view the modalities distinctively, no one modality truly operates alone. They are interconnected, and this interconnectivity is realized in linguistic expressions (see, for instance, phrases that describe vision as a

Since COGNITION IS PERCEPTION is a universal metaphor that is realized in similar yet distinct fashions across the globe, the challenge lies in determining the specific cultural nuances of conceptual metaphors without assuming a priori that they are identical to modern perceptual sensibilities. As a solution, Iraide Ibarretxe-Antuñano proposes establishing a "typology of prototypical properties," a culturally relative paradigm based not only on the phenomenology of perception but also the psychology of perception with which a given culture operates.[8]

Table 3.2. Distribution of Prototypical Properties with Descriptions

Properties	Description (PR = Perceiver; OP = Object of Perception; P = Act of Perception)
<contact>	whether the PR must have physical contact with the OP in order to be perceived
<closeness>	whether the OP must be in the vicinity of the PR to be perceived
<internal>	whether the OP must go inside the PR to be perceived
<limits>	whether the PR is aware of the boundaries imposed by the OP when perceived
<location>	whether the PR is aware of the situation of the OP when perceiving
<detection>	how the PR performs the P: how PR discloses the presence of an object and distinguishes one object from another
<identification>	how well the PR can discriminate what the PR is perceiving, the P

tactile experience, such as "my eyes picked out the correct item"). Similarly, while there are passages in which the modalities are viewed synthetically in the Hebrew Bible (e.g., Ps 34:9; Prov 4:18), there are also multiple examples of the modalities operating independently and even in contrast to each other (Deut 4:12; Job 42:1–6). The difference between ancient and modern epistemology lies in the values each society assigns to the individual modalities and how their interconnectivity is realized, not in an innate difference between disjunctive and synthetic thought patterns.

8. The following chart has been reproduced with permission from Ibarretxe-Antuñano, "Vision Metaphors for the Intellect," 20. For a full discussion of each property, see Ibarretxe-Antuñano, "Polysemy and Metaphor in Perception Verbs," 143–56.

\<voluntary\>	whether the PR can choose when to perform a P
\<directness\>	whether the P depends on the PR directly or is mediated by another element
\<effects\>	whether the P causes any change in the OP
\<briefness\>	how long the relation between P and OP should be in order for the perception to be successful
\<evaluation\>	whether the P assesses the OP
\<correction of hypothesis\>	how correct and accurate the hypothesis formulated about the OP in the P is in comparison with the real object of P
\<subjectivity\>	how much influence the PR has on the OP

The property of <identification>, for instance, refers to the perceiver's ability to identify its object. When we see a dog or tree, we easily recognize the nature of the object, assuming we do not have visual impairments and we know what the object is. However, it is often difficult to identify an object solely by its odor. The property of <identification> is thus associated with sight but not with smell. The property of <correction of hypothesis> is somewhat more complicated. When we perceive an object, especially with vision, hearing, or smell, "we formulate hypotheses about the nature and character of the OP."[9] How close these hypotheses come to the actual nature of the object varies—with sight being the most accurate, followed by hearing, and then smell—but each forms a hypothesis. Touch and taste, however, actually come into contact with the object, so no hypothesis is necessary.[10]

According to Ibarretxe-Antuñano, the <effects> property refers to whether a perceptual modality causes any change in the perceived object. In Western epistemology, for instance, only touch is an affective sense. It physically alters the object it encounters by exerting pressure on it, moving it from one location to another, or inflicting pain.[11] However, perception can also affect the person engaging in a perceptual act, a fact that Ibarretxe-Antuñano fails to consider. Touch, for instance, not only alters

---

9. Ibarretxe-Antuñano, "Polysemy and Metaphor in Perception Verbs," 147–48, 153.
10. See, however, the discussion of this property in touch below, which suggests that the inapplicability of this modality to touch may not be universal.
11. Ibarretxe-Antuñano, "Polysemy and Metaphor in Perception Verbs," 150.

the perceived object but also the perceiver. As Hans Jonas argues, whether initiated by the perceiver or the object perceived, both perceiver and perceived "do something to each other" in the act of touching.[12] The bite of an insect or the touch of a fingertip will elicit, at the very least, a sensation of pressure in both the object perceived and the perceiver. Such pressure may even elicit a sensation of pain or pleasure. The exact effect on the perceiver may be hard to measure, since the degree to which we experience pressure, pleasure, and pain, for instance, varies from person to person, as do our responses to such stimuli (e.g., one person may cry out in pain when bitten by an insect, while another may barely notice the sensation).[13] However, the perceiver is still affected by the act of perception. Thus, the property of <effects> should also consider whether the act of perception causes any change in the perceiver.

Each culture can be evaluated according to this typology. Thus, Ibarretxe-Antuñano summarizes modern Western conceptions of perception as follows, with the tags $_{yes}$ or $_{no}$ indicating the role that the property plays in the evaluation of the modality. These properties are organized according to the relationship between the perceiver (PR), the object perceived (OP), and the act of perception (P). The first five properties reflect the relationship between the perceiver and the object perceived (PR → OP), the next seven between the perceiver and the act of perception (PR → P), and the final three between object perceived and the act of perception (OP → P).[14]

---

12. Hans Jonas, "The Nobility of Sight: A Study in the Phenomenology of the Senses," in *The Phenomenon of Life: Toward a Philosophical Biology* (New York: Harper & Row, 1966), 146.

13. Sweetser, *From Etymology to Pragmatics*, 44.

14. This chart follows the one in Ibarretxe-Antuñano, "Vision Metaphors for the Intellect," 21; reproduced with permission. In keeping with the previous discussion of <effects>, however, I have included this property in both the PR → P and OP → P categories. I have also corrected what seems to be an error in Ibarretxe-Antuñano's representation of <subjectivity> (see the next note). In her charts Ibarretxe-Antuñano further arranges the properties according to their distribution, whether all of the modalities exhibit the property (A) or only some of them do (B). The A/B distribution varies among cultures, so I have not included it here. Ibarretxe-Antuñano does not seem to discuss this possibility, but she only includes the A and B labels on culturally specific charts, suggesting that she also recognizes this variability.

Table 3.3. Distribution of Prototypical Properties in the Modern West

Properties	Vision	Hearing	Touch	Smell	Taste
PR → OP					
<contact>	no	no	yes	no	yes
<closeness>	no	no	yes	yes	yes
<internal>	no	yes	no	yes	yes
<limits>			yes		
<location>	yes	yes			
PR → P					
<detection>	yes	yes	yes	yes	yes
<identification>	yes	yes	yes	no	yes
<voluntary>	yes	no	yes	no	yes
<directness>	yes	no	yes	yes	yes
<effects>		yes	yes	yes	
<correction of hypothesis>	yes	yes		yes	
<subjectivity>[15]			yes	yes	yes
OP → P					
<effects>			yes		
<evaluation>	yes				yes
<briefness>			yes		yes

---

15. In her chart Ibarretxe-Antuñano places <subjectivity> under the category PR → OP; however, as she argues in her dissertation ("Polysemy and Metaphor in Perception Verbs," 155–56), the <subjectivity> property reflects the relationship between the perceiver and the act of perception, a conclusion she maintains in the description of the property in her later article ("Vision Metaphors for the Intellect," 20). The property thus properly belongs to the PR → P category. In the chart, Ibarretxe-Antuñano labels touch and taste as subjective, since both are contact senses. Based on the discussion in

3. PERCEPTION

In Western schemas, sight is considered a distant modality. The perceiver does not need to have physical contact with an object or be in close proximity to it for vision to occur. It thus receives a $_{no}$ tag for <contact> and <closeness>. Touch, on the other hand, requires physical contact and closeness, so it receives a $_{yes}$ tag in <contact> and <closeness>. Since touch and taste do not form hypotheses, they do not receive a tag for <correction of hypothesis>.

Some modalities vacillate between tags, depending upon the context of its usage. For instance, any modality can be voluntary (we can be conscious of seeing, hearing, smelling) or involuntary (we can passively receive light waves, sound waves, or olfactory stimuli without initiating the act). Ibarretxe-Antuñano recognizes this and discusses it in her dissertation, yet she does not note it in her chart, instead tagging a modality according to its default property (i.e., sight as <voluntary $_{yes}$> but hearing as <voluntary $_{no}$>).[16] I have generally preserved Ibarretxe-Antuñano's notation style here, except in cases where the assignation of a property is clearly debatable; however, one should keep in mind that, like any heuristic device, this typology is not as black and white as it first appears. Although one can assign default tags to the properties, one should remember that reality is often more complicated and thus allow for a certain amount of flexibility in the analysis of actual linguistic uses.

As Ibarretxe-Antuñano argues, this typology is influenced by both biology and culture. Biology, for instance, determines what properties are associated with perception in the first place. "Human beings have the same physical configuration and our organs work in the same way; therefore, these prototypical properties do not need to change."[17] Biology, in other words, constrains the properties inherent to the modalities. Cultures, however, determine how these properties are conceived and what values are assigned to them. For instance, in physiological terms, vision and touch are both <internal> processes. "Light waves enter into the eyes, and the skin vibrations ... also trigger the mechanoreceptors that will carry the neural input to the spinal cord."[18] However, while modern Westerners conceive of smell, hearing, and taste as <internal> processes—smells enter into

---

her dissertation ("Polysemy and Metaphor in Perception Verbs," 155–56, 161), subjectivity may also be associated with smell in Western epistemology.

16. Ibarretxe-Antuñano, "Polysemy and Metaphor in Perception Verbs," 149.
17. Ibarretxe-Antuñano, "Vision Metaphors for the Intellect," 27.
18. Ibarretxe-Antuñano, "Polysemy and Metaphor in Perception Verbs," 145.

the nose; sound enters into the ears; food must be put into the mouths to taste it—they do not conceive of vision or touch as <internal> processes. The cultural understanding of perception thus constrains the properties identified with sight and touch, creating a conception of these modalities that is unique to modern Western cultures. Moreover, the values assigned to the modalities are determined by the culture. Since Western cultures conceive of sight as a distant modality (<contact $_{no}$>, <closeness $_{no}$>), sight is considered comparable and thus an objective means of obtaining knowledge. "Objectivity" is a value assigned to sight by the culture, not a property inherent to it. One cannot automatically assume that cultures who do not assign the same properties to sight attribute the same values to it.

Cultures also determine which modalities should be included in the typology to begin with. While modern Western societies tend to follow Aristotle in delineating five senses, Western and non-Western subgroups throughout history have provided alternative schemas, identifying more or fewer perceptual modalities (e.g., two, four, six, or seven) and grouping them differently (e.g., linking touch and taste together). The Hausa of Nigeria, for instance, only recognize two modalities, visual and nonvisual.[19] Their typology would look much different than the one constructed by Ibarretxe-Antuñano for the modern West. In the case of ancient Israel, Yael Avrahami has identified at least seven modalities (sight, hearing, kinesthesia, speech, taste/eating, smell, and touch) and argues that there could be more (e.g., sexuality).[20] A full typology of the Israelite modalities must take this plethora into account.

According to Ibarretxe-Antuñano, these prototypical properties not only account for the concrete nuances of the modalities in different cultures but also help explain the range of metaphorical expressions derived from them. In English, for instance, the semantic range of the verb *to touch* covers not only the physical action of touching ("I *touched* the cat")

---

19. Constance Classen, "Foundations for an Anthropology of the Senses," *International Social Science Journal* 153 (1997): 401; Ian Ritchie, "Fusion of the Faculties: A Study of the Language of the Senses in Hausaland," in Howes, *Varieties of Sensory Experience*, 195.

20. Yael Avrahami, *The Senses of Scripture: Sensory Perception in the Hebrew Bible*, LHBOTS 545 (T&T Clark International, 2011), 109–12. Avrahami, however, notes that sexuality may instead be a "contextual pattern" that is illuminated by more than one sense, rather than a sense in itself (111). Given the strong multimodality of sexual experience and language, I tend to agree.

but also emotional experience ("the music *touched* us deeply") and the verbal treatment of a topic ("he *touched* upon the issue in his speech"). Such polysemy occurs because the prototypical properties associated with each modality are neurologically mapped to varying degrees onto abstract conceptual domains (e.g, emotion, intellectual expression), creating distinct sets of conceptual metaphors.[21] For instance, in the phrase "the music *touched* us," the modern Western conception of touch as a modality that affects its object through close physical contact (<closeness $_{yes}$>, <contact $_{yes}$>, <effects $_{yes}$> $^{OP \rightarrow P}$) is mapped onto the abstract domain of emotion, thereby creating a conceptual metaphor in which emotional change is conceptualized as an act of touching (FEELING IS TOUCHING). The idea that touch is a close modality that requires contact with its object also influences the creation of the phrase "he *touched* upon the incident in his speech" (DEALING WITH IS TOUCHING). Here, however, the <effects> property does not map, while the idea that touch can occur briefly does (<briefness $_{yes}$>).[22] In each case, other properties are not negated, but they do not substantially influence the nuance of the final metaphor. The result is two phrases based on touch that have very different nuances.

Ibarretxe-Antuñano's model is helpful in explaining not only why certain metaphors for perception exist cross-culturally but also why the specific nuances of perceptually based conceptual metaphors for cognition vary across cultures. On the one hand, since biology determines the prototypical properties associated with the modalities, certain typologies of perception will occur cross-culturally, and the mappings based on them will be similar (COGNITION IS SEEING, COGNITION IS HEARING, etc.). On the other hand, since cultures determine which properties and values are assigned to the modalities, typologies will differ, as will the mappings based upon them (e.g., KNOWING IS SMELLING versus GUESSING IS SMELLING).[23]

---

21. Ibarretxe-Antuñano refers to this process as "property selection." Lakoff argues that this selectivity adheres to what he calls the "invariance principle," that is, the idea that in mapping properties, "metaphorical mappings preserve the cognitive typology (that is, the image-schema structure) of the source domain, in a way consistent with the inherent structure of the target domain" (George Lakoff, "The Contemporary Theory of Metaphor," in *Metaphor and Thought*, ed. Andrew Ortony [Cambridge: Cambridge University Press, 1993], 215).

22. See Ibarretxe-Antuñano, "Polysemy and Metaphor in Perception Verbs," 170–72.

23. For a discussion of these examples, see Ibarretxe-Antuñano, "Vision Metaphors for the Intellect," 29.

Cultures that are closer to each other in their conception of the modalities are more likely to attribute similar properties to them and map those properties onto cognition in similar ways. For example, Western cultures in general perceive sight to be the most direct and reliable modality for engaging the environment (<directness $_{yes}$>, <identification $_{yes}$>); hearing, however, is a mediated modality, still capable of identifying objects in the environment but doing so indirectly (i.e., through a sound wave; so <directness $_{no}$>, <identification $_{yes}$>). Since they come from similar cultures, both Spanish and English tend to map these properties of sight onto their conception of cognition. In each locale, the relatively universal metaphor COGNITION IS SEEING is realized as the culturally specific metaphor KNOWING IS SEEING in which knowledge is direct and objective. COGNITION IS HEARING remains an interpersonal form of knowledge (PAYING ATTENTION IS HEARING).[24] Those cultures that vary in their evaluation of the modalities tend to vary in their assignment of properties and the subsequent nuances of their conceptual metaphors. Unlike Western cultures, aboriginal Australian languages conceptualize *hearing* as the most direct mode of engaging the environment (<directness $_{yes}$>, <identification $_{yes}$>). Instead of viewing intellection as sight, these Australian languages view intellection as hearing. The relatively universal metaphor COGNITION IS HEARING is realized as the culturally specific metaphor KNOWING IS HEARING, while COGNITION IS SIGHT remains an interpersonal form of knowledge (e.g., DESIRE IS SIGHT).[25] A typology of prototypical properties can thus help evaluate how a given culture views the modalities, how cognitive metaphors based upon the modalities develop, and how those metaphors differ among cultures.

3.2. A Biblical Paradigm

In the chapters that follow, I use Ibarretxe-Antuñano's model to uncover the nuances of biblical sapiential conceptions of the perceptual modalities and the primary metaphors based upon them. In each chapter I first develop a typology for the modalities among Israelite scribes by outlining the emic conceptualizations of each modality. Admittedly, Israelite literature is not exceedingly forthcoming with its conception of perception. As

---

24. Ibarretxe-Antuñano, "Polysemy and Metaphor in Perception Verbs," 64.
25. Ibarretxe-Antuñano, "Vision Metaphors for the Intellect," 24–28; Caballero and Ibarretxe-Antuñano, "Ways of Perceiving, Moving, and Thinking," 278.

3. PERCEPTION

Avrahami points out, the Israelite conception of the modalities was clearly "somatic," with each modal experience being connected to particular physical organs and their embodied experiences, but the Israelites lacked abstract terminology for each modality and do not detail the mechanisms by which each modality was thought to operate.[26] It is thus difficult to determine what their conception of each modality was. However, by analyzing how the major Hebrew terms for perception are used in the Hebrew Bible and comparing those usages to ancient and modern explanations of perception, the basic contours of the sapiential understanding of the modalities can be deduced.[27]

After outlining its typology, I examine how each modality maps onto conceptions of wisdom in the books of Proverbs, Job, and Qoheleth. Although scholars often use *wisdom* as a standard translation for the Hebrew term חכמה, wisdom here is best understood as a broad semantic domain denoting a range of interrelated Hebrew terms that, when combined, constitute the Israelite and early Jewish conception of cognition. In his commentary on Proverbs, for instance, Fox classifies eleven Hebrew nouns as wisdom terms, and their meanings range from technical expertise (חכמה), discipline (מוסר), and the ability to devise plans (עצה, תחבלות) to intellectual acumen (בינה, שכל, תבונה, תושיה), shrewdness (ערמה, מזמה), and "cognition itself" (דעת).[28] Wisdom, in other words, describes the ability to obtain and retain knowledge about

---

26. As Avrahami states, "the Hebrew Bible offers no nouns that relate to the senses, such as 'sight' or 'smell,' nor does it offer any general terms that describe the sensorium." Only occasionally is an infinitive used in a manner similar to our abstract conception of the senses (e.g., "the seeing [ראות] of the eyes," Qoh 5:10; "walking" [הליכה], Nah 2:6), and these seem to stem from contextual considerations rather than "cultural reasoning (as if there is no abstract perception of action in biblical thought)" (Avrahami, *Senses of Scripture*, 114).

27. As Ibarretxe-Antuñano argues, a perception word alone does not reveal the semantic field of the modality; one must also look at the context in which the term occurs. For example, auditory terms themselves do not mean obey, but "it is in the context of conversation, hence interpersonal relation, that they acquire that meaning." Thus, "I told you to listen" does not imply obedience, while "I told you to listen to your mother" does (Ibarretxe-Antuñano, "Polysemy and Metaphor in Perception Verbs," 66, 117). Therefore, although this study is based upon occurrences of modality terms, it also examines the context in which those terms occur to determine the conception of the modality and mapping that is being put forth.

28. Fox, *Proverbs 1–9*, 28–38.

the world and the understanding of how that knowledge applies to practical, everyday situations.

As Fox has pointed out, Hebrew wisdom terms—as well as their corresponding verbs (e.g., ידע, בין) and other associated terms (e.g., למד, חסב)—are often not sharply distinguished in their applications. The terms בינה and תבונה, for instance, are often used interchangeably and do not reflect distinct forms of cognition. Likewise, although חכמה is frequently used as a general term for wisdom, it is virtually indistinguishable in application from terms such as דעת and תבונה, which often stand parallel to it (e.g., Prov 2:2, 6, 10; 3:13, 19; 5:1; 8:1).[29] To a certain extent, such terminological slippage is to be expected. As Michael Fortescue notes, the semantic fields of cognitive terms throughout the world tend to overlap. In English, for example, we routinely conceptualize cognition as *knowing, considering, recognizing, understanding, thinking*, and so forth without conscious reflection on how these terms vary.[30] So, too, in Hebrew, where any given wisdom term itself can denote a range of cognitive activities, including the faculties of cognition, the cognitive process itself, and the by-products of such cognitive activities. For instance, עצה can denote the ability to "plan" (Job 12:13; 38:2; 42:3), the actual process of "planning" (Prov 20:18), and the result of such planning, that is, "a plan" (Job 29:21; Prov 12:15; 19:20). Similarly, בינה can refer to the individual's ability to reason (Prov 3:5; Sir 38:6) as well as the content produced by that reasoning (Prov 9:10; 30:2–3; Job 28:12, 20; 38:4; Sir 6:35). As Fox notes, such "applications" are not "separate meanings" but rather different "possible realizations of a single meaning."[31] The term בינה *means* reason, but that reason can be realized in an individual's innate ability or in one's words and actions. Thus, although recognizing that there is a semantic distinction between various Hebrew terms for wisdom, it is best to think of wisdom as a cohesive "network of experiential categories" used to conceptualize a wide range of cognitive activities, rather than a specific term (חכמה) or a series of distinct terms (בינה, חכמה, etc.) each representing different forms of cognition.[32]

---

29. Ibid., 28; Fox, "Words for Wisdom," *ZAH* 6 (1993): 150.

30. Michael Fortescue, "Thoughts about Thought," *Cognitive Linguistics* 12 (2001): 16.

31. Fox, "Words for Wisdom," 151; see also the discussion on 154–58, 160.

32. Fortescue ("Thoughts about Thought," 32) uses this phrase with respect to cognition in general. As he states, with cognition "we are dealing with a network of experiential categories that are intertwined in such a way that words used to refer

At the same time, wisdom in ancient scribal circles was not simply a biological process. Although wisdom terms did describe the physiological means by which an individual processed information about the world, they also reflected the expectation that the individual would apply the resulting knowledge to his or her daily interactions. As Fox states, terms such as חכמה and תבונה involve more than "inert knowledge"; one must also "carry out what one knows."[33] Wisdom was an attitude, a moral character, and a practice as much as it was an intellectual capacity, and it required the individual to be willing to embody that attitude in everyday situations.[34] As such, wisdom was a normative concept; that is, it was good to have wisdom, and there was an appropriate way to obtain and use it. Scribal attempts to describe wisdom and the appropriate means of obtaining it are, therefore, epistemological endeavors. They are attempts to describe how human cognition works, how knowledge itself can be acquired, and to what ends it should be put.

Like other abstract terms, biblical wisdom terms describe experiences that are imperceptible to daily perceptual experience. One cannot actually see points, hear thoughts, or grasp a concept. One cannot buy בינה (Prov 4:5), seize מוסר (4:13), or walk on paths of הכמה (4:11). Yet like us, ancient scribes routinely spoke of cognition by means of these concrete experiences. Proverbs 4, for instance, frequently describes the abstract concept of wisdom as something that comes forth from the "mouth" of the teacher (4:5), enters the body of the student through the "ear" (4:20), and is stored in the "heart" (4:4, 21, 23). Wisdom is "heard" (4:1, 10), "seen" (4:21, 25), "grasped" (4:13), and experienced through "walking" (4:11–12, 26–27). In other words, biblical authors relied on metaphors to describe abstract cognitive processes.

Many of these metaphors are primary metaphors; that is, they are basic metaphors derived directly from a "subjective (phenomenological) experience of a basic event" (e.g., MORE IS UP, ANGER IS HEAT, DESIRE IS

---

to them will also tend to overlap in meaning and interact in terms of mutual implications." In his discussion of Qoheleth's epistemology, Fox speaks of a similar "unitary conception of wisdom." Despite its various nuances, wisdom is "a single, known attribute that can be praised, described, and personified without further definition" (Michael V. Fox, "Qohelet's Epistemology," *HUCA* 58 [1987]: 139).

33. Fox, *Proverbs 1–9*, 33.
34. Michael V. Fox, "Ideas of Wisdom in Proverbs 1–9," *JBL* 116 (1997): 620.

HUNGER).³⁵ In the case of wisdom metaphors, primary metaphors often describe the general acquisition and contemplation of factual information, namely, the color of objects, the workings of the human body, or the properties of food. This is information that can be obtained directly through the perceptual modalities and is therefore, at least in theory, accessible to everyone regardless of social class or station. In Proverbs, Job, and Qoheleth, such metaphors tend to fall into one of three semantic categories: (1) those related to learning, understanding, and knowledge (e.g., UNDERSTANDING IS SEEING, KNOWLEDGE IS A WORD); (2) those related to emotional experience (e.g., ENJOYING IS SEEING, FEAR IS A SOFT HEART); and (3) those related to moral judgment (e.g., JUDGING IS TASTING, DISTRESS IS A BITTER SELF).³⁶ The discussion that follows explores these different nuances and examines how the underlying perceptual foundation of these wisdom metaphors contributes to the ability of sages to develop and communicate meaning.

---

35. Grady, "Foundations of Meaning," 27.

36. This distinction between these three sematic categories follows the schema of Avrahami. In her examination of the senses, Avrahami (*Senses of Scripture*, 130–88) identifies six overarching "contextual patterns" (or semantic nuances) associated with each of the senses: (1) the power to help; (2) the power to harm; (3) learning, understanding, and knowledge; (4) emotional experience; (5) moral judgment; and (6) life, experience, and ability. Since the primary metaphors for wisdom tend to fall into the third, fourth, and fifth categories, I limit my discussion in the pages that follow to these three categories, although I recognize that the modalities discussed have other semantic associations.

4
Seeing

In the early twentieth century, scholars commonly dismissed the visual dimension of Israelite culture. The Israelites, they argued, were audiocentric, not visiocentric.[1] However, even a cursory examination of the Hebrew Bible reveals a culture permeated with sight. Not only did the Israelites rely upon sight for their daily functions: they saw the world, people, God, and so on; they also described cognition with visual metaphors. Due to the unique properties associated with sight, the COGNITION IS SEEING metaphor reflected a distinct conception of cognition, one in which cognition was conceived of as a direct, immediate experience.

4.1. Typology of Sight

In the Hebrew Bible, physical sight is clearly connected to the human eye (עין). Visual verbs (ראה, נבט, שזף, etc.) frequently appear in conjunction with עין to denote an individual's physical encounter with the environment. The eyes of miners see precious stones (כל־יקר ראתה עינו, Job 28:10), and the eyes of the scribe see the behavior of his fellow courtiers (אשר ראו עיניך אל־תצא לרב מהר, Prov 25:7–8).[2] Beyond this connec-

---

1. Although scholars did not deny that the Israelites could see, they argued that vision was less important to the Israelite culture, textual production, and religion than audition was. See, for instance, the dismissal of visual cognition by Thorleif Boman, *Hebrew Thought Compared to the Greek*, trans. Jules Moreau, The Library of History and Doctrine (Philadelphia: Westminster, 1961). Michael Carasik and Avrahami, however, have both sufficiently demonstrated that sight was not only valued in ancient Israel but that it was also a prominent modality for engaging the environment. See Michael Carasik, *Theologies of the Mind in Biblical Israel*, StBibLit 85 (New York: Lang, 2006), 32–42; Avrahami, *Senses of Scripture*, 223–76.

2. The examples provided here and in the following discussions are intended to be

tion, however, the Hebrew Bible is unclear about the exact mechanisms of sight. Contemporaneous Greek thinkers such as Alcmaeon of Croton, Empedocles, and Plato described vision as an intraocular light that extends from the eye, connects with an object, and then returns to the eye,[3] and it seems as though some subgroups of Israelite and early Jewish society may have ascribed to a similar extramission theory of vision (<contact yes>, <internal no>). For instance, Philo describes the eyes as "moving forward to meet" (προυπαντιάζω) objects in the environment and "emitting" (ἐκλάμπω) a light toward them (see *Abr.* 150; 157), and the Testament of Job describes the eye as a "lamp" (λύχνος) that looks about (18:3). A few earlier biblical passages also connect the brightening or darkening of the eye to its ability to see (עין + כהה: Gen 27:1; Deut 34:7; 1 Sam 3:2; Job 17:7; Zech 11:17; עין + חשׁך: Ps 69:24; Lam 5:17), which may suggest a belief in the presence of an intraocular light fluctuating within each individual.[4] It

---

illustrative, not exhaustive. For instance, on the connection between the eye and visual verbs in Job, Proverbs, and Qoheleth, one might also see: עין + ראה in Job 7:7, 8; 10:4, 18; 13:1; 19:27; 21:20; 29:11; 34:21; 42:5; Prov 20:12; 23:33; 24:18; Qoh 1:8; 11:7; עין + נבט in Job 39:29; Prov 4:25; עין + שׁזף in Job 20:9; עין + שׁור in Job 24:15; עין + שׁמר in Job 24:15; עין + נצר in Prov 22:12.

3. For a discussion of these Greek thinkers, see David Chidester, *Word and Light: Seeing, Hearing, and Religious Discourse* (Urbana: University of Illinois Press, 1992), 3–4; Francois Viljoen, "A Contextualised Reading of Matthew 6:22-23: 'Your Eye is the Lamp of Your Body,'" *HvTSt* 65 (2009), doi:10.4102/hts.v65i1.152. Other theories also circulated in ancient Greece, such as the intromission theory of the Atomists (in which images of the objects enter into the eyes of the perceiver) or the theory of Aristotle (in which vision resulted from a change in the state of the eye from transparent to light) (Chidester, *Word and Light*, 3–5). These latter theories, however, do not seem reflected in ancient Israel.

4. See also the various passages in which the light of the eyes is connected to life, benefit, or desire, each of which presupposes a conception of the eye as a container for light (e.g., 1 Sam 14:27, 29; Pss 13:4; 38:11; Prov 29:13; see also the discussion in Avrahami, *Senses of Scripture*, 176). To this one might add Job 41:10, in which Leviathan's eyes are described as the "eyelids of dawn," the implication being that light would issue forth from them just as the sun emits light. However, the cosmological nature of the creature, as well as the nonhuman characteristics that are attributed to it (e.g., light issuing forth from its sneezes and mouth, smoke coming from the nostrils, see Job 41:12) make it an unhelpful example for determining how human eyes functioned. Similarly, Daniel's vision of the angelic man with "eyes like torches of fire" (Dan 10:6) does not seem to reflect how Israelites perceived the normal functions of the human eyes. Various scholars use such evidence to argue in favor of an Israelite extramission theory; see, for instance, Viljoen, "Contextualised Reading of Matthew 6:22-23," 3;

is unclear, however, if this light emanated from the eye. Even if it did, the evidence is too sparse to be certain how widespread such a theory may have been.

There was, however, a common belief in antiquity that the eye had the power to adversely affect the object it was directed at (<effects $_{yes}$> $^{OP \rightarrow P}$).[5] Various Sumerian and Akkadian incantations, for instance, promise to protect the individual from eyes that "roam" about, strangle infants, incite discord, and inflict illnesses (e.g., *KTU* 1.96; *CT* 17.33; *VAT* 10018.15).[6] Such incantations presume that the eye had the ability to negatively affect

---

see also studies on the "evil eye" in ancient Israel (see the next note below), most of which assume an extramission theory. The evidence is indeed suggestive but hardly conclusive.

5. I purposefully refrain from referring to this phenomenon as the "evil eye." Scholars commonly assume that the Hebrew Bible had a concept of the evil eye, a belief that "certain individuals, animals, demons, or gods had the power of casting a spell or causing some damaging effect upon every object, animate or inanimate, upon which their glance fell" (John Elliott, "The Evil Eye in the First Testament: The Ecology and Culture of a Pervasive Belief," in *The Bible and the Politics of Exegesis: Essays in Honor of Norman K. Gottwald on His Sixty-Fifth Birthday*, ed. David Jobling, Peggy L. Day, and Gerald T. Shepperd [Cleveland: Pilgrim, 1991], 148). See also Malul, *Knowledge, Control, and Sex*, 209, 286–87, 351; Viljoen, "A Contextualised Reading of Matthew 6:22–23," 3; Schroer and Stabli, *Body Symbolism in the Bible*, 118–21; Nili Wazana, "A Case of the Evil Eye: Qohelet 4:4–8," *JBL* 126 (2007): 685–86. Yet as scholars have increasingly argued, a concept of an evil eye—as a malevolent force with independent agency—is lacking from Hebrew Bible. Passages that mention an "evil eye" (רעע עין/עין רע) (most notably Prov 23:6–8; 28:22; Deut 15:9; 28:54, 56) reflect the character of the individual and his or her inclination to refrain from helping another rather than the eye's ability to physically inflict harm (Avrahami, *Senses of Scripture*, 153; Rivka Ulmer, *The Evil Eye in the Bible and Rabbinic Literature* [Hoboken, NJ: Ktav, 1994], 1–4). Indeed, as Avrahami argues, "it is difficult to determine whether belief in the evil eye was widespread during the biblical period" (*Senses of Scripture*, 152). That said, sight (like touch or hearing) did have the ability to affect, for good or ill, the perceiver and the object perceived (see the following discussion). Thus, while the evil eye may be an inappropriate way of describing the phenomenon, the affective nature of the eye cannot be ignored. For more on the affective nature of sight and the other senses, see Nicole L. Tilford, "The Affective Eye: Re-examining a Biblical Idiom," *BibInt* 23 (2015): 207–21.

6. James Nathan Ford, "Ninety-Nine by the Evil Eye and One from Natural Causes: KTU² 1.96 in Its Near Eastern Context," *UF* 30 (1998): 201–78. For more on Mesopotamian beliefs in the evil eye, see John H. Elliott, *Introduction, Mesopotamia, and Egypt*, vol. 1 of *Beware the Evil Eye: The Evil Eye in the Bible and the Ancient World* (Eugene, OR: Cascade, 2015). But see Marie-Louis Thomsen, "The Evil Eye in Meso-

external objects. Similarly, when Saul "sets his eye upon David" (ויהי ... עוין) in 1 Sam 18:9, he does so with malicious intent, and when Balaam wishes to curse the Israelites in Num 23:13, he must first "look" (ראה) at them. The glances of deities in particular are said to affect the individual. Egyptian coffin texts, for instance, frequently describe the "eye of Horus" as an aggressive agent that "attacks" and "harms" humans in various ways (e.g., CT 3.300f-g; 4.325c; 6.175g-j; 7.60h, 97q, 142b).[7] It is thus no surprise that, when faced with adversity, the biblical Job asks God to "look away" (שעה) from him so that he can have a brief respite from his troubles (Job 7:19; see also 14:16; 40:11-12). According to Meir Malul, this affective nature of sight might also help explain why women needed to be veiled; veils protected women from male gazes while also protecting men from female gazes (e.g., Gen 24:65; Song 4:1, 3; 6:7).[8]

Sight also had the power to affect the perceiver (<effects $_{yes}$> $^{PR \rightarrow P}$). It could elicit emotional responses, as when the sight of a woman evoked desire in a man or vice versa (Gen 29:10-11; 34:2-3; 39:7; Deut 21:11; 2 Sam 11:2-4; Ezek 23:14-17; see, conversely, the elicitation of contempt, madness, envy, or horror in, e.g., Gen 16:4; Deut 28:34; 1 Sam 18:9; Nah 3:7). Sight could also transfer physical properties between entities. As Malul states, "by looking one can not only exert power upon the object of looking (as in the case of the evil eye, e.g.), but also absorb the power [good or ill] of the object that is looked at."[9] Thus, in 2 Kgs 2:9-15 Elisha absorbs the prophetic power of Elijah by seeing him ascend (see also the transference of healing by sight in Num 21:9). By the same rationale, the sight of God had the power to overwhelm the individual, and stories are told of people who were surprised when they saw God and lived (Gen 16:13; 32:30). While the affective nature of sight does not necessitate an extramission theory of vision, it does suggest that sight facilitated the necessary contact for such properties to transfer, even if the mechanics of that contact are unclear (<contact $_{yes?}$>).

More importantly, sight is understood to be a direct experience capable of detecting objects in the external world. Unlike hearing, which

---

potamia," *JNES* 51 (1992): 19-32, who argues that a belief in the malicious effect of the eye may not have been as widespread as it is commonly assumed.

7. Rune Nyord, *Breathing Flesh: Conceptions of the Body in the Ancient Egyptian Coffin Texts*, CNI Publications 37 (Copenhagen: Museum Tusculanum Press, 2009), 194.

8. Malul, *Knowledge, Control, and Sex*, 209, 286-87, 351.

9. Ibid., 351.

provides the listener with secondhand information about the world, sight provides an instantaneous connection between the perceiver and the object perceived, such that no mediating agent is required (<directness $_{yes}$>).[10] The Israelites know what God did to the Egyptians because they saw it with their own eyes (Exod 14:30–31; see the similar appeals to direct experience in Deut 3:21; 4:3; Qoh 5:10; etc.); the sage knows what happens to young men when they are seduced by a "strange woman," because he has seen it happen through his window (Prov 7:6–27). Events consistently happen "before" (‑ל) the eyes, not "in" (‑ב) them (Gen 23:11, 18; 47:19; Exod 7:20; etc.), and this same exterior focus is reflected when 1 Sam 16:7 states that "humans *see before the eyes* [יראה לעינים], but the Lord *sees* according to the heart [יראה ללבב]" (<internal $_{no}$>). The perceiver does not need to be near the object perceived as long as his field of vision remains unobscured by smoke, clouds, or other obstacles (Prov 10:26; Job 22:14) and there is the right amount of external light (Gen 44:3; Exod 10:23; Job 24:15; 28:11; 37:21; 38:15–17) (<closeness $_{no}$>).[11] Abraham can see the entire land of Canaan from a distant mountaintop (Gen 13:14; see also 13:10; 19:28), and Job can see to the highest heavens (Job 22:12; 35:5; see also 2:12; 36:25).

Sight is also distinguished by its "simultaneity of presentation." As Jonas explains, "one glance, an opening of the eyes, discloses a world of co-present qualities spread out in space, ranged in depth, continuing into indefinite distance."[12] With one glance, Lot sees the entire region of the Jordan (וישא־לוט את־עיניו וירא, Gen 13:10), and Abraham sees three

---

10. This <directness> property of sight is well recognized by scholars. See, for instance, Carasik, *Theologies of the Mind*, 39–40; Avrahami, *Senses of Scripture*, 158; Gregory Schmidt Goering, "Sapiential Synesthesia: The Conceptual Blending of Light and Word in Ben Sira's Wisdom Literature," in *Cognitive Linguistic Explorations in Biblical Texts*, ed. Bonnie Howe and Joel B. Green (Berlin: de Gruyter, 2014), 121–44.

11. The need for external light does not preclude an extramission theory. Plato, who advocated for extramission, also stressed the necessity of an external light source for the connection between perceiver and object to be maintained (Chidester, *Word and Light*, 3–4).

12. Hans Jonas, "The Nobility of Sight: A Study in the Phenomenology of the Senses," in *The Phenomenon of Life: Toward a Philosophical Biology* (New York: Harper & Row, 1966), 136; see also 142, 144–45. Jonas draws upon the Greek model of sight to speak of the universal (i.e., Western) properties of sight. However, as the examples above illustrate, the conclusions he reaches in this respect are applicable to Israelite conceptions of sight as well.

distinct visitors approaching (וישא עיניו וירא, Gen 18:2) (so <detection _{yes}> [simultaneity]). Such disclosure is instantaneous and complete. Although he must lift his eyes, Lot does not first see the river and then the hills and vegetation; rather, he sees the entire plain at once (<briefness _{yes}>).[13] Because everything within the field of vision is instantly revealed, space is the primary structuring device for vision.[14] Sight not only detects the location of the object perceived (up, down, left, right, etc.; e.g., Gen 13:14; Prov 4:25) (<location _{yes}>); sight relates the object spatially to other objects within the field of vision (e.g., the youth is "near" [אצל] the strange woman's corner, Prov 7:8). In doing so, sight provides an "instantaneous now," a "continued present" that extends infinitely as long as the eyes are open.[15]

Unlike other modalities, which require conscious effort to focus on particular stimuli (e.g., one voice or one smell among many), sight can easily "pick out ... and attend to one stimuli amid a multitude of input stimuli" (e.g., the sage identifies one youth among many, Prov 7:6–27).[16] Because of this, sight is generally understood to be an effective means of identifying objects and evaluating the environment. Thus Moses sends men into Canaan to "see" (ראה) what the land is like and who lives there (Num 13:1–14:10). Each of these men sees the same thing; each sees a land flowing with milk and honey and identifies the inhabitants as strong men (<identification _{yes}>). Based on this sight, however, they come to different conclusions. Most of the men decide that the people of Canaan are too

---

13. Although the use of two visual phrases "look up" (נשא עין) and "see" (ראה) in these verses indicates two stages of the visual process (opening the eyes and seeing), it does not imply that sight relies on a sequential presentation of material (as hearing or touch do; see below). Once opened, the eyes perceive the entire scene at once, rather than in sequential stages. Ibarretxe-Antuñano ("Polysemy and Metaphor in Perception Verbs," 150–51) argues that, although sight gives the impression of briefness, it is actually "the context and our familiarity with the object perceived" that allows us to recognize items by sight quickly, not the act of perception itself. However, as the Abraham and Lot examples illustrate, context does not always provide us with the sight we expect, and sight cannot always be trusted to provide accurate information. Thus, at least in antiquity, sight could occur quickly (so <briefness _{yes}>).

14. Jonas, "Nobility of Sight," 149–52.

15. Ibid., 144.

16. Sweetser, *From Etymology to Pragmatics*, 32, 38–39. Sweetser's statement is based on the modern understanding of vision's biological processes, but it is confirmed by the biblical data.

strong and that the land is too difficult to occupy (Num 13:32–33); Joshua and Caleb, on the other hand, determine that the land is fair and should be occupied (Num 13:30; 14:6–9). In other words, each party evaluates the situation based on their own sight of it (<evaluation $_{yes}$>).[17] Although the evaluation differs, the sight itself remains the same: the land is fair, and the people are strong (<subjectivity $_{no}$>).

While certain passages extol sight as the most accurate of modalities, especially when compared to hearing (e.g., 1 Kgs 10:7; Job 42:5) (<correction of hypothesis $_{yes}$>), other passages doubt the veracity of sight or recognize its limitations (<correction of hypothesis $_{no}$>).[18] Judah sees Tamar but mistakes her for a prostitute (ויראה יהודה ויחשבה לזונה, Gen 38:15; see also 1 Sam 21:14–16); Job's friends see him but do not recognize him (וישא את־עיניהם מרחוק ולא הכירהו, Job 2:12). In particular, sight has limited value for identifying God and other otherworldly beings. God can pass by the human and not be perceived by sight (e.g., הן יעבר עלי ולא אראה, Job 9:11; see also Gen 18:2; Job 4:16; 23:8–9; 33:14; 34:29), and it often takes a transformative experience to perceive God (e.g., ואחר עורי נקפו־זאת ומבשרי אחזה אלוה, Job 19:25–26).

Finally, sight can be either a voluntary or an involuntary action. On the one hand, the individual must open (פקח) his or her eyes (Job 27:19; 2 Kgs 4:35) and direct them toward the object perceived (see especially the idiom "lift the eyes," נשא עין;[19] e.g., Gen 24:64; Josh 5:13; Ps 121:1; Job 2:12) (<voluntary $_{yes}$>). At the same time, the eye can be opened for the person (Gen 21:19; 2 Kgs 6:17, 20; Isa 35:5; 42:7), and then the object perceived can appear before the individual without his or her volition (Gen 9:14; Song 2:12; esp. with appearances of a divine figure, e.g., Gen 12:7; 17:1; 18:1; Exod 3:16; Num 16:19). People must move away or avert their

---

17. Each party then uses this visual observation to verbally sway the opinions of the Israelites by the report they give. For this secondary step, see the discussion of <evaluation> in hearing below.

18. Ibarretxe-Antuñano ("Polysemy and Metaphor in Perception Verbs," 153) argues that a modality must receive a $_{no}$ tag in <contact> for <correction of hypothesis> to be a property associated with it. As shall be seen in the discussion of touch and ingestion below, this is not always true, which means that an affirmative answer for <correction of hypothesis> cannot determine whether <contact> was perceived to be negative or positive.

19. This idiom is often used in narrative as a "stylistic device to introduce a new episode." See H. F. Fuhs, "מַרְאָה, מַרְאֶה, רְאוּת, רְאִי, רֹאֶה, רָאָה," TDOT 13:215.

eyes; they cannot help but see what happens in front of them (e.g., Gen 21:16) (<voluntary $_{no}$>).

The following typology of sight thus emerges.[20]

Table 4.1. Biblical Typology of Sight

<contact $_{yes?}$>	<directness $_{yes}$>
<closeness $_{no}$>	<effects $_{yes}$> $^{PR \rightarrow P}$
<internal $_{no}$>	<correction of hypothesis $_{yes/no}$>
<location $_{yes}$>	<subjectivity $_{no}$>
<detection $_{yes}$> ^{simultaneity}	<effects $_{yes}$> $^{OP \rightarrow P}$
<identification $_{yes}$>	<evaluation $_{yes}$>
<voluntary $_{yes/no}$>	<briefness $_{yes}$>

4.2. COGNITION IS SEEING

As Grady states, across the globe "virtually any term which conventionally refers to the domain of vision can be used to refer to the domain of intellection: see, blind, obscure, eyes, light, etc."[21] Ancient Israel was no exception. Scribal circles frequently conceptualized cognition as a visual experience, mapping the properties of sight onto the target domains of knowledge acquisition, emotional experience, and moral judgment.

4.2.1. Knowledge Metaphors

Because it is an effective means of identifying objects in the environment, sight is a common source domain for metaphors of knowing and understanding. Take, for example, the book of Qoheleth, one of the clearest epistemological reflections in the Hebrew Bible. As noted above, Qoheleth presents itself as the personal quest of the king of Israel (the Teacher) to analyze the world and understand its contents. According to the Teacher, sight is a direct means of acquiring information about

---

20. As with Western epistemology, <limits> does not seem to be a property associated with sight in ancient Israel.
21. Grady, "Foundations of Meaning," 7.

the world. The Teacher himself "*sees* [ראה]" all the works that are done under the sun" (Qoh 1:14). He sees the activities of human beings and God (3:10; 4:4; 8:16–17), the dichotomy between justice and wickedness (3:16; 4:1, 3; 5:7, 12; 6:1; 7:15; 8:10; 10:5, 7), and life in general (4:15). "By day or by night," he declares, "there is no end of *seeing* [לראות] with the eyes" (8:16).[22] No one has told the Teacher of these things; he has seen them for himself.

While some of these visual passages could refer to concrete observations, they generally connote abstract cognitive activities such as thinking or understanding (CONSIDERING IS SEEING, UNDERSTANDING IS SEEING):

Qoh 2:12   And I turned to *see* [לראות] wisdom, madness, and folly; for who is the person who comes after me? Shall he control[23] that which has already been done?

Qoh 3:10   I have *seen* [ראיתי] the occupations that God has given to the children of humanity to occupy themselves with.

Qoh 8:16–17   When I gave my heart to know [לדעת] wisdom and *to see* [לראות] the work that is done upon the earth … I *saw* [ראה] all the work of God, that no one is able to find out the work that is done under the sun.

The Teacher cannot actually see *every* action that humans take or *every* wicked deed that occurs (Qoh 3:10; 8:16–17). He cannot physically *see* abstract concepts such as wisdom (הכמה), madness (הוללות), or folly (סכלות) (Qoh 2:12; see also 10:5–6). Rather, the visual terminology indicates that the Teacher has *considered* wisdom, folly, and the divine origin

---

22. Literally: "by day or night, they do not see sleep with their eyes." As Seow (*Ecclesiastes*, 289) notes, the phrase is awkward in its present location. At best it is intended as a parenthetical comment in anticipation of the next verse; at worst, it has been "inadvertently transposed" from the following verse. This makes it difficult to interpret. Still, the phrase itself seems to imply that the eyes never close; that is, they do not cease from viewing the world around them.

23. The second half of this verse is awkward in the MT: כי מה האדאם שיבוא אחרי הַמֶּלֶךְ את אשר־כבר עשוהו (lit.: "for what is the man who comes after the king, that which they already do?"). Because the construction המלך את is unusual, Seow emends the MT's noun הַמֶּלֶךְ ("king") to the verb הַמֹּלֵךְ ("to rule, control") (Seow, *Ecclesiastes*, 134).

of human occupations (2:12; 3:10; 8:17) and that he desires to *understand* the work done upon the earth (8:16). As Michael Carasik notes, the term ראה frequently parallels ידע in the Hebrew Bible, often as a near synonym (1 Sam 12:17; 14:38; 23:22, 23; 25:17; 2 Sam 24:13; 1 Kgs 20:7, 22; 2 Kgs 5:7; Jer 2:19; 12:3; Pss 74:9; 138:6; Job 11:11; Isa 29:15) and sometimes as a preliminary stage to it in the epistemological process (1 Sam 24:12; Jer 2:23; 5:1; Ps 31:8).[24] Thus Qoh 3:10 introduces a unit of text in which ראה leads to ידע (see Qoh 3:12, 14). First the Teacher *considers* human occupation; then he *knows* about God and the world (see also ראה וידע in Qoh 6:5). These and other frequent references to sight refer to cognitive perception, to the intellectual endeavor to comprehend and to catalogue the world, not to physical observation.

Such metaphors function by mapping select prototypical properties associated with sight onto the target domain of cognitive knowledge, in this case, sight's properties of <detection $_{yes}$> [simultaneity], <voluntary $_{yes}$>, <directness $_{yes}$>, and <subjectivity $_{no}$>. The Teacher chooses which matters to pursue; he turns to *see* (ראה) the work that is done under the sun (Qoh 2:12; 8:16–17; see also 8:9) (<voluntary $_{yes}$>), but the assumption is that anyone who so chooses can consider the same matters and will have the same information available to him or her (<subjectivity $_{no}$>). Generally, there is no indication that the individual approaches these matters sequentially. The Teacher considers multiple items at once (e.g., wisdom, madness, and folly; *everything* that is done under the sun), which are revealed simultaneously before him (<detection $_{yes}$> [simultaneity]). Moreover, the frequent appeal to the personal nature of the cognitive experience highlights the <directness $_{yes}$> property inherent to the CONSIDERING IS SEEING metaphor. "*I* have seen the occupations of humanity," says the Teacher (Qoh 3:10); "*I* have seen each work of God" (8:17; see also 1:14; 3:16; 4:1, 4; etc.). No one has seen it for him; the Teacher has seen it for himself.

Sight is also used to refer to the individual's ability to draw conclusions from thinking (CONCLUDING IS SEEING).

---

24. Carasik, *Theologies of the Mind*, 39 including nn. 96, 97. The verbs ראה and ידע are not always synonyms, however, since one can see but not know (e.g., Exod 6:3). This supports the idea that the choice to use ראה in Qoheleth and other such literature to indicate knowledge carries with it a set of distinct connotations.

4. SEEING

Qoh 1:10   Is there a matter of which it is said, "*See* [ראה], this is new"? It has already been, in the ages that were before us.[25]

Qoh 2:24   There is nothing better than to eat and drink and enjoy one's work.[26] This, too, I *saw* [ראיתי] is from the hand of God.

Qoh 4:4   And I *saw* [וראיתי] that all toil and all achievement is from one's envy of another.[27]

Again, visual terms reflect the contemplative process. Thus the Teacher *concludes* that all food and drink come from God (e.g., Qoh 2:24; see also 7:14) and that envy causes a person to work hard and succeed (4:4). Similarly, the hypothetical speaker in Qoh 1:10 *concludes* (ראה) that a particular event is new. As Seow states, in these passages ראה does not mean "just to 'look at,' but to recognize as reality."[28] The use of visual terms to mean *conclude* relies on sight's ability to directly identify elements in the environment and evaluate the information it provides (<directness $_{yes}$>, <identification $_{yes}$>, <evaluation $_{yes}$>). The metaphor, however, plays with the dual nature of sight's <correction of hypothesis> property. On the one hand, the Teacher recognizes that people are capable of producing erroneous conclusions (Qoh 1:10) (<correction of hypothesis $_{no}$>). On the other hand, the Teacher uses the directness of sight to lend credibility to his conclusions. Just as he has *seen* directly (ראה, i.e., *considered*) everything that is done under the sun, so his audience should believe his conclusions (2:24; 4:4; see also 2:13; 9:11; etc.). The Teacher's conclusions, the book insists, are correct because they are based on his direct experience (<correction of hypothesis $_{yes}$>).

Sight can also be used as a source domain for the transference of knowledge from one person to the next (TEACHING IS SHOWING).

Qoh 3:18   I said in my heart with regard to human beings that God is testing them to *show* [ולראות] that they are but animals.

---

25. For the difficulties surrounding the construction of this verse, see Seow, *Ecclesiastes*, 110–11.
26. והראה את־נפשו טוב בעמלו (lit. "to see the *nepeš* good in its work").
27. Here following the translation of Seow, *Ecclesiastes*, 179.
28. Ibid., 240.

To teach a person, one "shows" him or her a point. Thus in Qoh 3:18 the Teacher concludes that God tests individuals in order to *teach* (ראה) them that they are the same as animals. As with other knowledge metaphors, this passage maps the <directness $_{yes}$> property of sight onto the domain of knowledge. Just as the Teacher has concluded these matters for himself from direct contemplation, humans understand their bestial nature because God has *shown* it to them directly.

Fox argues that Qoheleth is "revolutionary" in that a "sage chooses to seek out sensory experience as a path to insight."[29] Only rarely, he states, do other sages present their activities as visual observations.[30] While it is certainly true that the book of Qoheleth presents itself as the result of empirical inquiry and favors visually derived cognitive metaphors, other sapiential writers also appeal to visual experience to describe cognitive experience. For instance, in the Babylonian Theodicy, an ancient Near Eastern acrostic poem at least five hundred years older than the book of Qoheleth, the act of seeing a person's distress is equated to the cognitive comprehension of it: "You are kind, my friend; behold my grief. Help me; *look on* [*a-mur*] my distress; know it [*lu-ú ti-i-du*]" (CONSIDERING IS SEEING: Babylonian Theodicy 287–288).[31] Similarly, in Egyptian wisdom literature, where the type of personal experiences valued by Qoheleth is rarely seen as an effective means to obtain knowledge, sight can still be used as a source domain for thinking and learning (CONSIDERING IS SEEING): one is to "search out" (*dʿr*) the nature of humanity (Instruction of Ptahhotep), the advice of one's companions (Amenhetep), and the sayings of one's teachers (Khakheperre-seneb); that is, one is to think about

---

29. Fox, "Qohelet's Epistemology," 142. In making this statement, Fox is commenting particularly on the empirical nature of the Teacher's investigations, who "proceed[s] by seeking experience, observing it, and judging it, and then reporting his perceptions or reactions" (142). While I do not wish to deny the empirical nature of the Teacher's inquiry (he drank wine, acquired wealth, etc.) vis-à-vis a book such as Proverbs, it is my contention that much of Qoheleth's visual language refers to abstract contemplation and in this he was not unique among the sages.

30. Fox, "Qohelet's Epistemology," 145–46. Fox notes, for instance, the observation of a field in Prov 24:30–34 and the observation of a youth's seduction in Prov 7. These, he claims, differ from Qoheleth's position in that they "are not claimed as the source of knowledge or even as its proof" (146).

31. The translation here follows that of Wilfred G. Lambert, "The Babylonian Theodicy," in *Babylonian Wisdom Literature* (Winona Lake, IN: Eisenbrauns, 1996), 63–91.

them and investigate their implications.³² In the biblical book of Job, cognitive metaphors based on sight appear repeatedly as Job and his friends debate their respective positions (e.g., CONSIDERING IS SEEING: Job 5:9, 27; 8:8; 32:11; UNDERSTANDING IS SEEING: 9:10; 11:7; 13:1; 15:17; 24:1; 27:12; 31:21; 34:32; 36:26; CONCLUDING IS SEEING: 4:8; 32:5). Even the biblical book of Proverbs, which is generally considered to have a strong auditory focus, commands its listener to *consider* (ראה) the behavior of ants or the field of the lazy in order to learn about the value of prudence (CONSIDERING IS SEEING: Prov 6:6; 24:32). In fact, the occurrences of עין (eye) in Proverbs outnumber those of אזן (ear) almost four to one.³³ While only a fraction of those are used in cognitive metaphors, it does suggest that Proverbs is not as antivisual as Fox supposes. Indeed, it seems as though vision serves as a natural source domain for the acquisition of knowledge throughout ancient Near Eastern wisdom literature.

4.2.2. Emotion Metaphors

Sight also serves as a source domain for emotional experience. For instance, a person who is happy has a "satisfied" eye (Qoh 2:10; 11:9); a person who is unhappy has an "insatiable" eye (Qoh 1:8; 4:8; Prov 27:20) (SATISFACTION IS A GOOD EYE/DISSATISFACTION IS A BAD EYE). Similarly, to "see good" or "see life" (ראה טוב[ה]/חיים) is to be happy (ENJOYING IS SEEING).³⁴

Job 7:7   Remember that my life is a breath; *my eye* will not again *see good* [לא תשוב עיני לראות טוב].

---

32. Nili Shupak, *Where Can Wisdom Be Found? The Sage's Language in the Bible and in Ancient Egyptian Literature*, OBO 130 (Göttingen: Vandenhoeck & Ruprecht, 1993), 71. For the Instruction of Ptahhotep, see *ANET*, 414, line 463; for the Amenhetep text, see Wolfgang Helck, ed., *Inschriften von Zeitgenossen Amenophis' III*, vol. 21 of *Urkunden der 18. Dynastie*, Urkunden des ægyptischen Altertums 4 (Berlin: Akademie, 1958), 1817, lines 8–9; for a translation of Khakheperre-seneb, see *COS* 1.44:104, recto 1 with n. 5.

33. Carasik, *Theologies of the Mind*, 150–51. See nn. 49–50 therein for specific textual examples.

34. Avrahami, *Senses of Scripture*, 163–64; Fuhs, *TDOT* 13:222. See also sight as a metaphor for hope: "the ways of Tema *look* [הביט]; the ones who travel Sheba wait for them" (Job 6:19) (EXPECTATION IS SEEING).

> Qoh 3:13 It is a gift of God that every human eat and drink and *see good* [ראה טוב] in his toil.

> Qoh 5:17-18 It is fair to eat and drink and *see good* in all the work [ולראות טובה בכל־עמלו] that one works under the sun ... to eat from it [wealth] and to carry his lot and to enjoy his work—this is a gift from God.

> Qoh 9:9 *See* life [ראה חיים] with the wife whom you love.

In his dejected state, Job frets at ever *enjoying* (ראה טוב) life again (Job 7:7; see also 9:25; Qoh 6:6), whereas the Teacher commands his listener to *enjoy* (ראה) life with a good wife (Qoh 9:9; see also 11:7; Prov 15:30).[35] Testing the different aspects of human experience, the Teacher determines that eating and drinking and working are gifts from God; like eating or drinking, one should thus *enjoy* work (Qoh 3:13; 5:17; see also 2:1, 24; 3:22). That ראה [ה]טוב implies enjoyment is made clear in Qoh 5:18, where the phrase "enjoy work" (בעמלו ולשמח) replaces the standard ראה [ה]טוב. The "satisfied eye" or the "eye that sees good," then, indicates the individual's enjoyment of a situation. Such metaphors select the properties <directness $_{yes}$> and <effects $_{yes}$> $^{PR \rightarrow P}$ and map them onto emotional experience. The individual's own, direct experience of events affects his or her emotional state.

4.2.3. Judgment Metaphors

Related to the use of vision to describe mental conclusions, sight also serves as a source domain for evaluative moral judgments (JUDGING IS SEEING).

> Qoh 3:22 I *saw* [וראיתי] that there is nothing better than that an individual enjoy his work, for it is his lot.

> Job 15:15 The stars are not pure *in his eyes* [לא־זכו בעיניו].

> Prov 3:4 And you will find favor and good insight *in the eyes of* God and humanity [בעיני אלהים ואדם].

---

35. This latter example is probably a shortened version of ראה טובה.

Job 32:1 And these three men ceased from answering Job, because he was righteous *in his own eyes* [כי הוא צדיק בעיניו].

Just as the Teacher *concludes* (ראה) that work comes from God (Qoh 2:24), he *judges* (ראה) that it is good, that there is nothing better than that one enjoy one's work (3:22; see also 2:3, 13; 5:17; 10:5). Throughout the Hebrew Bible, "to see that" a matter is good or bad (ראה כי ... טוב/רעה) indicates that one has not only arrived at a conclusion but also formed an opinion or moral judgment based on that conclusion (see, for instance, the positive examples in the first creation story Gen 1:4, 10, 12, 18, 21, 25; and the negative example in Gen 6:5). Similarly, the expression "in the eye(s)" (בעין/בעיני) indicates a personal evaluation of a situation, an opinion about the inherent moral qualities of a thing. The stars are impure "in God's eyes" (לא־זכו בעיניו, Job 15:15; see also 25:5; Prov 24:18); that is, God *judges* them to be so. A person is favorable and wise "in the eyes of God and humanity" (בעיני אלהים ואדם, Prov 3:4). A person can also evaluate his own actions, being wise "in his own eyes" (בעיניו, Prov 26:12; 28:11; see also Job 11:4; 32:1) but not necessarily in the eye of his companions.

As with the CONCLUDING IS SEEING metaphor, JUDGING IS SEEING maps sight's properties of <evaluation $_{yes}$> and <directness $_{yes}$> onto the domain of mental judgment. The Teacher *evaluates* the situation (Qoh 3:22); God *judges* (Job 15:15). With this metaphorical mapping, however, other properties shift. Although physical sight is understood to occur outside the eyes, moral sight occurs "within" (ב־) the eyes (e.g., Prov 3:4; Job 32:1). The property <internal $_{no}$> becomes <internal $_{yes}$>. Similarly, although sight itself is understood to remain consistent across individuals (<subjective $_{no}$>), moral sight is subjective (<subjective $_{yes}$>). As Avrahami argues, such phrases as "in the eyes of" "often indicate the existence of an opinion that is personal, subjective, and unconventional."[36] Thus, individuals are described as having opinions that deviate from others, and such deviations are often condemned as erroneous (Prov 3:7; 12:15; 21:2; 26:5, 12, 16; 28:11; 30:12; Job 19:15; 32:1) (<correction of hypothesis $_{no}$>). Why these properties shift is unclear, although perhaps the possibility is inherent in the ancient conception of sight itself. Although sight was generally perceived to be an external modality, the references to an intraocular light noted above suggest that there was also an inter-

---

36. Avrahami, *Senses of Scripture*, 168; see also the discussion on 258–62.

nal component to sight, at least in the initial stages. If so, this might help explain the mapping of <internal ~yes~> as well as <subjectivity ~yes~>.[37] As Sweetser and Ibarretxe-Antuñano both argue, across cultures internal modalities tend toward the subjective. In fact, Ibarretxe-Antuñano argues that a modality can only be subjective if it is also <internal> and <close>.[38] Given that closeness is not required in ancient Israel, it seems likely that the presence of only one of these properties (<internal> or <close>) is enough to allow for the possibility of <subjectivity>, although having both properties would make <subjectivity ~yes~> much more probable.[39] At any rate, if the evaluative qualities of vision were linked to the internal components of the eye when they were mapped onto the target domain of judgment, then it is reasonable to suggest that <subjectivity ~yes~> developed as a natural by-product of this mapping. What is clear is that JUDGING IS SEEING, unlike CONCLUDING IS SEEING, presupposes a certain degree of internal subjectivity that may or may not have been beneficial to the individual.

4.3. SUMMARY

In summation, there are at least seven common iterations of the cognition is seeing metaphor among Israelite and early Jewish scribes, each of which maps certain properties onto cognition.[40]

Table 4.2. Metaphorical Mappings: COGNITION IS SEEING

CONSIDERING IS SEEING
    <detection ~yes~> [simultaneity], <voluntary ~yes~>, <directness ~yes~>, <subjectivity ~no~>

UNDERSTANDING IS SEEING
    <detection ~yes~> [simultaneity], <voluntary ~yes~>, <directness ~yes~>, <subjectivity ~no~>

---

37. The reversal in <subjectivity> might also stem from the idea that people see different things if their location is different.

38. Ibarretxe-Antuñano, "Polysemy and Metaphor in Perception Verbs," 156.

39. So also Sweetser, *From Etymology to Pragmatics*, 41–44.

40. This chart and those in the following chapters are modeled after similar ones in Ibarretxe-Antuñano, "Polysemy and Metaphor in Perception Verbs," 177.

CONCLUDING IS SEEING
   <directness $_{yes}$>, <identification $_{yes}$>, <evaluation $_{yes}$>, <correction of hypothesis $_{yes/no}$>
TEACHING IS SHOWING
   <directness $_{yes}$>
SATISFACTION IS A GOOD EYE/DISSATISFACTION IS A BAD EYE
   <directness $_{yes}$>, <effects $_{yes}$> $^{PR \to P}$
ENJOYING IS SEEING
   <directness $_{yes}$>, <effects $_{yes}$> $^{PR \to P}$
JUDGING IS SEEING
   <evaluation $_{yes}$>, <directness $_{yes}$>, <internal $_{yes}$>, <subjective $_{yes}$>

The specific nuances of these metaphors vary depending upon which properties are selected. The mapping of <effects $_{yes}$> $^{PR \to P}$ develops emotive metaphors, while <evaluation $_{yes}$> develops metaphors of concluding and judging. Common to them all, however, is the mapping of sight's <directness $_{yes}$> property onto the cognitive domain. Considering, emoting, and judging are all personal events that an individual engages in directly. The COGNITION IS SEEING metaphor in ancient sapiential literature is thus characterized by its directness, and its local iterations form a distinct collection of metaphors by which Israelites and early Jewish scribes expressed their understanding of cognition as a direct, immediate experience.

5
Hearing/Speaking

Early twentieth-century scholars focused almost exclusively on the oral-auditory dimension of Hebrew epistemology, and for good reason.[1] From the first chapter in Genesis, speech and hearing pervade the biblical text. God speaks creation into existence, and people discover their world through speech and sound. Not surprisingly, then, hearing and speech each serve as a source domain for cognition, especially cognition that is indirect and sequential.

As Avrahami rightly notes, hearing and speaking were two distinct modalities in Hebrew epistemology.[2] Each had its own way of engaging the environment and its own properties associated with it. However, hearing and speech were closely linked, physically and conceptually. More than any other two modalities, hearing and speech routinely functioned as an integrated unit, such that the two modalities were effectively two sides of the same perceptual process.[3] Consequently, cognitive metaphors based upon hearing and speaking are closely related and in some cases even draw upon the properties of each without discrimination. It is thus appropriate to discuss hearing and speaking as a unit, recognizing their distinctiveness as well as their areas of convergence.

---

1. See, for example, the auditory focus of Boman, *Hebrew Thought Compared to the Greek*.
2. Avrahami, *Senses of Scripture*, 84–93.
3. Malul (*Knowledge, Control, and Sex*, 102 n. 2) argues that speech is "not strictly a sense" but a "sub-sense" of hearing; however, in his discussion and charts he still separates it from hearing, perhaps because of the "substantial role" the modality plays in Israelite epistemology. Avrahami (*Senses of Scripture*, 85–90) also acknowledges these linkages, especially in the semantic domains of cognition, obedience, and divine help.

5.1. Typology of Hearing and Speaking

As with sight, hearing in the Hebrew Bible is clearly connected to a specific physical organ, the ear (אזן), which commonly appears together with auditory verbs such as שמע and קשב (Gen 23:13; Num 11:1; Deut 5:1; 2 Chr 6:40; Ps 17:6; etc.). Like sight, the exact mechanisms of hearing are unclear. According to the ancient Greeks, hearing resulted "from a blow [*plēgē*] that struck the air, traveled over some distance, and impacted upon the ear,"[4] and it is possible that the Israelites held similar theories. What is at least clear is that hearing was thought to be an involuntary, internal modality. An external sound enters "into the ears" of its own volition (Gen 20:8; 23:10, 13, 16; 44:18; 50:4; etc.) (<internal $_{yes}$>), and the perceiver generally has no control over its production or reception (Gen 12:1–3; 1 Sam 3:4–18; Job 4:12) (<voluntary $_{no}$>).[5] More importantly, in hearing the perceiver does not engage the object itself but a third party, the קול ("sound") (<directness $_{no}$>). There is no contact between the perceiver and the object perceived (<contact $_{no}$>), and, as Jonas states, "what the sound immediately discloses is not an object but a dynamical event [walking, speaking, etc.] at the locus of the object."[6] Thus the first humans do not experience God himself in the garden but the קול of God walking (Gen 3:8, 10), and Lamech's wives do not experience their husband but the קול of their husband's voice (Gen 4:23). Unlike the spatial modality of sight, then, hearing

---

4. Chidester, *Word and Light*, 6. Thus, Empedocles likened the ear to a "bell" or "gong" that reverberated when struck by sound, and Anaxagoras described speech as an "echo" created when breath crashed into the air.

5. Jonas, "Nobility of Sight," 139. The phrase "uncover the ear" (גלה אזן) indicates an act of speech that is voluntary on the part of the speaker but not on the part of the listener (e.g., Ruth 4:4; 1 Sam 9:15; 20:2, 12, 13). On the other hand, passages that mention "opening" (פתח, Isa 35:5; 48:8; 50:5), "closing" (עלם, Lam 3:56), or "turning" (נטה, 2 Kgs 19:16; Ps 17:6; Prov 4:20; 5:1, 13; 22:17) the ear generally appear to be metaphorical in nature, referring either to an act of help or to a state of cognitive readiness (or a combination of the two) and not the physical status of the ear itself. The one possible exception is Isa 35:5, where God "opens" (פתח) the ear of the deaf. This event, however, is beyond the volition of the individual receiving the healing and does not represent a voluntary condition. For more information on these phrases as metaphors of help, see Avrahami, *Senses of Scripture*, 131. For their use as metaphors for cognition, see the discussion of PAYING ATTENTION IS HEARING below.

6. Jonas, "Nobility of Sight," 137. The indirectness of hearing in Israelite literature has been well recognized. See, for instance, Avrahami, *Senses of Scripture*, 158; Carasik, *Theologies of the Mind*, 154; Goering, "Sapiential Synesthesia."

provides a temporal orientation to the environment. One detects the sound of one footstep and then another; one hears one word and then the next (<detection ₍yes₎> [sequence]). Because of this, the amount of time it takes to hear a sound varies according to the duration of the sound. A trumpet blast, for instance, can be "long" (משך, lit. "drawn out," Exod 19:13; Josh 6:5), while a "word" (דבר) can be a brief "whisper" (שמץ, Job 26:14) or a "small" (קטן) or "great" (גדול) sound (1 Sam 22:15; 25:36).[7] Hearing, then, is not an inherently brief modality (<briefness ₍no₎>).

Like hearing, speech is connected to a particular physical organ (פה, "mouth") and its component parts (שפה, "lip"; לשון, "tongue"), each of which frequently appears with verbs of saying, especially אמר and דבר (Gen 45:12; Exod 4:12; Ps 12:4; etc.). As the obverse of hearing, speech occurs when a sound issues forth from the mouth of the individual and is directed outward (<internal ₍no₎>). Unlike hearing, speech is a voluntary modality (<voluntary ₍yes₎>). The individual can choose when to speak and when to remain silent (Gen 50:4; Judg 18:25; 1 Sam 3:10, 18), and an individual's character is often measured by his or her ability to know which action is appropriate at any given moment (Prov 10:19; 11:13; Qoh 3:7; 5:1, 3). However, in speech there is still no contact between the speaker and the object of perception, the listener.[8] Like hearing, speech is an indirect modality, connecting the speaker to the listener only via sound (<contact ₍no₎>, <direct ₍no₎>). It, too, then is temporal, interacting with the listener through the sequential production of דברים, אמרים, or מלין ("words"; see, for instance, the sequential dialogue between Abraham and the Lord in Gen 18:20–33 or the litany of Judah's questions in Gen 44:16). However, although speech is temporal, the property of <detection> itself does not

---

7. While 1 Sam 22:15 could use דבר in a more generic sense to mean "anything," 1 Sam 25:36 clearly uses דבר to refer to a verbal action that Abigail decided not to take: "she did not declare to him a word, small or great [לא־הגידה לו דבר קטן וגדול], until the light of morning." It is plausible that Ahimelech's declaration in 1 Sam 22:15—"your servant did not know any of this דבר, small or great"—similarly refers to the idea that Ahimelech had not heard even a whisper of David's activities, especially when Saul condemns the priests two verses later for failing to disclose (גלה) the matter to him.

8. Unlike ordinary sound, the modality of speech operates under the presumption that there is an entity waiting to receive it, the listener. Under Ibarretxe-Antuñano's rubric, this listener seems most appropriately classified as the object perceived. Ibarretxe-Antuñano, however, does not seem to discuss speech as a separate modality, incorporating it instead into her discussions of hearing.

apply to the modality, as the goal of speech is not to acquire information about the environment but to transmit information into it.

Since neither speech nor hearing requires contact between the perceiver and object perceived, closeness is a negative property in both (<closeness $_{no}$>). The Egyptians can "hear" (שמע) Joseph weeping, even though they are in an entirely different room (Gen 45:2; see also Ezra 3:13), and an Assyrian messenger can "call" (קרא) to the people of Judah from outside the city walls (2 Kgs 18:17–36, esp. v. 28). Likewise, God can hear humanity's cries from the highest heavens (Gen 21:17; 1 Kgs 8:32, 34, 36, 39, 43; etc.) and speak to them from the same (Gen 21:17; 22:11, 15). Hearing can identify and locate the object perceived, although it is not as precise as sight. Hearing, for instance, can detect footsteps entering a room and identify them as such, but not to whom those footsteps belong (1 Kgs 14:6;[9] see also Num 7:89; 1 Sam 4:6; 2 Sam 5:24 // 1 Chr 14:15; 1 Kgs 1:41–45; 6:7) (<identification $_{yes}$>, <location $_{yes}$>). Speech, on the other hand, has no such need, and the properties are irrelevant to it.

Moreover, hearing often provides only indirect information about a situation. For instance, Job knows about the death of his livestock, servants, and children only because another person has reported it him (Job 1:14–19; see also Gen 14:14; 24:30; 29:13; etc.). Because it does not directly engage the object perceived, hearing is not as reliable of a source of information as sight or even touch. Hearing can, for instance, correctly identify a sound of a trumpet blast as the sound of a successful campaign (e.g., 1 Sam 13:3–4) or misidentify the sound of revelry in the Israelite camp as a sound of war (Exod 32:17) (<correction of hypothesis $_{yes/no}$>). This is particularly problematic when multiple stimuli are present, for, unlike sight, hearing has difficulty distinguishing one sound from the next (e.g., sounds of weeping from sounds of joy, Ezra 3:12–13). Speech in particular can be manipulated, providing the hearer with false information (Gen 34:13; 39:19; Prov 20:14; 26:19; 28:24; Job 13:7; 27:4). For this reason, passages frequently value other modalities more than hearing. Job, for instance, proclaims that, although he has heard of God by the "hearing of the ear" (לשמע־אזן), now he is vindicated, because he has seen God directly with his eye (עיני ראתך, Job 42:5; see also Gen 18:21; 42:20). Similarly, in Gen

---

9. In 1 Kgs 14:6 the blind Ahijah identifies Jeroboam's wife not because he heard her footsteps but because the Lord told her he was coming. In this case, one form of hearing is reliable (God's report), while another (the sound of footsteps) only allows him to identify that type of sound (footsteps) but not the creator of the sound.

27:22 Isaac mistrusts the information provided by hearing ("the voice is the voice of Jacob," הקל קול יעקב) in favor of what his hands tell him ("the hands are the hands of Esau," הידים ידי עשו). Still, some passages validate hearing, privileging information provided by hearing, especially when visual data is lacking. Thus Deut 4:12 declares that when God spoke to the Israelites from the fire they "heard the *sound of words* [קול דברים] but saw no form [ותמונה אינכם ראים], only a *sound* [זולתי קול]" (see also the value of teaching future generations about God, e.g., Deut 6:4–7).

Although speech itself does not evaluate or formulate hypotheses about the object perceived,[10] it can sway the impression of those who hear it, for good or for ill. Thus the prophets use speech to encourage certain behaviors among the Israelites (e.g., care for the poor, Amos 2:6–8; trust in God's saving power, Nah 1:12–15) and discourage others (e.g., following foreign deities, 1 Kgs 18:17–40; migrating to Egypt, Jer 42:1–22). Based on these and other sounds, hearers assess their environment (<evaluation $_{yes}$>), and false information can lead to adverse judgments. Listening to the words of the spies, the Israelites decide not to go to war with the Canaanites, which incites God's anger against them (Num 13:26–14:23).[11] Speech, then, is a subjective modality; the speaker influences the act of speaking (<subjective $_{yes}$>). Hearing, however, is not subjective; like sight, the listener can formulate hypotheses and evaluations based on hearing, but the listener cannot influence the act of hearing itself (<subjective $_{no}$>).

Finally, like sight, hearing often elicits an emotional response. Thus the hearts of the Canaanite kings are dismayed when they hear of the Lord's activities on behalf of his people (Josh 2:11; 5:1; 10:1–2), and God is wrathful when he hears the rebellious words of the Israelites (Deut 1:34) (<effects $_{yes}$> $^{PR \to P}$). Conversely, because the one who hears is the object of speech, speech can affect its object (Gen 50:21; Ruth 2:13) (<effects $_{yes}$> $^{OP \to P}$). Thus, "a gentle answer averts rage, but a harsh word [דבר] kindles anger" (Prov 15:1; see also 15:23). Speech can also affect the speaker (<effects $_{yes}$> $^{PR \to P}$). For instance, Elihu feels compelled to speak so that he might find relief (וירוח־לי, lit. "it be wide for me," Job 32:20; see also 1 Sam 1:16 and, conversely, Job 16:6). Because speech could affect the listener, the Israelites took care to regulate it. Thus Proverbs advises the student to

---

10. That is, the properties <correction of hypothesis> and <evaluation> are not applicable.

11. See also the discussion of this passage in §4.1 above.

"withhold speech" (e.g., חושך שפתיו, Prov 10:19), and Qoheleth counsels his audience to "let [their] words be few" (יהיו דבריך מעטים, Qoh 5:1).

The properties of hearing and speech can be summarized as follows.[12]

Table 5.1. Biblical Typology of Hearing and Speaking

Hearing		Speech	
<contact $_{no}$>	<directness $_{no}$>	<contact $_{no}$>	<directness $_{no}$>
<closeness $_{no}$>	<effects $_{yes}$> $^{PR \to P}$	<closeness $_{no}$>	<effects $_{yes}$> $^{PR \to P}$
<internal $_{yes}$>	< cor. hyp. $_{yes/no}$>	<internal $_{no}$>	
<location $_{yes}$>	<subjectivity $_{no}$>		<subjectivity $_{yes}$>
<detection $_{yes}$> ^{sequence}	<effects $_{no}$> $^{OP \to P}$		<effects $_{yes}$> $^{OP \to P}$
<identification $_{yes}$>	<evaluation $_{yes}$>		
<voluntary $_{no}$>	<briefness $_{no}$>	<voluntary $_{yes}$>	<briefness $_{no}$>

5.2. COGNITION IS HEARING/SPEAKING

According to Carasik, in the Hebrew Bible "the directive 'hear!' [שמע] is always used in its literal sense, indicating an instruction or request to listen to actual sounds, ordinarily words." He goes on to state that "the Israelite metaphor for thought was a *visual image*. It gives a dimension to ראה that שמע does not have."[13] Speech, Carasik argues, could have metaphorical dimensions in certain contexts, but hearing referred only to a physical act.[14] On the one hand, Carasik is operating with a different conception of meta-

---

12. Again, the property of <limits> does not seem applicable for hearing or speech. As noted above, since speech does not detect objects, other properties are also not applicable to speech: <location>, <correctness of hypothesis>, and <evaluation>.

13. Carasik, *Theologies of the Mind*, 41, emphasis original. Carasik briefly mentions (in a note) that the imperative of שמע could mean "heed" or "obey." He also notes that hearing could "bring knowledge" and "serve as a model for mental representations of the world" (as when God commands Ezekiel to hear words in his ear, ובאזניך שמע, Ezek 3:10). To him, however, these exceptions are trivial when compared to vision. Vision, he declares, was by far the primary means of conceptualizing thought in ancient Israel; hearing was not (38–39).

14. Ibid., 93–104.

phor than the one presumed in this study, which leads him to interpret the data differently. For him, the imperative of ראה is metaphorical because it can refer to "an invitation to be aware of an intangible situation," while שמע is literal because it is always connected to physical hearing.[15] However, as this study has already shown, the sharp distinction between literal and metaphorical that Carasik presumes does not adequately represent how humans develop meaning. There is an intimate connection between the physical and abstract dimensions of human thought, such that even the most abstract metaphorical phrase flows naturally from and reflects concrete experiences. Although one cannot deny the prevalence of sight and speech as source domains for cognition, hearing itself did not lack metaphorical extensions. In sapiential literature, both speech and hearing could serve as a source domain for metaphors of cognition, especially metaphors of knowing.

5.2.1. Knowledge Metaphors

As Carasik recognizes, in the Hebrew Bible cognition is often conceptualized as a mental dialogue (THINKING IS SPEAKING).

> Job 1:5   For Job *said* [אמר], "Perhaps my sons have sinned and cursed[16] God in their hearts."
>
> Job 7:4   If I lie down and *say* [ואמרתי], "When will I rise?"
>
> Job 32:7   I *said* [אמרתי], "Let days speak and many years make known wisdom."

In each of these verses the verb אמר ("to say") introduces the internal dialogue of the speaker. In Job 1:5, for instance, Job rationalizes his daily sacrificial practices, arguing that he should perform a sacrifice in case his children have sinned. No external listener is specified,[17] and it is unlikely

---

15. Ibid., 41.
16. Literally "bless" (ברך). According to Habel (*Book of Job*, 88), the use of the term ברך here is a "deliberate literary technique to heighten the radical nature of this unmentionable sin by employing an antonym to describe it." On the other hand, it could be a euphemism inserted by ancient scribes to "soften" the language of the text.
17. This statement occurs in the narrative portion of Job before his friends arrive.

that Job would feel the need to justify his sacrificial actions to another; rather, the passage records the internal thoughts of Job as he conducts his affairs. Similarly, Job's nocturnal musings, although they could theoretically be directed at his wife, do not specify a listener and probably refer to his own internal dialogue (Job 7:4). Elihu's comment in Job 32:7 certainly refers to internal speech, since in the previous verse he states that he was afraid to declare his opinion to Job (see also Job 7:13; 9:27; 24:15; 29:18; Prov 5:12; Qoh 7:23; etc.).

While אמר by itself can indicate thought, according to Carasik, "when a biblical writer wishes to reveal the contents of someone's thought, it [typically] requires the combination of a verb of saying with some form of the word לב."[18] Thus, the לב speaks.

Prov 15:28 The heart [לב] of the righteous *utters* [יהגה] to *answer* [לענות], but the mouth of the wicked pours out evil.

Prov 23:33 Your heart [ולבך] will *speak* [ידבר] perversities.

As in the Job passages above, these Proverb passages indicate cognitive speech, not concrete speech. In Prov 15:28, for instance, the heart of the righteous הגה ("utters under one's breath"). While הגה could imply an

---

18. Carasik, *Theologies of the Mind*, 93. Carasik uses a variety of indicators to determine when a verb of speech refers to concrete speech and when it refers to thought: (1) the presence of an interlocutor/listener indicates concrete action; the absence indicates thought; (2) speech within speech indicates thought; (3) the use of an introductory particle (e.g., כי, הנה, אשר, פן) often indicates thought; (4) when all else fails, context often provides the indication of whether thought or physical action is implied (100). By such criteria Carasik identifies about 350 occurrences (of the 5,298 in the Hebrew Bible) in which אמר serves as a mental function. Those in wisdom literature include: Job 1:5; 7:4, 13; 9:27; 22:29; 24:15; 29:18; 31:24; 32:7, 13; 38:11; Prov 5:12; 20:9, 22; 24:29; 28:24; 30:9, 20; Qoh 1:16; 2:1, 2, 15; 3:17, 18; 6:3; 7:10, 23; 8:14, 17; 9:16; 12:1. For Carasik's complete list, see Michael Carasik, "Theologies of the Mind in Biblical Israel" (PhD diss., Brandies University, 1996), 120 n. 41. According to Carasik, however, the clearest indicator of cognitive speech is often the organ that performs the speech act. When the verb occurs with a physical organ (mouth, lips, etc.), it refers to physical action; when it occurs with לב, it indicates thought (94–96). This is especially true of verbal passages without אמר (i.e., with דבר, הגה, שיח, etc.). Carasik admits, however, that such a control is not always present or accurate. For instance, of the 350 occurrences of אמר that indicate cognitive functions, only thirty-four are paired with לב (102).

intelligible sound, here it probably refers to an internal activity, a uttering of the לב to itself (see also Prov 24:2).[19] Unlike the wicked, who are quick with their words, the righteous deliberately *consider* how they should answer. Similarly, when the לב "speaks" (דבר) in Prov 23:33, it *thinks* perversities. In such cases, the לב is the speaker of the discourse and functions as a metonymy for the person as a whole. Elsewhere, however, the לב is the one who hears the cognitive discourse.

> Qoh 1:16   I *spoke* [דברתי], I with my heart [אני עם־לבי], *saying* [לאמר], "Indeed, I have grown great and added wisdom."

> Qoh 2:1   I *said* [אמרתי], I in my heart [אני בלבי], "Let us go; let us test joy and see good. But indeed, this, too, vanity."

Here the Teacher is conceptualized as a bifurcated entity made up of a core Essence ("that which makes [him] unique," his "I") and a separate Self (a לב, a rational center).[20] This Self is conceptualized as a person capable of hearing audible discourse (THE SELF IS A PERSON). When the Teacher thinks, his Essence speaks to his Self, giving it information about the world that it cannot directly access. Thus the Teacher describes thought as a conversation "with" (עם) or "in" (ב־) his לב (Qoh 1:16; 2:1; see also Qoh 2:15a). These passages, then, reflect a simple compound metaphor in which the THINKING IS SPEAKING metaphor has combined with the conceptualization of THE SELF IS A PERSON to convey the idea that THINKING IS SPEAKING TO ONE'S SELF.

---

19. Carasik, *Theologies of the Mind*, 94. For physical "uttering" in wisdom literature, see also Job 27:4, 37:2, and Prov 8:7, although the last could possibly refer to thought as well (95).

20. As Lakoff and Johnson (*Philosophy in the Flesh*, 267–89) argue, this bifurcation is a common cross-cultural conception for the human individual. According to this conceptualization, the individual consists of a basic Subject—"that aspect of a person that is the experiencing consciousness and locus of reason, will, and judgment" (269)—and various Selves (a moral self, a physical self, a social self, etc.). The Essence of the individual (that which "makes you unique, that make you *you*," 282) is part of the Subject. The Subject and Selves of an individual relate to another as one person would relate to another, as in this case through speech. According to Lakoff and Johnson, the Subject/Essence takes the dominant position in this metaphor, controlling its various Selves. See also Kathleen Ahrens, "Conceptual Metaphors of the 'Self,'" *HPKU Papers in Applied Language Studies* 12 (2008): 47–67.

Yet with or without לב, a verb indicating cognitive speech is frequently followed by the content of that speech, most commonly in the form of a direct quotation.[21] Thus Qoh 1:16, 2:1, Job 1:5, 7:4, and Prov 23:33 are each followed by a direct recitation of the words that the individual thinks.[22] Job *thinks*, "Perhaps my sons have sinned..." (Job 1:5), and the Teacher *thinks*, "I have grown great and added wisdom" (Qoh 1:16). The nominal forms of אמר, דבר, and מלין themselves seem to be reserved for cases where a sound is directed externally to another person; however, the content of cognition is clearly conceived of as words produced in a sequential order, one thought after another (IDEAS ARE WORDS). Such words can stay within the individual, with only the heart listening (Prov 23:33; Qoh 2:1; 1:16), or they can be externalized (i.e., one can "think out loud"), and it is not always clear which is intended. Job 1:5 and 7:4 could each refer to Job's internal dialogue, or they could reflect his vocalized thoughts. The same ambiguity is also present with the noun שיח, with which it is not always clear if the "complaint" or "musing" of the individual occurs audibly or silently (see Job 7:11, 13; 9:27; 23:2; Prov 23:29).[23] As Carasik states, "unless a specific point is to be made, it is left indeterminate whether this speech was audible or internal"; that is, the Hebrew lacked "interest in the rigorous separation of the two categories."[24]

As with visual metaphors of cognition, such oral metaphors function by mapping the properties of speech onto the target domain of cognition. First, cognitive speech is voluntary; as with physical speech, the individual chooses of his or her own volition when to initiate the act of thinking (e.g., Job 1:5; 7:4) (<voluntary $_{yes}$>). It is also subjective; the לב can speak truth or

---

21. Exceptions to this general trend include Prov 15:28, where cognitive speech is clearly implied but the content is not recorded, probably because the point of the proverb is to indicate that the wise person considers his or her words before speaking them. See also the use of שיח (discussed below) and Qoh 8:17, where individuals are discredited who "claim to know wisdom (אמר־יאמר החכם לדעת)." Qoheleth 3:18 introduces the content of the Teacher's thought process with the particle -ש, but this verse may be more illustrative of the CONCLUDING IS SPEAKING metaphor (see below) than THINKING IS SPEAKING.

22. Proverbs 23:33 is initially followed by the noun תהפכות ("perversities"), but the content of these perversities is recorded two verses later in Prov 23:35.

23. Carasik, *Theologies of the Mind*, 96–98. The clearest example of שיח as internal speech, noted by Carasik, is found in the story of Hannah, whose silent prayer is described as her שיח (1 Sam 1:10–18, esp. 1:16).

24. Ibid., 98.

falsehood (e.g., Prov 23:33; 24:2; see also Job 1:5) (<subjective ᵧₑₛ>). More importantly, cognitive speech is sequential and indirect (<directness ₙₒ>). Like verbal speech, cognitive speech relays information word by word, question by question, to the intended object (the thinker) that it otherwise would not have access to; that is, the word itself is a mediator of knowledge. Job, for instance, reveals the reason for his actions through the sequence of his words (Job 1:5), and the heart of the righteous ponders what it is to answer through a sequence of utterances (Prov 15:28). THINKING IS SPEAKING TO ONE'S SELF preserves this metaphorical mapping. The לב itself does not know of the great wisdom of the Teacher (Qoh 1:16) or that it should test joy (2:1), save that the I of the Teacher tells it so.[25] Metaphors of cognitive speech also preserve the <internal ₙₒ> property of physical speaking. Although cognitive speech occurs within the individual, the activity itself is conceptualized as an external action. Thus, in THINKING IS SPEAKING the thought is directed *out* of its point of origin (the thinker) toward an unspecified object, while in THINKING IS SPEAKING TO ONE'S SELF it is directed toward another part of the individual (the לב).

Like vision, speech can also serve as a source domain for conclusions drawn from thinking (CONCLUDING IS SPEAKING).

Job 22:29   When [others] are humiliated, then you will *say* [ותאמר], "It is pride; the lowly of eyes are saved."

Qoh 6:3   I *said* [אמרתי], "A stillborn is better than he."

Qoh 9:16   And I *said* [ואמרתי אני], "Wisdom is better than might."

According to Eliphaz, if Job accepted traditional wisdom, he would *conclude* (אמר) that humiliation is the result of pride (Job 22:29). On the other hand, the Teacher's own investigations led him to *conclude* that it is better to be stillborn than to live a long life without enjoying it (Qoh 6:3) and that having wisdom is better than being strong (9:16; see also 8:14; 12:1; etc.).

---

25. Compare, for instance, the verbal and visual dimension of Qoh 1:16. In the first half of the verse the Teacher informs (דבר) his heart that he has great wisdom. In the second half of the verse the heart itself has seen (ראה) wisdom and knowledge. For an example of the sequential nature of cognitive speech, see the series of thoughts in Qoh 1–2.

As with THINKING IS SPEAKING, this metaphor can combine with THE SELF IS A PERSON metaphor (CONCLUDING IS SPEAKING TO ONE'S SELF).

> Qoh 2:15   I *said* [ואמרת], I in my heart [אני בלבי], "This, too, is vanity."

> Qoh 2:2   I *said* [אמרתי] concerning laughter, "What does it boast?"[26] and concerning gladness, "What does it do?"

In Qoh 2:15 the conclusion of the Teacher's thinking—that the wise die like the foolish and that this is vanity—is that which he spoke "in" (ב-) his לב (see also Qoh 3:17, 18). So, too, in Qoh 2:2, where the object of the thought, the לב, is specified in the previous verse. The CONCLUDING IS SPEAKING metaphor follows the same pattern as THINKING IS SPEAKING, mapping the properties of <internal $_{no}$>, <voluntary $_{yes}$>, and <directness $_{no}$> onto the domain of cognition. It adds, however, an evaluative element from hearing; that is, it assumes that the individual is capable of hearing the cognitive speech and evaluating the situation based upon it (i.e., that being wise is a futile endeavor, Qoh 2:15) (<evaluation $_{yes}$>).

Even when not spoken to one's Self, a person's knowledge, theological position, or general outlook on life is frequently conceptualized as his or her word (KNOWLEDGE IS A WORD). Thus already in ancient Near Eastern literature one's knowledge is one's words: "Give your heart; listen [*sḏm*] to my *words* [*mḏ.wt*]" (P.Anastasi 3.4, 3; see also 5.23, 6); "Listen [*sḏm*] to my *words* [*mḏ.wt*]; do not neglect my *words* [*mḏ.wt*]" (Instruction by a Man for His Son).[27] Similarly, in the book of Job the listener is commanded to "listen" to the knowledge that the speaker proclaims.

> Job 32:10   Therefore, I say [אמרתי], "Listen [שמעה] to me, I, too, will *declare* [אחוה] my *knowledge* [דעי]."

---

26. מהולל. Typically this term is read as a *poal* participle from הלל and is thus translated "it is mad." However, based on the Syriac translation and the syntactical structure of the sentence, Seow (*Ecclesiastes*, 126) makes the convincing argument that a textual corruption has likely occurred and that the original text probably read מה הלל, "What does it boast?" This would bring the first half of the sentence into parallel with the syntax of the latter half of the sentence, מה־זה עשה, "What does it do?"

27. The translations here follow those of Shupak, *Where Can Wisdom Be Found?*, 52–53, with slight modifications.

5. HEARING/SPEAKING

> Job 32:11 Indeed, I waited for your *words* [לדבריכם]; I *gave ear* [אזין] to your *understanding* [תבונותיכם] while you searched out *words* [מלין].

On the one hand, such passages hardly seem metaphorical. It seems perfectly natural to say that Elihu can "declare" (אהוה) his דעת (Job 32:10; see also 32:6, 17) or "give ear to" (אזין) Job's תבונה (32:11). However, such expressions are not physical realities; rather, they rely upon a metaphorical conception of the spoken word. Physically, when people speak they emit only a sound, a קול. Conceptually, however, people understand this קול to have meaning because the spoken word is understood to convey the verbal thoughts of an individual (IDEAS ARE WORDS). Thus Elihu's perspective is contained within the words that he "utters" (חוה, Job 32:10), while Job's opinion is preserved in the words that Elihu "hears" (אזן, 32:11). The pervasiveness of such passages and the easy slippage between abstract cognitive terms and oral terms attest to how deeply ingrained this metaphor was in the Israelite and early Jewish conceptual system. In any given passage cognitive terms and oral terms are practically interchangeable, as seen in the following examples.

> Prov 1:23 I will make known [אודיע] my *words* [דברי] to you.

> Job 34:33 *Speak* [דבר] what you know [מה־ידעת]!

Proverbs 1:23 could just as easily be written, "I will make known my *knowledge* [לדעתי] to you," and Job 34:33, "Speak your *words* [דבריכם]" (see also the parallel between דברים and תבונה in Job 32:11). Sometimes a modifier specifically marks the speaker's words as his knowledge (see, e.g., Prov 1:2; 19:27; 23:12). However, even by itself the "word" of the speaker is clearly what he or she knows (e.g., Prov 1:23; Job 32:11; 34:33).

As with cognitive speech, the depiction of knowledge as a verbal utterance functions by mapping the features of physical experience onto the abstract domain of knowledge. This verbal utterance, however, can be spoken *or* heard, such that KNOWLEDGE IS A WORD draws upon properties of both speech *and* hearing. When the focus is on the act of transmitting knowledge, the properties of speech map onto cognition, as in the דעת that Elihu declares is voluntarily directed outside himself toward Job (Job 32:10; see also 34:33; Prov 1:23) (<internal $_{no}$>, <voluntary $_{yes}$>). On the other hand, when the focus is on the act of receiving knowledge, the properties of hearing map. Elihu, for instance, must wait (יחל) for Job's words of understanding to reach his ear; he cannot hear until Job has discovered what to say (Job 32:11) (<detection $_{yes}$> [sequence], <voluntary $_{no}$>, <internal $_{yes}$>).[28] In either case, however, the shared property of <directness $_{no}$> takes precedence. Like other cognitive metaphors that draw on speech and hearing, these metaphors refer to knowledge that is indirectly obtained. Job, Elihu, or the student knows the knowledge in question only because he has been given it by another (Job 32:10, 11; 34:33; Prov 1:23).

Given the importance that the spoken word had for the transmission of knowledge, one might expect that hearing would become a natural source domain for understanding. In many cultures this is in fact what one finds. In ancient Sumerian, for instance, the word for "understanding" (geštu) was written with the sign for an ear,[29] and in Akkadian the word for "ear" (ḫasīsu) also meant "understanding."[30] Thus in the Babylonian Theodicy hearing indicates cognitive attention: "Pay attention [qú-lam-mu] for a moment; *hear my words* [ši-mi qa-ba-[a]-[a]]" (Babylonian Theodicy 26; see also 265).[31] Similarly, in ancient Egyptian the verb *sḏm* could indicate physical hearing, "understanding," or "obeying" that which is heard. Thus in the Story of Sinuhe the one who "hears" (*sḏm*) the language of Egypt is the one who "understands" it (B 30). Likewise, the dog who "hears" (*sḏm*) his master's words "obeys" and follows (Instruction of Ani 10.3–4; see also Instruction by a Man for His Son 1.2).[32] The heart in particular is designated as the entity that hears: "it is the heart which makes of its owner a hearer or non-hearer. Man's heart is his life, prosperity, and health! The hearer is one who *obeys* [*sḏm*; lit. "listens to"] what is said" (Instruction of Ptahhotep 550–556; see also the Biography of Amenhetep 4.1817.8–17).[33] Speaking is thinking; hearing is understanding and obeying.

---

28. Job 32:11 does not specifically state that the knowledge of Job enters into Elihu's ear. However, the choice of the verb אזן here, rather than שמע, draws attention to the biological apparatus through which a word enters into the body of an individual and thus, arguably, to the internal dimension of hearing (see also Prov 5:1).

29. Julia Asher-Greve, "The Essential Body: Mesopotamian Conceptions of the Gendered Body," *Gender and History* 9 (1997): 434.

30. Shupak, *Where Can Wisdom Be Found?*, 280.

31. The translation here follows that of Wilfred Lambert, "Babylonian *Theodicy*," in *Bablyonian Wisdom Literature* (Winona Lake, IN: Eisenbrauns, 1996), 73.

32. Shupak, *Where Can Wisdom Be Found?*, 52–53.

33. Ibid., 55. The translation here follows Shupak.

5. HEARING/SPEAKING

Israelite and early Jewish sapiential literature, however, does not typically describe thought itself as an act of hearing. The לב, for instance, rarely appears as the subject of an auditory verb, although it is sometimes implied (Qoh 1:16; 2:1).³⁴ In this regard, Carasik's evaluation is correct: שמע does not have the same intangible cognitive nuance as ראה does. However, this does not mean that hearing is devoid of metaphorical derivations. As in other ancient Near Eastern cultures, the frequent exhortations to "hear" (שמע) that one finds in Israelite and early Jewish sapiential literature (particularly in Proverbs) do not simply request a biological response. Sometimes, for instance, they exhort the listener to pay attention to or heed the speaker (PAYING ATTENTION IS HEARING).³⁵

Job 13:17   *Hear, hear!* [שמעו שמוע], my words [מלתי], and let my declaration be *in your ears* [באזניכם].

Job 33:31   *Heed* [הקשב], Job. *Hear me* [שמע־לי]!

Prov 7:24   And now, my child, *listen* to me [שמעו־לי]; *heed* [והקשיבו] the words of my mouth [לאמרי־פי].

As elsewhere in the Hebrew Bible, the use of the infinitive absolute in Job 13:17 emphasizes the act of the main verb, in this case, the act of hearing (see also Job 21:2). But here, as in Job 33:31 and Prov 7:24, the speaker is not simply asking the listener to physically hear him, although that is part of the request, but to *pay attention* to what he is about to say (see also Job 9:16; 37:14; Prov 1:8; 4:10; 5:7, 13; 8:32; 15:31; 17:4). Like שמע, the more forceful command to קשב also indicates more than a simple physical act; it carries a corresponding cognitive focus. Thus Job is to *heed* the words of Elihu (Job 33:31; see also 13:6), and the student is to *heed* the words of

---

34. The only exception of note occurs outside of sapiential literature in 1 Kgs 3:9, where the לב acts as the subject of the participle שמע in order to describe Solomon's capacity to judge wisely: "Give to your servant *a heart that hears* [לב שמע] to judge your people, to discern between good and evil." Although this passage is part of the Deuteronomic History, it is noteworthy that the heart's capacity to judge is connected here to Solomon, the quintessential wisdom figure in Israelite literature.

35. As Avrahami notes (*Senses of Scripture*, 131–35), in ancient Israel this metaphor also corresponds to the contextual pattern of "power to help," in that an individual (esp. God) "pays attention" to the suffering of another in order to help them.

the sage (Prov 7:24; see also 2:2). Similarly, exhortations for words to be "in your ears" (באזניכם, Job 13:17) and commands that the listener "turn the ear" (נטה אזן, Prov 4:20; 5:1, 13; 22:17) do not only refer to a physical process but rather to the cognitive process of attending to the words of the speaker.[36] As Nili Shupak states, the ear is not "merely a passive organ.... [It is] an instrument for understanding and evaluating words."[37]

Because it is based on hearing, this metaphor maps hearing's properties onto cognition, most notably its indirectness, sequential detection, and internal orientation (<internal $_{yes}$>, <detection $_{yes}$> [sequence], <directness $_{no}$>). Thus external information indirectly enters *into* the ears through a sequential acquisition of words. However, as with the JUDGING IS SEEING metaphor above, the PAYING ATTENTION IS HEARING metaphor shifts an inherent property of hearing; in this case the <voluntary> property shifts from a negative to a positive value. In physical hearing, a person cannot choose whether or not to hear a sound; one cannot actually "open" the ear. A sound either reaches the ears or not, regardless of the individual's preference (<voluntary $_{no}$>). However, the PAYING ATTENTION IS HEARING metaphor presumes a choice on the part of the listener. The student can choose not to heed the words of the teacher and must therefore be commanded to pay attention (<voluntary $_{yes}$>). The reason for this shift probably lies in the biological nature of hearing itself. Like sight, hearing has the capacity to focus on one particular sound among a host of stimuli, although it does so with much greater difficulty than vision.[38] While this capacity does not seem to factor into the Israelite and early Jewish conception of hearing to any great extent, it does help account for its reap-

---

36. Similarly, "closing the ear" (אטם אזן) in Prov 21:13 means "to not heed." The phrase "uncover the ear" (גלה אזן) in Job 36:10, 15 also seems to carry metaphorical undertones, meaning not simply to speak to (as in Job 33:16) but "to cause someone to heed." However, unlike the "turning of the ear," which is likely based on physical reality (one can turn the head and thus the ear toward a sound), the description of cognitive attention as an "uncovering" or "closing" of the ear cannot derive from physical reality (the ear cannot be "uncovered" or "closed"). Rather, these phrases are probably based on an analogy to the physical opening and closing of the eye (Avrahami, *Senses of Scripture*, 72–73). They thus reflect a more complex metaphorical process than the metaphors discussed here.

37. Shupak, *Where Can Wisdom Be Found?*, 278.

38. That is, through hearing the individual cannot choose whether or not to receive a sound, but one can choose to focus on one particular sound among many that reaches one's ears (Sweetser, *From Etymology to Pragmatics*, 38–39).

pearance in the metaphorical extensions of hearing here. The student can choose whether or not to listen to the sage, and although Proverbs presents this choice as a foregone conclusion, it is this choice on the part of the student that determines his or her ability to acquire wisdom.

A person who gives the proper attention to a word acknowledges its validity and accepts it as true; that person understands and knows it.[39] In this way, hearing become a source domain for understanding; the one who *hears* knowledge *knows* it (UNDERSTANDING IS HEARING).

Prov 4:1   *Be attentive* [והקשיבו] to know insight.

Job 5:27   Thus it is; *hear* it [שמענה] and know it for yourself.

Job 13:1   Indeed, all of this my eye has seen; *my ear has heard* [שמעה אזני] and understood it.

While PAYING ATTENTION IS HEARING inherently contains the concept that hearing leads to understanding, UNDERSTANDING IS HEARING draws this out more explicitly. Thus in Job 5:27 the imperative of שמע is equivalent to that of ידע, while in Prov 4:1 קשב is. In Job 13:1 both eye (עין) and ear (אזן) are used to indicate the cognitive perception of the matters being debated, with the ear in particular paralleling understanding (בינה), not merely as a prerequisite to it but as its functional equivalent (see also Job 23:5; 26:14; 36:12; 37:14).[40] As Carasik points out, שמע and ידי are rarely linked, a notable fact when compared to the prolific equation of ראה and ידע.[41] Yet this scarcity should not suggest that hearing is only superficially con-

---

39. Malul, *Knowledge, Control, and Sex*, 194. For a discussion of the legal ramifications of שמע, see 194–97.

40. G. Johannes Botterwick ("ידי," *TDOT* 5:462) argues that "in such parallelisms, *yāda'* can function as the superior term, summarizing the sensory perception and processing it intellectually"; that is, first one hears and then one knows. Yet as he goes on to argue, this combination (as well as the combination of ידי and ראה) "do not always point to a deliberate distinction between sensory and intellectual apperception; more generally, the totality of human knowledge is addressed." I would argue that this latter statement is generally the case, at least in wisdom literature. Avrahami (*Senses of Scripture*, 158) argues a similar point, stating that both "sight and hearing express knowing and learning when they are not parallel to the heart/mind."

41. For examples of the pairing of שמע and ידי, Carasik (*Theologies of the Mind*, 39–40) lists Deut 9:2; 29:3; 31:13; Num 24:16; Ps 78:3; Job 5:27; Isa 40:21, 28; 41:22, 26;

nected to cognition, as Carasik would argue.⁴² Elsewhere in the Hebrew Bible auditory terms and terms of knowing commonly appear in conjunction with one another, most notably שמע with בין (e.g., Deut 4:6; 1 Kgs 3:9, 11; Neh 8:2; see also Isa 6:9, 10; 52:15; Dan 12:8). Hearing, speech, and cognitive terms (שמע, דברים, לשין, ידע, בין), for instance, are virtually interchangeable when referring to the comprehension of languages (Gen 11:7; Deut 28:49; Jer 5:15; Isa 33:19; Ezek 3:6).⁴³ In such cases hearing does not refer simply to a physical action, even if it is closely tied to it, but also to cognitive comprehension. As Ibarretxe-Antuñano states, "when we use hearing verbs in these situations, we are not simply saying that we heard somebody saying something, we imply that we 'know' something, and that the information that we have is second hand—although the informant does not necessarily have to be mentioned."⁴⁴ Thus, like other oral or auditory metaphors, UNDERSTANDING IS HEARING is principally governed by hearing's <directness $_{no}$> property, such that the nominal form of שמע can even refer simply to second-hand information, a "report" (e.g., Job 28:22). Like PAYING ATTENTION IS HEARING, however, it also witnesses a shift in the <voluntary> property from a negative value to a positive one; one can choose to hear and thus understand a concept.

Given that a speaker often expects a particular response from the individual, hearing also comes to indicate obedience (OBEYING IS HEARING).⁴⁵

> Prov 5:7–8   And now, my child, *listen* [שמע] to me … keep your way far from her; do not approach the door of her house.

48:6–8; 50:4; Jer 6:18. To these, I might add Gen 42:23; Exod 3:7; Isa 33:13; Jer 5:15; Mic 3:1; Ps 81:6. For ראה and ידע, see §4.2.1 above.

42. Carasik (*Theologies of the Mind*, 40) concludes that שמע means "'understanding' only in a specific and limited sense: comprehending verbal information."

43. Malul, *Knowledge, Control, Sex*, 145. Malul (145, 196) also points to the phrase לשמע הטוב והרע ("to hear good and bad") in 2 Sam 14:17, which functions like the phrase לדעת טוב ורע ("to know good and bad," Gen 3:22; see also 2:9, 17; 3:5; 2 Sam 19:36; etc.). See also אזן + בין in Ps 5:2. קשב appears with ידע only in Prov 4:1; it does not appear with בין. Carasik (*Theologies of the Mind*, 40) argues that the use of בין with שמע is more common than that of ידע with שמע, but by my reading the evidence from the Hebrew Bible does not suggest a great difference statistically between the two.

44. Ibarretxe-Antuñano, "Mind as Body," 102.

45. Thus, Ibarretxe-Antuñano ("Polysemy and Metaphor in Perception Verbs," 65) argues that the OBEYING IS HEARING metaphor is, in many respects, an extension or specialized form of the PAYING ATTENTION IS HEARING metaphor.

Job 3:18–19 The prisoners are at ease together; they do not *hear* [שמעו] the voice of the one who confines them. The small and the great are there, and servants are free from their lords.

In such cases one not only pays attention to the speaker's word but cognitively assents to it and acts upon its advice. Thus the prisoners of Job 3:18 are normally expected to *obey* (שמע) their taskmaster, but in death they, like servants, are free from such expectations. Similarly, the sage of Prov 5:7–8 commands his student to *obey* (שמע) his word and not enter into the house of the strange woman. Elsewhere in the Hebrew Bible it is God's voice that the individual or community heeds and acts upon (Exod 19:5; 24:7; Judg 2:20; Jer 11:3, 6; etc.); in Proverbs, however, it is the sage's voice that the listener is directed to obey. The frequent appeals to "hear" in Proverbs (e.g., Prov 1:8; 4:10; 5:13; 7:24; 15:31; 17:4) also implicitly carry this connotation. The student should not only heed the words of his teacher; he should behave as his teacher prescribes. Like the PAYING ATTENTION IS HEARING metaphor, OBEYING IS HEARING is governed by hearing's properties of <internal $_{yes}$>, <detection $_{yes}$> $^{[sequence]}$, <voluntary $_{yes}$>, <directness $_{no}$>. It also relies, however, upon the notion that hearing is capable of affecting its listener (<effects $_{yes}$> $^{PR \to P}$). The words of the sage are intended to elicit a response in the individual, a corresponding action or the adoption of a particular worldview.

In other words, while Carasik is certainly correct to note that hearing is not used to refer to the internal dimensions of thought in the same way that sight or speech are, hearing is not devoid of abstract metaphorical extensions. As the above survey indicates, together oral and auditory metaphors for cognition are as prolific as visual metaphors and exhibit a similar range of nuances.

5.2.2. Emotion Metaphors

While hearing and speaking can affect the participants (e.g., Prov 15:30; 23:16; Job 7:11; 16:6; 32:20), hearing and speaking do not seem to serve as source domains for emotional experience itself in Israelite and early Jewish sapiential literature.[46] For instance, unlike the phrase to "see

---

46. For the connection between hearing/speaking and the emotions throughout the Hebrew Bible, see Avrahami, *Senses of Scripture*, 165–66. Although not framed in terms of conceptual metaphor, Avrahami's conclusions would seem to argue in favor

good" ([ראה טוב]ה), the phrase to "hear good" or to "hear bad" does not indicate satisfaction, enjoyment, or lack thereof. Similarly, a "good" or "bad" דבר may elicit an emotional state in an individual (Prov 12:25; 15:1, 23; Qoh 8:5), but it does not itself refer to that emotional experience. Rather, it indicates the "eloquence" of the speaker or the "morality" of its content.[47]

5.2.3. Judgment Metaphors

Elsewhere in the Hebrew Bible speaking and hearing can be used to signify the act of judgment. Solomon, for instance, asks for a לב שמע (a "heart that hears") so that he may judge wisely (1 Kgs 3:9).[48] Kings speak judgment (דבר משפט, 2 Kgs 25:6; see also Jer 1:16; 4:12; 39:5; 52:9). This nuance is not prevalent in Proverbs, Job, and Qoheleth, yet the results of judgment—specifically, conclusions about the moral character of an individual or situation—are described in terms of oral experience (MORAL QUALITIES ARE WORDS). For instance, as already seen above, perversity is something that can be spoken:

> Prov 23:33   Your heart [ולבך] will *speak* [ידבר] perversities.

Similarly:

> Prov 8:6   *Hear* [שמעו], for I will *speak* [אדבר] candid things,[49] and *from the opening of my lips* [ומפתח שפתי] will be straightness.

---

of hearing/speaking as source domains for emotions. She states, for instance, that "just as listening to a song (2 Sam 19:36), speech (Prov 23:16), or good tidings (Prov 15:30) denotes enjoyment and happiness, so evil tidings denote sadness and pain" (166; see her example of Hab 3:16). However, from my reading, unlike visual phrases, which do appear as the equivalent of emotional experience, hearing and speaking only cause emotional states; they do not stand in for them.

47. See, e.g., Shupak (*Where Can Wisdom Be Found?*, 332–33), who notes that דבר טוב "denotes the eloquent speech of the sage and the poet" or its "moral perfection."

48. Contrast this with the Egyptian texts mentioned above, where the heart that "hears" is one that "understands."

49. So Fox, *Proverbs 1–9*, 263, 269. According to Fox, נגידים means "honest or forthright things, things that are directly before (*neged*) a person" (269).

Job 13:7   Will you *speak* [תדברו] falsehood to God or *speak* [תדברו] deceit to him?

As Avrahami states, "falsehood and truth are presented as verbal entities."[50] Truth is spoken (Prov 8:6; see also Qoh 12:10), as are falsehood and deceit (Job 13:7; see also 27:4), perversity (Prov 23:33; see also 2:12; 24:2), and righteousness (Prov 8:6; see also 16:13; 23:16). Although such qualities could theoretically be heard (Prov 8:6 commands as much), the focus of these passages is on the *spoken* aspect of these qualities. As such, speech's properties dominate the mapping. Moral qualities are conceptualized as words that indirectly convey information to an external object (<internal $_{no}$>, <directness $_{no}$>). More importantly, the speaker can choose when to speak and what to speak, a choice that reflects both the voluntary nature of the act and the speaker's influence over it (<voluntary $_{yes}$>, <subjective $_{yes}$>). However, the metaphor also presumes that the listener will be able to judge the value of what is spoken, its truth or falsity; as such, it adopts hearing's evaluative property (<evaluation $_{yes}$>).

5.3. Summary

In sum, there are various metaphors of cognition in Israelite and early Jewish sapiential circles derived from the oral/auditory domain of human experience, some of which derive directly from the experience of speaking, others from hearing, and others from a combination of the two. As with visual metaphors, each of these maps the properties of their respective modalities onto the target domain of cognition.

Table 5.2. Metaphorical Mappings: COGNITION IS HEARING/SPEAKING

THINKING IS SPEAKING
    <internal $_{no}$>, <voluntary $_{yes}$>, <directness $_{no}$>, <subjective $_{yes}$>
THINKING IS SPEAKING TO ONE'S SELF
    <internal $_{no}$>, <voluntary $_{yes}$>, <directness $_{no}$>, <subjective $_{yes}$>
CONCLUDING IS SPEAKING
    <internal $_{no}$> , <voluntary $_{yes}$>, <directness $_{no}$>, <evaluation $_{yes}$>

---

50. Avrahami, *Senses of Scripture*, 173.

CONCLUDING IS SPEAKING TO ONE'S SELF
    <internal $_{no}$>, <voluntary $_{yes}$>, <directness $_{no}$>, <evaluation $_{yes}$>
KNOWLEDGE IS A WORD
    <directness $_{no}$> + <internal $_{no}$>, <voluntary $_{yes}$> or <detection $_{yes}$> ^{sequence}, <voluntary $_{no}$>, <internal $_{yes}$>
PAYING ATTENTION IS HEARING
    <internal $_{yes}$>, <detection $_{yes}$> ^{sequence}, <voluntary $_{yes}$>, <directness $_{no}$>
UNDERSTANDING IS HEARING
    <voluntary $_{yes}$>, <directness $_{no}$>
OBEYING IS HEARING
    <internal $_{yes}$>, <detection $_{yes}$> ^{sequence}, <voluntary $_{yes}$>, <directness $_{no}$>, <effects $_{yes}$> $^{PR \rightarrow P}$
MORAL QUALITIES ARE WORDS
    <internal $_{no}$>, <voluntary $_{yes}$>, <directness $_{no}$>, <subjectivity $_{yes}$>, <evaluation $_{yes}$>

As with sight, the specific metaphors vary depending upon which properties map. THINKING IS SPEAKING is a subjective enterprise, while CONCLUDING IS SPEAKING is evaluative. Yet there is also a good deal of continuity across these metaphors, with the same properties consistently mapping onto cognition: a concern for cognition's voluntary nature, the sequential nature of the detection or revelation, and its indirectness. These last two properties are especially important. Unlike sight, hearing and speaking provide an indirect, sequential engagement with the environment, and this translates into a conception of knowledge that is similarly indirect and sequential.

6
Touching

To include a section on tactility in a discussion of Israelite and early Jewish epistemology may strike some readers as odd. As Constance Classen notes, "the sense of touch, like the body in general, has been positioned in opposition to the intellect and assumed to be merely the subject of mindless pleasures and pains."[1] Yet touch is as fundamental to universal conceptions of knowledge as sight and sound. Like vision, orality, and audition, tactility provides individuals an important means of engaging their environment and serves as a natural source domain for how people conceptualize cognition.[2] As with other perception-based metaphors, conceptual metaphors

---

1. Constance Classen, "Fingerprints: Writing about Touch," in *The Book of Touch*, ed. Constance Classen (Oxford: Berg, 2005), 5. For instance, until recently antiquity studies have ignored touch and the other "lower senses" (taste, smell), preferring to focus instead on the opposition between hearing and seeing. See, for instance, Chidester, *Word and Light*; Carasik, *Theologies of the Mind*; George W. Savran, "Seeing Is Believing: On the Relative Priority of Visual and Verbal Perception of the Divine," *BibInt* 17 (2009): 320–61. Exceptions to this tendency include Susan Ashbrook Harvey, *Scenting Salvation: Ancient Christianity and the Olfactory Imagination* (Berkeley: University of California Press, 2006); and Deborah Green, *The Aroma of Righteousness: Scent and Seduction in Rabbinic Life and Literature* (University Park: Pennsylvania State University Press, 2011).

2. Taste could be considered part of the tactile domain. As A. D. Smith states, "we can taste *objects* in our mouths ... only because we *feel* them there" ("Taste, Temperatures, and Pains," in *The Senses: Classical and Contemporary Philosophical Perspectives*, ed. Fiona Macpherson [New York: Oxford University Press, 2011], 343). The Hebrew Bible even occasionally refers to the act of eating as an act of touching. "My appetite [נפשי] refuses to *touch* [לנגוע] them; my food is like a disease" (Job 6:7; see also Lev 7:21). However, although taste is closely related to touch, I argue in favor of preserving ingestion's relative autonomy. As discussed in ch. 7 below, it has different properties associated with it, relies on different processes for its acquisition of knowledge, and is generally distinguished as a separate modality across cultures. Moreover, although

based on tactility reflect a distinct conception of knowledge, one in which knowledge is conceived of as a direct, manipulable experience.

6.1. Typology of Touch

Tactility is a difficult modality to analyze. Although we often associate it with the hand, touch is not limited to any one part of the body; it can be experienced by the hand, the head, the arm, the foot, and the skin more generally. Ancient philosophers recognized this. Aristotle, for instance, discusses at length the indeterminate nature of touch, that is, how its location is often left unspecified and how it utilizes various means to convey its perception (*De an.* 422b17–423b15). Similar discussions of the "nonlocalization" of touch can be found in theories of Plato, the Hippocratics, and Cleidemus.[3] Tactility is also associated with a range of complex functions, from grasping, kissing, and simply coming into contact with an object to assessing temperature and evaluating pressure.[4] For the purposes of understanding cognitive metaphors in ancient wisdom literature, however, two types of actions are particularly relevant: the generic act of touching (frequently represented by the verb נגע, "touch"; see also משש/מוש, "feel") and specific acts of object manipulation (לקח, "to take"; אחז, "to seize, hold"; תמך, "to grasp"; תפש, "to seize"; חזיק, "grip strongly";[5] נתן, "to give"; and שים, "to put, place"). While both types of actions are commonly associated with the hand (the יד or כף; Gen 3:22; Exod 19:13; 1 Sam 6:9; Ps 115:7; etc.), they can also be experienced by any part of the body (the רגלים, "feet," Exod 4:25; the ירך, "thigh," Gen 32:26; the עבק, "heel," Gen 25:26; Job 18:9; and the ראש, "head," Gen 28:11, 18; 48:17; 2 Sam 18:9).

Regardless of the apparatus used, touch is a direct modality. Like sight, touch requires a direct connection between the perceiver and the object

---

there is some overlap between the semantic realms of touch and taste in the Hebrew Bible, tactile terms (e.g., נגע, לקח, אחז) are not generally interchangeable with ingestive terms (e.g., אבל, שתה, טעם), suggesting that they are conceptualized as separate modalities. Thus I discuss taste below as a separate category.

3. See Richard Sorabji, "Aristotle on Demarcating the Five Senses," in Macpherson, *Senses*, 78–79.

4. Jonas, "Nobility of Sight," 140.

5. Although the meaning of the *hiphil* itself is derivative from חזק, which in the *qal* means "to be strong," the *hiphil* clearly refers to the concrete experience of "grip strongly" with the hand (see, for instance, 2 Sam 15:5, where הזיק is parallel to שלח את־ידו, "sending forth his hand").

perceived (<directness ~yes~>).⁶ Thus when describing his angelic vision, Isaiah appeals to touch (the seraph ויגע על־פי, "touched me upon the mouth," with a coal) to indicate that he has personally experienced the cleansing power of God (Isa 6:7; see also 1 Kgs 19:5, 7; Jer 1:9). Similarly, Jacob experiences God directly when he "wrestles" (אבק) a divine man by the side of a wadi at night (Gen 32:23–33).⁷ Even more so than sight, however, touch involves actual contact between the perceiver and the object perceived (<contact ~yes~>). The perceiver physically connects with another individual (Gen 32:23–33; Exod 19:13; Lev 12:4; 15:7; Num 19:11; etc.), the carcass of an animal (Lev 11:24, 27, 31; etc.), or an object (Isa 6:7; Exod 7:9, 15; 9:10; 19:12; Lev 15:21–23; etc.).⁸ Touch, therefore, requires the perceiver and its object to be in close proximity to one another (<closeness ~yes~>). Abraham must "approach" (הלך) the ram that is caught in a

---

6. Even if the exact nature of touch was debated, it was commonly assumed by ancient philosophers (including Aristotle) that touch was a direct modality, requiring the perceiver to come into physical contact with the object perceived (Sorabji, "Aristotle on Demarcating the Five Senses," 78–79).

7. The exact meaning of אבק is uncertain; the verb occurs only within these two verses and likely originated as a wordplay on the wadi Jabbok (יבק) and Jacob (יעקב). Given the other actions in this section, a possible connection with the root חבק ("to embrace"), and the earlier brotherly contest in Gen 25:19–26, אבק probably refers to a physical, tactile experience between the two characters, somewhat akin to the modern idea of wrestling. For the connection of אבק and חבק, see Gordan Wenham, *Genesis 16–50*, WBC 2 (Dallas: Word, 1994), 295. Alternatively, since אבק elsewhere has the connotation of "dust," the verb might carry the connotation of "wrestling in the dust" (Allen P. Ross, "Studies in the Life of Jacob, Pt 2: Jacob at the Jabbok, Israel at Peniel," *BSac* 142 [1985]: 344). Interestingly, the end of the narrative recasts this episode as a visual encounter. In 32:31 Jacob articulates and understands his experience, not as having "touched" the body of God, but as having "seen God face-to-face" (כי־ראיתי אלהים פנים אל־פנים).

8. Touch can also occur through the use of a mediating object, such as when an angel of God "touches" (נגע) meat and bread with a staff (Judg 6:21). In such cases touch (like hearing or speech) has an indirect component to it in that the perceiver (e.g., the angel) indirectly experiences an object (e.g., meat and bread). Unlike hearing or speech, however, this indirect perception is the result of two separate perceptual acts: (1) the perceiver (e.g., the angel) touches an object (e.g., a staff), and (2) an object (e.g., a staff) touches another object (e.g., meat and bread). It is only when these two separate tactile acts are combined that an indirect experience arises. The two primary acts of perception, however, remain experiences of direct contact (between, for instance, the angel and the staff and the staff and the meat/bread). As such, <direct ~yes~> and <contact ~yes~> are the default properties for touch.

bush in order to "seize" (לקח) it (Gen 22:13; see also 1 Kgs 1:50; 2:28; Esth 5:2). Touch does not, however, require the object to enter into the body. Although the hand can serve as a temporary container for an object (e.g., ביד, Gen 38:18; 39:13; 1 Sam 14:43; בכף, Exod 4:4; 2 Sam 18:14), the object itself remains outside the body, and the perceiver's attention is directed toward elements outside himself or herself (<internal $_{no}$>).

Like other modalities, touch is capable of detecting and identifying objects within the environment (<detection $_{yes}$>, <identification $_{yes}$>), although this dimension of touch is underrepresented in the Hebrew Bible. In fact, it seems to surface only when sight is unable to assess the situation adequately, for instance, in the middle of the night (Gen 32:23-33; Deut 28:29) or after an individual has become blind (Gen 27:21-30).[9] Modern theorists have demonstrated, however, that touch is capable of identifying the same core characteristics of an object as sight—namely, its size (e.g., big, small), its dimensions (e.g., where the edge of an object is), and its relative orientation (e.g., vertical, horizontal, left, or right of the perceiver)—a capacity hinted at in a few biblical passages (see, for instance, the story of Jacob's blessing below).[10] More important for the Hebrew Bible, touch can also identify the "material properties" of an object (e.g., weight, texture, temperature),[11] and it is this felt quality in

---

9. One might also consider the odd tactile experience of Zipporah, which occurs at night (Exod 4:24-25).

10. For a modern discussion of tactile manipulation and its capacity to identify, see Roberta Klatzky and Susan Lederman, "The Haptic Identification of Everyday Life Objects," in *Touching for Knowing: Cognitive Psychology of Haptic Manual Perception*, ed. Yvette Hatwell (Amsterdam: Benjamins, 2003), 105-22, as well as the other essays in that edited volume. According to Ibarretxe-Antuñano ("Polysemy and Metaphor in Perception Verbs," 146), touch also has the capacity to recognize the boundaries between the perceiver and the object perceived, such that when the perceiver touches an object it invades its space (<limits $_{yes}$>). It is unclear, however, if this property was associated with touch in the Hebrew Bible. Similarly, modern theorists such as Klatzky and Lederman ("Haptic Identification," 112-13) note that touch is capable of determining the relative location of an object vis-à-vis the perceiver, though not as precisely or as quickly as sight (so <location $_{yes}$ >). Ibarretxe-Antuñano ("Polysemy and Metaphor in Perception Verbs," 146) disagrees, assigning this property only to vision and audition. While from a modern standpoint the former position seems closer to the way touch interacts with the environment (at least in its haptic capacity), it is again unclear what value the Israelites would have assigned to the modality.

11. According to Klatzky and Lederman ("Haptic Identification," 117), it is this dimension of touch that is the defining feature of haptic identification. "Haptic object

particular that can be found hovering below the surface of many biblical passages. Thus, Gen 27 specifically connects touch to its ability to determine the relative smoothness (חלק) or hairiness (שעיר) of an individual (see 27:11–12, 23), while other passages simply label objects as "smooth" (חלק, 1 Sam 17:40; Ps 55:22; Prov 5:3; Isa 57:6), "soft" (רכך, Ps 55:22; Isa 1:6), "sharp" (חד, Job 41:22; Ps 57:5; Prov 5:4; מלטש, Ps 52:4), "heavy" (כבד, Prov 27:3), "cold" (צנה, Prov 25:13), and so forth.[12]

Unlike sight, however, the scope of touch is limited to its "zone of contact" with the object perceived.[13] A single touch gives only a partial impression of an object, that the tip of an arrow is "sharp" (שנן, Pss 45:6; 120:4; Isa 5:28) or that the hand of an individual is "hairy" (שעיר, Gen 27:23). It takes the additive experience of multiple touching sensations to construct a complete impression of an object.[14] Thus Laban must "feel" (משש) Rachel's entire tent in order to determine if his stolen *teraphim* are in it (Gen 31:34, 37), and an individual must "grope" (משש) in the dark in order to determine how he or she should go (e.g., Deut 28:29). Like hearing and speaking, then, touch acquires its information in successive stages and is thus a sequential modality.

It is not, however, a temporal modality. Touch can engage the constituent parts of its object in any order and then arrange that information into a static spatial presentation of its object.[15] Thus Laban acquires a full impression of the interior of Rachel's tent by combining his multiple tac-

---

identification cannot rely virtually entirely on information about the spatial layout of edges … because spatial information is extracted coarsely and slowly by means of touch. Material information [is] suggested as a potential supplement, if not alternative, to information about spatial layout, and material properties [are] shown to be more available than spatially coded properties under haptic exploration."

12. In many of these passages a physical object (curd, oil, path, etc.) is physically described as חלק, רכך, or חד in order to form the basis for the metaphorical extension in which words are conceived of as smooth, soft, or sharp. For a discussion of this metaphor in wisdom literature, see below.

13. Yvette Hatwell, "Introduction: Touch and Cognition," in Hatwell, *Touching for Knowing*, 2.

14. Jonas, "Nobility of Sight," 140; Klatzky and Lederman, "Haptic Identification," 2.

15. As Hatwell ("Introduction," 2) notes, "although touch is highly sequential, it is nevertheless a spatial modality because it does not explore in a linear way and in an imposed order. In audition, the order of the sequence of stimuli cannot be changed since its carries meaning (in speech, music, etc.) By contrast, touch can explore the stimulus in any order and it can contact several times the same part of the object or set of objects.… Therefore, touch provides information about the spatial properties of the

tile sensations of it. Even if only a single touch occurs, the individual can extrapolate based on memory what the rest of the object feels like. The blind Isaac, for instance, "feels" (משׁשׁ) only Jacob's hands, which have been covered with goat skin to make them feel like the hands of his brother Esau (Gen 27:21–30). Isaac then extrapolates, based on that single touch and his prior knowledge of Esau, that the entire person who stands before him is Esau. In such cases the individual does not physically experience the entire object; Isaac does not feel his son's neck, torso, or head. Rather, one's brain fills in the gaps in perception based on the information obtained from the first experience.[16] The end result, however, is the same; a static impression of the object (in Isaac's case, a person) is achieved. By way of comparison to vision and audition, Jonas calls this process a "presentation of simultaneity through sequence" (so, <detection $_{yes}$> [simultaneity through sequence]).[17]

However, no matter how complete the impression constructed by touch, it is still an "elaborate synthesis of many single perceptions." Unlike sight, touch provides an impression of an object that is bound to have "blank spaces" and remain incomplete.[18] Because of this, the hypotheses that touch forms about the environment may or may not be correct (<correction of hypothesis $_{yes/no}$>).[19] Since it comes into contact with the object, touch is generally thought to be reliable; both Isaac and Laban trust their hands as if it is appropriate to do so. Yet as these examples demonstrate, touch can provide false information, misleading Laban about the status of his *teraphim* and Isaac about the identity of his son. Thus individuals often rely on other modalities to confirm the information provided by touch. Isaac, for instance, relies upon smell (וירח את־ריח בגדיו, "he smelled the smell of his garments," Gen 27:27) to confirm his impression that Esau stands before him. Correct or not, like sight or hearing, touch provides the individual with information by which to evaluate the environment (<eval-

---

environment." See, however, Klatzky and Lederman, "Haptic Identification," esp. 113, 117 (and note 11 above) for the relative spatiality of touch.

16. Hatwell ("Touch and Cognition," 2), for instance, notes that haptic manipulation requires "a mental integration and synthesis in order to obtain a unified representation of the whole." See also Jonas, "Nobility of Sight," 141.

17. Jonas, "Nobility of Sight," 142.

18. Ibid., 143.

19. Contrary to Ibarretxe-Antuñano, I argue that touch does form a hypothesis, even in modern conceptions of tactility. For Ibarretxe-Antuñano's position, see "Polysemy and Metaphor in Perception Verbs," 153–54, and her chart summarizing the typologies of Western modalities, reproduced in chapter 3 above.

uation ~yes~>). Based on their tactile experiences, Isaac determines that it is appropriate to bless Jacob and Laban decides to capitulate to Jacob and form a covenant with him (Gen 31:44).

More important, in the Hebrew Bible touch is connected to the individual's ability to affect the environment and be affected by it. Through touch, the individual is able to physically manipulate the object perceived (<effects ~yes~> ^OP → P^). One can grab bread and water (Gen 6:21; 18:4, 8; 21:14), animals (8:9; 22:13), jewelry and clothing (24:22, 65), plants (30:37), sharp instruments (22:10), and so forth and move them from one place to the next. One can hold onto parts of a building and shake them until the structure collapses (Judg 16:3, 26–30). One can also seize people, moving them from one spot to another (Gen 19:16) or holding them stationary in order to injure them (Gen 34:2; Judg 1:6; 16:21; 20:6).[20] Touch can cause pain, as when a person "strikes" (נכה) a slave with a staff (Exod 21:20; see also Prov 23:13–14; Isa 10:24) or inflicts some other "wound" (מכה, Deut 25:3; 1 Kgs 22:35; פצע, Gen 4:23; Exod 21:25; 1 Kgs 20:37; etc.).[21] The degree to which individuals create and experience pressure, pleasure, and pain, however, varies from person to person, as do their responses to such stimuli (<subjective ~yes~>).[22] One blow may injure a person (Exod 21:18; Prov 23:13–14), while another might kill him or her (Exod 21:12, 20). Moreover, a person knows only the pain of his or her own body (Job 14:22), and while one person may cry out in pain when struck (Exod 3:7), another may be unaffected or choose to ignore it (Jer 5:3; Job 6:10). In such cases the degree to which a person is affected by a touch is not due to the individual's physiology but the force with which one is struck and the character of the individual. Thus a great blow kills (Exod 21:12), while a lesser blow only maims (Exod 21:18), and arrogance keeps people from feeling the blow of God (Jer 5:3), while faithfulness allows Job to endure it (Job 6:10). Wine can, however, dull the individual's sensations (Prov

---

20. Most references to "taking" (לקח) a woman or a person are not concrete actions but metaphorical extensions of the concrete action, meaning to "marry" (Gen 11:29; 16:3; 24:67) or to accompany from one geographic location to another (Gen 11:31; 12:5). Each depends upon the conception that PEOPLE ARE MANIPULABLE OBJECTS.

21. God's touch in particular is lethal, such DISEASE IS THE TOUCH OF GOD becomes a common metaphor in the Hebrew Bible. See, for instance, Gen 12:17, where God "touches" (נָגַע) Pharaoh's household and causes "plagues" (נֶגַע) in it (see also 2 Kgs 15:5; Job 1:11; 2:5; 19:21).

22. Sweetser, *From Etymology to Pragmatics*, 44.

23:35), in which case the chemical state of the person affects the degree to which one experiences environmental stimuli so that one has little influence over the act of perception.

Moreover, because touch brings the individual into contact with the object perceived, it also allows for the transference of inherent qualities from the object to the perceiver (<effects $_{yes}$> $^{PR \to P}$). Uncleanness, for instance, can be transferred by touch (טמא, Lev 5:2, 3; 7:19; etc.) as can holiness (קדש, Exod 29:37; 30:29; Lev 6:18; etc.). Unlike sight or speech, which also affects the object perceived, touch has the potential to create a more lasting effect on its participants such that, foregoing the performance of certain rituals, the same property can be transferred to any subsequently person or object who comes into contact with the contaminated entity (e.g., Lev 15:22–23, 26–27; 22:3–6).

Touch, then, has a permanence that sight and hearing do not have, and its improper or accidental usage must therefore be guarded against. The first woman reports that God has instructed the first humans not to "touch" (נגע) the fruit of the tree in the middle of the garden, lest their touch result in death (Gen 3:3; see also Exod 19:12, 13).[23] Touch is also assumed to be a voluntary modality (<voluntary $_{yes}$>). Moses can choose to "send out his hand" (וישלח ידו) and "seize" (ויחזק) a serpent by its tail (Exod 4:4; see also Gen 7:2; Deut 25:11; 1 Sam 15:27; 2 Sam 1:11), and Jael can choose to "take" (לקח) a tent peg and hammer it into Sisera's skull (Judg 4:21).[24] As this latter example illustrates, the individual can also be on the receiving end of a touch, in which case the act is not initiated by him or her (see also Gen 19:16; 21:18; Isa 6:7) (<voluntary $_{no}$>). Touch can also happen accidently (ונעלם ממנו, Lev 5:2–4; see also 2 Sam 18:9; <briefness $_{yes}$>),[25] and the individual must therefore be careful lest he or she involuntarily comes into contact with the object perceived. A good inten-

---

23. According to Gen 2:16–17, God tells the first humans that they may not eat of the tree of knowledge of good and evil; he says nothing about touching it, although the first woman later reports that he does in Gen 3:3.

24. The individual can also choose how much force to apply when moving an object and how far that object is moved, which further supports the conclusion that touch is a subjective modality.

25. Ibarretxe-Antuñano ("Polysemy and Metaphor in Perception Verbs," 150) notes that with even a brief touch one can determine the texture and temperature of an object. That the inherent properties of an object can transfer to a person without a person being aware that he or she touched the object suggests that briefness was also a property associated with touch in ancient Israel.

tion can even result in a negative effect. Uzzah touches the ark to steady it but is killed for the action anyway (2 Sam 6:6–7; see also Lev 5:2–4). Regardless of intent or volition, touch affects the individual.

The properties of touch can be summarized as follows.[26]

Table 6.1. Biblical Typology of Touch

<contact $_{yes}$>	<directness $_{yes}$>
<closeness $_{yes}$>	<effects $_{yes}$> $^{PR \rightarrow P}$
<internal $_{no}$>	<correction of hypothesis $_{yes/no}$>
<limits $_{???}$>	<subjectivity $_{yes}$>
<location $_{???}$>	<effects $_{yes}$> $^{OP \rightarrow P}$
<detection $_{yes}$> $^{simultaneity\ through\ sequence}$	<evaluation $_{yes}$>
<identification $_{yes}$>	<briefness $_{yes}$>
<voluntary $_{yes/no}$>	

6.2. COGNITION IS TOUCHING

Given that the Hebrew Bible shows little interest in tactility as a modality by which to identify items in the environment, it is not surprising that metaphors derived from tactility do not focus on <identification>. As with its physical counterpart, the only notable occurrences of this dimension of tactility among sapiential metaphors for cognition occur in complex metaphors in which sight's failure to identify objects in the environment is also a prominent feature.[27] However, like vision, hearing, and speech, tactility frequently serves as a source domain for cognitive experience, particularly

---

26. Although the properties of <limits $_{???}$> and <location $_{???}$> below are applicable to tactility, the values of these properties in ancient Israel remain unclear.

27. IGNORANCE IS GROPING IN THE DARK. See, for instance, Job 5:14 and 12:25, in which "twisted" individuals (נפתלים, 5:13) and self-aggrandizing leaders are described as "groping" (משש) in the dark. Here the idea that UNDERSTANDING IS SEEING and UNDERSTANDING IS FEELING combine to create the metaphor IGNORANCE IS GROPING IN THE DARK. Although UNDERSTANDING IS FEELING is not attested independently, it seems to be the primary metaphor upon which this complex metaphor is based.

in its capacity to manipulate the environment and experience the material properties of objects.

6.2.1. Knowledge Metaphors

Just as thought is conceived of as an internal dialogue or a visual observation, thinking is also conceptualized as an act of cognitive manipulation (THINKING IS MANIPULATING OBJECTS). For instance, etymological studies suggest that various Hebrew terms for cognition conceptualize thought as a process of "binding" or "twisting" ideas within oneself. The term זמם ("to think, devise"), for instance, may derive from the same root as the Arabic *zamma, zimām* ("rein") and the Modern Hebrew זמם, זמום ("muzzle"), which suggests that its original meaning was "to bind." If so, the wisdom term זמם (e.g., Prov 30:32; 31:16) may indicate thoughts that are "bound" within the individual. Similarly, the term חשב ("to think," e.g., Prov 17:28) may literally mean to "bind within oneself knowledge," since its nominal form (חֵשֶׁב) indicates a decorative band that binds the priest's ephod (Exod 28:28). The term שכל ("to examine," noun: "insight, discretion") is probably related to the root שָׁכֵל, which means "to overcross [the legs, hands, etc.]" (see, e.g., Gen 48:14). To speak without שכל (Job 17:4; 34:27, 35) may thus indicate speech that occurs without first having "crossed ideas over within oneself."[28] The same tactile connotations can be conjectured for תחבלות ("guidance, plan"). Related to the Hebrew noun חבל ("rope"), a תחבלות (Prov 1:5; 11:14; 12:5) may be a "bound" thought, a "saying that is tightly phrased, well constructed, a pithy maxim made like a series of knots and loops" that directs the behavior of the individual.[29]

Admittedly, such readings are based on conjectured etymologies,[30] and even if they are correct the terms may have lost some of their tactile

---

28. Malul, *Knowledge, Control, and Sex*, 107 n. 33, 113 n. 38; see also Juda Lion Palache, *Semantic Notes on the Hebrew Lexicon* (Leiden: Brill, 1959), 26, 35. Although Malul and Palache do not go so far as to suggest a tactile definition for thought like the ones provided in the discussion here, Malul argues that these and similar etymologies clearly reflect the "sensory concrete nature of the epistemic process" of ancient Israel (107).

29. Shupak, *Where Can Wisdom Be Found?*, 315–16. The definition proposed here is that provided by Shupak, with some slight modifications.

30. The term זמם, for instance, has also been connected with the Arabic *zāmam* ("murmer, hum"), in which case it would reflect an oral connotation rather than a tactile one (Malul, *Knowledge, Control, and Sex*, 107 n. 33).

associations by the time they were included in Israelite and early Jewish sapiential literature, becoming instead abstract constructs. As James Barr argues in his examination of biblical semantics, root meaning does not always indicate the actual semantic value of a term: "hundreds of examples could be adduced where words have come to be used in a sense widely divergent from, or even opposed to, the sense of the forms from which they were derived."[31] The English term *comprehend*, for instance, derives from the Latin *comprehendre* ("to seize"), but few English speakers would consider it to have a tactile orientation. Because of this, Barr argues that it is a complete "fallacy" to use etymology or word roots to speak about the meaning of individual words or the conceptual systems of ancient peoples more generally. Language, he argues, cannot reveal *how* a people thought.[32]

However, as demonstrated throughout the present study language *is* closely linked to the cognitive systems of individuals. The meanings of words derive from the embodied experiences of the people who use them and convey specific conceptions of the world to the people who hear or read them. As Enino Mueller states, "we have 'words'; 'we have 'concepts'; and we have 'entities in the world.'… The whole structure of human language and thought supposes that there is a relation between them, and that it is this relation that allows us to know something."[33] Etymology and semantics studies more generally can help uncover these meanings when

---

31. James Barr, *The Semantics of Biblical Language* (London: Oxford University Press, 1961), 107; see also his critique of specific etymologies on 108–60.

32. Ibid., 33–45, 100–106. Barr's critique was directed particularly at scholars such as Johannes Pedersen and Thorleif Boman, who used etymology and the semantics of Biblical Hebrew more generally to argue for the distinctive nature of Israelite thought (esp. when compared to the ancient Greeks). See Johannes Pedersen, *Israel: Its Life and Culture*, trans. A. Møller and A. I. Fausbell, 2 vols. (London: Oxford University Press, 1926–1947); Boman, *Hebrew Thought Compared to the Greek*. As such, many of Barr's critiques were valid. These nineteenth-and early twentieth-century scholars did have the tendency to haphazardly project modern theological assumptions onto ancient languages and thus falsely assert the distinctiveness of the biblical data. However, as will be discussed momentarily, it may be time to reevaluate Barr's vehement critiques in light of more recent theories about the formation and cognitive dimensions of language.

33. For more on the modern linguistic challenges to Barr, see Enio Mueller, "The Semantics of Biblical Hebrew: Some Remarks from a Cognitive Perspective," 8–12, http://tinyurl.com/SBL2634a.

direct experience is unavailable. In fact, in many cases we find ancient language users playing with the perceptual nuances of a term's etymology, which suggests that the metaphorical nuances of the abstract term may not have been completely lost. For instance, in Egyptian literature *ts* ("wise saying") literally refers to a "knot," as indicated by its hieroglyphic representation: a "tied belt with the determinative for rope." When the Egyptian sage uses the term *ts*, he or she thus visually conjures up the image of words that are "tied and bound together" (see, e.g., Instruction of Ptahhotep 42; Prophecies of Neferti 7). Similarly, the verb *wḥʿ* ("explain") derives from the physical act of "untying a knot." Thus when the Instruction of Amenemope tells the student to become a man who can "explain" his teacher's words to others, he literally tells him to be "a man who *unties* [his teacher's] *knots*" (*rmṯ n wḥʿw.w*) (27.13–15). Consider also the Instruction of Ptahhotep, where the student is cautioned against "loosening the cords" (*wni ini im.k*) within him before he has enough wisdom to do so properly (608–611).[34] In each case, the sage plays with the tactile nuances of the term's etymology to convey his or her message.

Similarly, when translating Prov 1:5 into Greek, the Septuagint renders תחבלות with κυβέρνησις.

Prov 1:5 Let the wise hear and add learning and those who have understanding acquire תחבלות [MT] / κυβέρνησιν [LXX].

Prov 12:5 The thoughts of the righteous are just; the תחבלות [MT] / κυβερνῶσιν [LXX] of the wicked are treacherous.

Such a translation not only preserves the tactile nuances of the Hebrew term but also injects a nautical connotation into the passage. Like the rope that allows a navigator to steer a boat, the proverb becomes a tightly phrased maxim that *steers* the life of the individual to safety (LXX Prov 1:5), while the thoughts of the wicked become tightly bound thoughts that steer him or her astray (LXX Prov 12:5). Philo makes this connection even more explicit. Like a skilled "navigator" (κυβερνήτης), he argues, the properly trained intellect "steers" (κυβερνάω) the individual through the trials of life (*Leg.* 3.80; see also *Abr.* 84; *Agr.* 69; *Sacr.* 105).[35] In such cases the

---

34. Shupak, *Where Can Wisdom Be Found?*, 63–64, 315–17. The translations here follow Shupak.

35. In making this assertion, Philo was largely drawing upon the prevailing Greek

metaphor represented in the etymology is itself not "dead" but has merely become so entrenched in the society's conceptual system that its usage is "so automatic as to be unconscious and effortless."[36] We must, of course, be careful when using etymology to determine the metaphorical nuances of a given term, especially in ancient contexts where the data is limited; still, etymology can suggest possible embodied nuances behind abstract terms that may otherwise remain hidden. At any rate, that similar tactile conceptualizations can be found throughout ancient Near Eastern wisdom literature suggests that thought was frequently conceptualized as a tactile event. Thus in Egyptian literature to "give" or "put" a matter to one's heart is to think about it. The student is commanded to "give your ears, hear what is said; *give your heart* [*imi ḥty r*] to understand them" (Instruction of Amenemope 3.9–10); he is to "be a scribe; *put this in your heart* [*rdi m ib*] and your fame will be similar [to that of the great scribes]" (Papyrus Chester Beatty 4, pl. 18, verso 2, 13). The heart is the locus of understanding; bringing ideas to it increases one's knowledge.[37] Similar resonances can be found in the Hebrew Bible, where thought is conceptualized as an act of "transferring" information *to* the לב (THINKING IS TRANSFERRING AN OBJECT TO ONE'S SELF).

> Qoh 7:2   [Death] is the end of every person, and the living *give* it to heart [יתן אל־לבו].

> Qoh 9:1   For I *gave* [נתתי] all of this to my heart [אל־לבי].

According to Qoheleth, people should "give" it to heart (יתן אל־לבו) that death is their end (7:2); that is, they should *consider* it, just as the Teacher *considers* (נתתי אל־לבי) the nature of human toil (9:1). As with THINKING IS SPEAKING, these passages assume a bifurcated person, one in which the core essence of the individual can interact with his or her component self, which is again conceptualized as a person (SELF IS A PERSON). Like its verbal counterpart, then, this metaphor probably results from a

---

philosophical concepts of his day, yet steeped as he was in the Jewish traditions of his community, Philo was probably also influenced by the Septuagint's treatment of Proverbs here.

36. Lakoff and Turner, *More Than Cool Reason*, 129.

37. Shupak, *Where Can Wisdom Be Found?*, 57–58. The translation of these passages follow Shupak. See also P.Anastasi 3.4, 1, 3; 5.8, 6; 23, 6.

simple combination of its primary metaphor, THINKING IS MANIPULATING OBJECTS, and a SELF metaphor. Here, however, abstract concepts are not conceptualized as words but as objects that can be physically manipulated (IDEAS ARE MANIPULABLE OBJECTS).

Israelite and early Jewish sapiential texts also frequently conceptualize thought as an act of manipulating one's self (THINKING IS MANIPULATING ONE'S SELF).

> Qoh 1:17   And I *gave my heart* [ואתנה לבי] to know wisdom and to know foolishness and folly.

> Job 1:8   And the Lord said to the satan,[38] "Have you *put your heart* [השמת לבך] upon my servant Job?"

Like THINKING IS TRANSFERRING AN OBJECT TO ONE'S SELF, these passages combine THINKING IS MANIPULATING OBJECTS with an assumption of a bifurcated person, a core essence and a self. Here, however, the self is conceptualized not as a person but as the object itself that can be "given" or "put" to a matter (THE SELF IS AN OBJECT). Thus, the Teacher "gives" his heart (ואתנה לבי ל-) to understand wisdom and folly; that is, he *thinks* about the nature of these categories (see also Qoh 1:13; 8:9, 16). Similarly, in Job 1:8 God asks the satan if he has "put" his heart upon (השמת לבך על-) the behavior of Job, that is, if has he *considered* it (see also Job 2:3; 7:17; Prov 22:17; 24:32; 27:23). The notion that IDEAS ARE MANIPULABLE OBJECTS is thus superseded by the idea that the self is itself an object that can be manipulated in the cognitive process.

As with other perception-based metaphors, THINKING IS MANIPULATING OBJECTS and its compound iterations function by mapping the properties of their concrete modality onto cognition. Like concrete tactile experience, cognition is conceptualized as an experience of direct contact between the individual (or his or her לב) and the matter under consideration, such as wisdom, the nature of human conduct, and death (<contact _{yes}>, <directness _{yes}>). Since these concepts are considered to be objects that can be physically manipulated, these metaphors presume tactility's ability to manipulate the environment, to move the לב

---

38. השטן. As is well recognized, השטן is not equivalent to the Christian Satan figure but is rather a title meaning "adversary" or "opponent."

or abstract concepts (<effects $_{yes}$> $^{OP \rightarrow P}$). Cognition is also considered to be voluntary (<voluntary $_{yes}$>); the Teacher can choose whether or not to consider human toil (Qoh 9:1), and the satan can choose whether or not to consider Job's behaviors (Job 1:8). When this metaphor combines with a SELF metaphor, tactility's <internal $_{no}$> property is emphasized. Cognition becomes a process that involves concepts that originate outside and remain external to the self (<internal $_{no}$>), although the relative position of the לב during the cognitive process varies; either it is moved toward an external concept (THINKING IS MANIPULATING ONE'S SELF), or an external concept is moved toward it (THINKING IS TRANSFERRING AN OBJECT TO ONE'S SELF).

The notion that IDEAS ARE MANIPULABLE OBJECTS also surfaces in conceptualizations of understanding, which view cognition as an act of grasping or taking a concept (UNDERSTANDING IS GRASPING).

> Prov 1:3 for *taking* [לקחת] discipline of discretion, righteousness, judgment, and uprightness
>
> Qoh 2:3 I scouted about with my לב … [how] to *seize* [לאחז] folly.

According to the superscription of Proverbs, one of the reasons for recording the proverbs of Solomon is so that the wise might *understand* (לקח) such abstract qualities as discretion, righteousness, and justice. Likewise, the Teacher of Qoheleth sets out to consider how best to *understand* (אחז) the nature of folly (2:3; see also 7:17–18). Again, such passages presume a conception of ideas as objects that can be grasped (IDEAS ARE MANIPULABLE OBJECTS). As Avrahami states, such associations make sense "in a culture where all learning is by way of apprenticeship and participation."[39] Just as one must first "grasp" a lyre or an oar in order to understand how to use it, one must "grasp" a concept in order to *understand* it.

---

39. Avrahami, *Senses of Scripture*, 160. In making this statement, Avrahami is speaking particularly of the way that verbs such as תפש ("to grasp") and אחז ("to seize") are used to describe professions, such as lyre players (תפש כנור ועוגב, "the one who holds a lyre and pipe," e.g., Gen 4:21), mariners (תפש משוט, "the one who holds an oar," e.g., Ezek 27:29), and soldiers (אחזי חרב, "the one who holds a sword," e.g., Song 3:8). Yet, her larger point—that tactility and learning are closely associated in apprenticeship cultures—is applicable to the broader discussion here.

Similarly, learning is depicted as an act of adding up, obtaining, or acquiring ideas (ACQUIRING KNOWLEDGE IS ACQUIRING OBJECTS).

Prov 1:5   Let the wise hear and *add* learning [וְיוֹסֶף לֶקַח]; let the ones who discern *acquire* [יִקְנֶה] guidance.

Prov 3:13   Happy the one who finds wisdom and the one who *obtains* [יָפִיק] understanding.

Prov 4:5   *Acquire* [קְנֵה] wisdom; *acquire* [קְנֵה] insight; do not turn away from the words of my mouth.

Prov 21:11   When the wise one is taught, he *takes* [לְקַח] knowledge.

Again, an abstract concept is described as an object experiencing physical manipulation (IDEAS ARE MANIPULABLE OBJECTS). Learning is "added up" (יָסַף, Prov 1:5), guidance and wisdom "acquired" (קנה, 1:5; 4:5), understanding "obtained" (פוק, 3:13), and knowledge "taken" (לקח, 21:11; see also Qoh 1:16, 18 and the loss of understanding in Job 12:24).[40] The noun לֶקַח ("learning, instruction") itself is related to the verb לקח ("to take") and probably carries the connotation of learning by taking.[41] Thus the phrase "adding לֶקַח" in Prov 1:5 is doubly tactile, with both noun and verb conceptualizing the cognitive process as a tactile experience (see also Prov 4:2; 9:9; 16:21, 23). The noun חכמה and its verbal equivalent חכם could also, according to Malul, carry a tactile connotation, due to a possible derivation from the Akkadian verb *ekēmu*, "to hold, grasp, appropriate."[42] If so, then the reference to "acquiring הכמה" in Prov 4:5 (see also 4:7; 16:16; 17:16) might also inherently refer to an act of "acquiring that which is known by grasping."

Like THINKING IS MANIPULATING OBJECTS, ACQUIRING KNOWLEDGE IS ACQUIRING OBJECTS can combine with a bifurcated conception of the

---

40. Compare this to Egyptian literature, where neglecting a teaching is equated to "setting it down" (ḫ3ʿ): "I am told that you have *set down* [ḫ3ʿ.k, i.e., neglected] the writing" (P.Anastasi 4.2, 4). See Shupak, *Where Can Wisdom Be Found?*, 80.

41. Malul, *Knowledge, Control, and Sex*, 135. The definition proposed here is my own.

42. Ibid., 138.

individual. Here again the self is conceptualized as an object that can itself be manipulated; in this case, it can be acquired (THE SELF IS AN OBJECT). Thus the possession of the heart itself (or lack thereof) is indicative of a person's cognitive abilities (HAVING KNOWLEDGE IS POSSESSING HEART).

Prov 6:32   The one who commits adultery *lacks heart* [חסר־לב]; he who ruins his נפש does it.

Prov 15:32 The one who hears an argument *acquires heart* [קונה לב].

Job 15:12   What has taken [יקחך] your לב from you?[43]

Whether the individual has a physical organ called the לב is not in question; presumably every individual has this organ. Rather, what is at stake is the individual's intellectual capabilities. Contrary to the modern Western idiom in which "having heart" indicates moral fortitude, "having heart" in sapiential literature is equivalent to having knowledge. Therefore, "acquiring heart" (קנה לב) is commended (Prov 15:32; see also 19:8), while "lacking heart" (חסר־לב) or having heart "taken" away (יקחך לבך) is equivalent to lacking knowledge, being foolish, and being destined for destruction (Prov 6:32; see also 7:7; 9:4, 16; 10:13, 21; 11:12; 12:11).[44]

Like the tactile THINKING metaphors above, ACQUIRING KNOWLEDGE IS ACQUIRING OBJECTS and UNDERSTANDING IS GRASPING map tactility's <effects $_{yes}$> $^{OP \rightarrow P}$, <contact $_{yes}$>, <internal $_{no}$>, <voluntary $_{yes}$>, and <directness $_{yes}$> properties onto cognition. The individual can choose to "acquire" or "seize" abstract concepts, as the frequent commands to do so make clear, and such actions require the individual to come into direct contact with external concepts to do so. More important, unlike visual cognition, this form of knowledge acquisition is by no means a distant, passive endeavor. As Classen writes, such tactile metaphors "acknowledge and grapple with the tangled, bumpy and sticky nature of the topic" in question such that a personal "active involvement with the subject matter"

---

43. As Habel argues, the לב can act as the subject or object of the verb here. Based on a comparison with Hos 4:11, he prefers the latter, suggesting that the meaning of the idiom is akin to the English expression to "take leave of one's senses" (*Book of Job*, 247). Given the other metaphors in this grouping, Habel's reading seems appropriate.

44. See also the phrase לב־אין, "there is no heart" in Prov 17:16.

forms.[45] One personally acquires knowledge (Prov 1:5), wrestles with folly (Qoh 2:3), and takes hold of discipline (Prov 1:3). There is nothing between the individual and the concept that one is trying to understand, not even space (so <closeness $_{yes}$>), which means that the degree of understanding is based on the amount of effort the individual puts into the endeavor (<subjectivity $_{yes}$>). In the case of HAVING KNOWLEDGE IS POSSESSING HEART, this <closeness $_{yes}$> property becomes the primary element in the metaphorical mapping, although the fact that the individual's actions affect whether or not one has heart suggests that tactility's <voluntary $_{yes}$> property also factors in.

Teaching is also conceptualized as a manipulative action, as one "gives" or "puts" a concept to another (TEACHING IS TRANSFERRING AN OBJECT TO ANOTHER).

> Prov 9:9   *Give* [תן] to the wise, and they will be wiser still; make known to the righteous, and they will *add learning* [ויסף לקח].

"Giving" (נתן) to the wise is equivalent to making something known (הודע) to them. God in particular is said to "put" knowledge within the human.

> Prov 2:6   For the Lord *gives* [יתן] wisdom; from his mouth is knowledge and understanding.

> Qoh 2:26   For to one who is good before him, [God] *gives* [נתן] wisdom and knowledge and joy, but to the one who sins he *gives* [נתן] the work of gathering and colleting; only to the one who is pleasing before God is it *given* [לתת].

According to Prov 2:6 and Qoh 2:26, God "gives" (נתן) wisdom, knowledge, and joy to the individual; that is, he endows the person with information about the world and the capacity to understand it (see also Qoh 3:11). Theoretically, God can also take this understanding away (see, e.g., the deity "carrying off" understanding in the Sumerian text A Diaologue between a Man and His God 35–45), although this nuance is not stressed in Israelite wisdom literature. Like the metaphor THINKING IS TRANSFERRING AN

---

45. Classen, "Fingerprints," 5. Classen is speaking of tactile knowledge in general, but the sentiments are well suited to these particular metaphors in Israelite culture and the complex metaphors formed from them.

OBJECT TO ONE'S SELF, such expressions function by mapping <contact $_{yes}$>, <internal $_{no}$>, <voluntary $_{yes}$>, <directness $_{yes}$>, and <effects $_{yes}$> $^{OP \rightarrow P}$ onto the target domain of instruction. Here, however, the focus is not on the information one can give to one's self but on information that can be given to and taken from another.

Teaching is also conceptualized as an act of physical discipline. Thus in ancient Egyptian striking a student with rod was praised as a useful method of instruction: "Thoth has placed the stick on earth in order to teach the fool by it."[46] Indeed, the common Egyptian verb of instruction (*sb3*), which indicated professional training or teaching more generally, was often "accompanied by the determinative of a man holding a stick." By "striking" the student, the teacher "taught" his pupil a lesson, just as a trainer "taught" a lion or a monkey how to dance by striking it with a rod.[47] So, too, in ancient Israel, where physical discipline was used as a means of instruction.

> Prov 13:24   The one who withholds his *rod* [שבטו] hates his son, but the one who loves him is diligent to *discipline* [מוסר] him.

> Prov 26:3   A whip for a horse, a switch for an ass, and a *rod* [שבט] for the back of fools.

According to Proverbs, the loving father is one who uses a rod to correct his child's behavior (Prov 13:24; see also 29:15, 19); fools cannot learn without the rod (26:3; see also 20:30). Whether in a school or at home, physical discipline becomes a means to teach the next generation how to behave properly. By extension, any act of instruction becomes conceptualized as an act of corporeal punishment (INSTRUCTION IS A LASHING).

> Prov 3:11–12   My son, do not reject the *discipline* [מוסר] of God, and do not loathe his reproof, for the LORD reproves the one whom he loves, like a father does to the son who pleases him.

---

46. Papyrus Insinger 9.6; see also 11.1–2; Shupak, *Where Can Wisdom Be Found?*, 49–50. The translation follows that of Shupak.

47. Shupak, *Where Can Wisdom Be Found?*, 31–32. See also P.Anastasi 3.3, 13; Bologna 1094 3, 10; P.Anastasi 4.8, 7; 5.8, 5–6, 7–8.

Prov 15:33 The fear of the Lord is the *discipline* [מוסר] of wisdom.

Prov 22:15 Folly is *bound* [קשורה] within the heart of a youth; *the rod of discipline* [שבט מוסר] sends it far from him.

In Prov 22:15 discipline is conceptualized as a physical rod that beats folly out of the heart of the youth where it is bound (קשר), while in 15:33 the abstract behavior "fear of the Lord" is conceptualized as physical discipline that brings wisdom. In Prov 3:11 the parent-child relationship found in 13:24 has been extended to God and the student; the "discipline" (מוסר) of the God-father becomes the means by which the student-child is taught. In each case the noun מוסר is a tactile term connected to the physical sensation of יסר, to "punish" an individual by striking him or her with a rod (e.g., Prov 13:24; 23:13). It invokes learning that is obtained through the tactile sensation of a beating.[48] Such passages presume that learning is not without a certain degree of pain; it takes effort to correct incorrect behaviors such as folly. Thus, in addition to mapping <contact $_{yes}$>, <internal $_{no}$>, <voluntary $_{yes/no}$>[49], <directness $_{yes}$>, and <effects $_{yes}$> $^{OP \rightarrow P}$, INSTRUCTION IS A LASHING relies upon tactility's ability to create a physiological response (pain) in the one who is on the receiving end of the touch.

6.2.2. Emotion Metaphors

Avrahami does not connect emotion to tactility, in part because she limits her examination to expressions of happiness/sadness and joy/suffering.[50] Indeed, the generic act of touching (e.g., "to touch" or "feel," נגע, משש/מוש) does not connote an emotive response as it does in English, which suggests that generic tactility was not as prominent of a source domain for

---

48. In many cases these instruction terms (*sb*ṭ, מוסר) also have verbal connotations, in that the "rod" is metaphorically replaced by a word that strikes the individual. See the discussion of WISDOM IS A VERBAL LASHING in Nicole L. Tilford, "Taste and See: Perceptual Metaphors in Israelite and Early Jewish Sapiential Epistemology" (PhD diss., Emory University, 2014), 220–22. The point, however, is that the primary metaphor INSTRUCTION IS A LASHING is, at its core, a tactile metaphor.

49. It is voluntary for the one who performs the lashing (the parent) but involuntary for the one who receives the lashing (the child).

50. Avrahami, *Senses of Scripture*, 163–67.

6. TOUCHING

conceptualizing emotion in sapiential literature as other modalities were.[51] Yet tactility does serve as a source domain for emotion, particularly its capacity to manipulate objects and identify their material properties. For instance, negative emotions can "seize" an individual (BEING AFRAID IS BEING SEIZED).

Job 18:20   Horror *seizes* [אחזו] those of the east.

Job 21:6   And if I remember, then I am disturbed, and a shuddering *seizes* [ואחז] my flesh.

In these examples a negative emotion is portrayed as a person who seizes the individual (EMOTIONS ARE PEOPLE). Horror (שער) and fear (represented by פלצות, "a shuddering") "seize" (אחז) people, effectively paralyzing them from action. Persistence is similarly described as a seizure (PERSISTENCE IS GRASPING).

Job 2:3   Still, he *seizes firmly* [מחזיק] his integrity.

Here, however, it is the individual who "seizes" an abstract concept (IDEAS ARE MANIPULABLE OBJECTS), and the action displays the steadfastness of that person's character. Thus, despite egregious affliction, Job *persists* (מחזיק) in his commitment to God (Job 2:3; see also 2:9; 27:6).[52] Such metaphors derive from tactility's ability to connect directly with an object and to hold it still (<contact $_{yes}$>, <directness $_{yes}$>, <closeness $_{yes}$>, and <effects $_{yes}$> $^{OP \rightarrow P}$). Given the subject matter of the literature, it is not surprising that these emotive metaphors in sapiential literature are concentrated in Job. However, these metaphors appear elsewhere in the Hebrew Bible (Exod 15:14, 15; Deut 1:38; Isa 13:8; 21:3; Ps 48:7), which indicates that they are not the unique invention of the author.[53]

---

51. By way of comparison, consider the English terms *feel* and *touch*, which refer not only to physical sensations but emotional responses (e.g., "I do not *feel* well"; "the music *touched* him"; "her *feelings* were hurt"). See also the discussion in Sweetser, *From Etymology to Pragmatics*, 37, 42.

52. Persistence seems to be a neutral quality. In Job it is commended but in Exodus (4:21; 7:13, 22; 8:15; etc.) it is condemned.

53. See also Ps 119:53, where "heat" (זלעפה) "seizes" (אחז) the speaker. In this latter example, temperature is used as a source domain for the emotion of anger.

Emotions are also conceptualized as objects with physically characteristics. Negative emotions, for instance, "weigh" a person down (ANGER IS HEAVY, SORROW IS HEAVY).

> Prov 27:3 A stone is heavy [כֹּבֶד], sand is weighty [נֵטֶל], but the anger of a fool is *heavier* [כָּבֵד] than both.

> Job 6:2–3 Oh, surely let my vexation be *weighed* [שקול ישקל]; let my misfortune[54] *be lifted* [ישאו] as one onto the *scales* [במאזנים]. For it would *be heavier* [יכבד] than the sands of the sea.

Just as an English speaker would speak of having a "heavy heart," the Hebrew speaker can say that he or she is burdened by heavy emotion. For instance, anger is as "heavy" as a stone, and anxiety is as "heavy" as sand (נטל, כבד, Prov 27:3; see also Job 6:2–3). Here emotions are conceptualized as manipulable objects that have material weight (EMOTIONS ARE MANIPULABLE OBJECTS), thus mapping tactility's ability to identify that quality onto abstract emotional experience (<identification $_{yes}$>). Similarly, the heart can be "hard" or "soft," qualities that reflect the emotional status of the individual (FEAR IS A SOFT HEART/STUBBORNNESS IS A HARD HEART).

> Prov 28:14 Happy the person who fears continually, but the one who *hardens* his heart [ומקשה לבו] will fall into evil.

> Job 23:16 God has *softened* my heart [הרך לבי]; the Almighty has terrified me.

Here the self is once again conceptualized as a material object with physical characteristics (THE SELF IS AN OBJECT).[55] In Job 23:16 fear is described as a "softening" (הרך) of the לב, while in Prov 28:14 the one who does not fear is described as having a "hardened" (מקשה) לב. While neither

---

54. Thus following Habel (*Book of Job*, 139) in reading the וְהָיָתִי of the *ketiv* rather than the וְהַוָּתִי ("my desire") of the *qere*.

55. By analogy with the THINKING metaphors above, which combine a primary cognitive metaphor with a SELF metaphor, one would assume that these FEAR metaphors are compound iterations of a simpler metaphor, perhaps FEAR IS SOFTNESS/STUBBORNNESS IS HARDNESS. That stubbornness is also described as a "hard neck" seems to support this suggestion (see STUBBORNNESS IS A HARD NECK below).

metaphor is positive, the latter metaphor in particular is condemned. Like the pharaoh of Exodus, who does not show proper fear toward God—he כבד ("made heavy") or חזק ("made firm") his לב to the words of God's messenger (see Exod 7:13, 14, 22; 8:11, 28)—the one who makes his or her heart "hard" is destined for destruction. Stubbornness is also described as a "hard" neck (STUBBORNNESS IS A HARD NECK).

> Prov 29:1 The chastised man who *hardens* his neck [מקשה־ערף] will be suddenly broken, and there will be no healing.

Again, the act of hardening part of one's body is equated to a negative emotion that condemns the individual to destruction (compare the condemnation of the עם־קשה־ערף, "stiff-necked people," in Exod 32:9; 33:3, 5; 34:9). Given the agricultural context of ancient Israel, the individual here may be envisioned as an animal that refuses to be properly harnessed (THE SELF IS A DOMESTICATED BEAST) rather than as an object or person.[56] Yet whether referring to the לב, the neck, or the entire person, such passages combine tactility's ability to identify the material properties of objects with its ability to affect the perceiver (<identification $_{yes}$>, <effects $_{yes}$> $^{PR \rightarrow P}$).

6.2.3. Judgment Metaphors

As with emotion, Avrahami does not identify judgment with touching, and for good reason.[57] In sapiential literature, at least, tactile manipulation does not play a prominent role as a source domain for moral judgment. There are, however, two notable exceptions. The first is the root חלק (verb "to make smooth"; adj. "smooth"), which appears frequently in Proverbs as an adverse judgment on the moral character of the individual in question (e.g., Prov 2:16; 5:3; 6:24; 7:5, 21; 26:28; 28:23; 29:5; see also Job 17:5). The term is used, however, only in complex metaphors in which words are deemed "smooth" and is probably a direct result of the combination of WISDOM IS WORD and IDEAS ARE MANIPULABLE OBJECTS. As such, a discussion of these examples is best reserved for elsewhere.[58]

---

56. Thanks to Carol Newsom (personal communication) for suggesting this possibility.
57. Avrahami, *Senses of Scripture*, 167–75.
58. See, for example, my discussion of FLATTERY IS A SMOOTH OIL in Tilford,

The second exception is found in passages that depict judgment as an act of "weighing" (JUDGING IS WEIGHING).[59]

> Prov 21:2 All the ways of a person are upright in his eyes, but the LORD *measures out* [ותכן] the heart.

> Job 31:6 Let me be *weighed* [ישקלני] in the scales of righteous; let God know my integrity.

Here the self is conceptualized as a manipulable object with weight that can be physically measured (THE SELF IS AN OBJECT) (see also Prov 16:2; 24:12). Such statements are reminiscent of Egyptian culture, where the god Anubis "weighs" the heart of the deceased upon a scale to determine its suitability for the afterlife (see the depictions of the scene in the various versions of the Book of the Dead).[60] Similarly, in the Proverbs and Job it is God who evaluates humanity, not humanity evaluating itself. This suggests that the evaluative aspect of this metaphor derives from more complex theological speculations about God's function as judge than more basic notions about human epistemology. Tactility, in other words, is not an important source domain for human evaluative cognition.

6.3. SUMMARY

Tactility provides a source domain for a plethora of cognitive metaphors, each of which envisions cognition as a manipulable experience.

Table 6.2. Metaphorical Mappings: COGNITION IS TOUCHING

THINKING IS MANIPULATING OBJECTS
    <contact $_{yes}$>, <internal $_{no}$>, <voluntary $_{yes}$>, <directness $_{yes}$>, <effects $_{yes}$> OP → P

"Taste and See," 236–39.

59. In this regard, one might also point to Job 1:22 and 4:8, each of which depicts judgment as an act of "putting" or "giving" a charge to another (see also Job 9:33, where the execution of judgment is a "laying on" of the hands). These passages, however, seem to derive from the legal sphere of Israelite life and envision judgment as a verbal charge brought against another. They are, in other words, complex legal metaphors rather than primary cognitive metaphors.

60. Habel, *Book of Job*, 432.

THINKING IS TRANSFERRING AN OBJECT TO ONE'S SELF
    <contact _{yes}>, <internal _{no}>, <voluntary _{yes}>, <directness _{yes}>, <effects _{yes}> ^{OP → P}

THINKING IS MANIPULATING ONE'S SELF
    <contact _{yes}>, <internal _{no}>, <voluntary _{yes}>, <directness _{yes}>, <effects _{yes}> ^{OP → P}

UNDERSTANDING IS GRASPING
    <closeness _{yes}>, <effects _{yes}> ^{OP → P}; also:<contact _{yes}>, <internal _{no}>, <voluntary _{yes}>, <directness _{yes}>, <subjectivity _{yes}>

ACQUIRING KNOWLEDGE IS ACQUIRING OBJECTS
    <closeness _{yes}>, <effects _{yes}> ^{OP → P}; also: <contact _{yes}>, <internal _{no}>, <voluntary _{yes}>, <directness _{yes}>, <subjectivity _{yes}>

HAVING KNOWLEDGE IS POSSESSING HEART
    <closeness _{yes}>, <voluntary _{yes}>

TEACHING IS TRANSFERRING AN OBJECT TO ANOTHER
    <contact _{yes}>, <internal _{no}>, <voluntary _{yes}>, <directness _{yes}>, <effects _{yes}> ^{OP → P}

INSTRUCTION IS A LASHING
    <contact _{yes}>, <internal _{no}>, <voluntary _{yes}>, <directness _{yes}>, <effects _{yes}> ^{OP → P}

BEING AFRAID IS BEING SEIZED
    <contact _{yes}>, <directness _{yes}>, <closeness _{yes}>, and <effects _{yes}> ^{OP → P}

PERSISTENCE IS GRASPING
    <contact _{yes}>, <directness _{yes}>, <closeness _{yes}>, and <effects _{yes}> ^{OP → P}

ANGER/SORROW IS HEAVY
    <identification _{yes}>

FEAR IS A SOFT HEART
    <identification _{yes}>, <effects _{yes}> ^{PR → P}

STUBBORNNESS IS A HARD HEART/NECK
    <identification _{yes}>, <effects _{yes}> ^{PR → P}

Since they each rely upon tactility's ability to manipulate objects, these metaphors consistently map tactility's properties of <contact _{yes}>, <internal _{no}>, <voluntary _{yes}>, <directness _{yes}>, <effects _{yes}> ^{OP → P} onto the target domain of cognition. What varies between them is the emphasis that those properties have and the object and direction of the manipulation, specifically whether the object is the לב (e.g., THINKING IS MANIPULATING ONE'S SELF) or an abstract concept (e.g., ACQUIRING KNOWLEDGE IS ACQUIRING OBJECTS) and whether it is moved toward (e.g., THINKING IS

TRANSFERRING AN OBJECT TO ONE'S SELF) or away from (e.g., TEACHING IS TRANSFERRING AN OBJECT TO ANOTHER) the perceiver. INSTRUCTION IS A LASHING and the emotive metaphors also rely upon tactility's ability to initiate physiology change (pain, terror, etc.) in the object perceived. Of utmost importance throughout, however, is the conception of cognition as an experience of direct, manipulable contact between the perceiver and its object.

7
INGESTING

Just as touch is commonly dismissed as an epistemological modality due to its associations with base sensations, taste has often been regulated to the realm of subjective preference and emotional experience. Such connotations are certainly not absent from the Hebrew Bible, where taste serves as a frequent source domain for emotive and evaluative metaphors, yet emotional experience and moral judgment are important components of the human cognitive system, and it is thus appropriate to include a discussion of this modality here. Like other modalities, conceptual metaphors based on taste reflect a distinct conception of cognition, in this case one in which cognition is understood as a personal, subjective experience.

7.1. Typology of Ingestion

As Avrahami notes, in biblical Hebrew there is not a "sharp semantic distinction ... between the common verb 'to eat' (אכל) and the rare verb 'to taste' (טעם), nor the tasting process and eating" more generally.[1] For instance, 1 Sam 14:24 equates the two functions: "'Cursed be the one who *eats* bread [אכל לחם] before evening.'... So none of the people *tasted* bread [טעם לחם]" (see also Jonah 3:7). Moreover, while אכל and שתה can respectively refer to the consumption of solid or liquid foods (e.g., Gen 27:25; Exod 34:28; Deut 2:6), they frequently operate in tandem to signify the entire process of ingestion (e.g., Gen 24:54; 25:34; 26:30). It is appropriate, therefore, to broaden the examination here to include the entire act of ingestion—the act of putting food or drink into the mouth,

---

1. Avrahami, *Senses of Scripture*, 93. Malul similarly notes an overlap between "taste" and the domain of eating (*Knowledge, Control, and Sex*, 131–32).

tasting it, and swallowing it—rather than limiting the discussion to "taste" specifically.

Like speech, ingestion is associated with the mouth (פה) and its component parts (חך, "roof of mouth, palate"; שפתים, "lips"; לשון, "tongue"; גרון, "throat"), which appear in conjunction with verbs of eating (אכל, לחם), drinking (שקה, שתה), swallowing (בלע), and tasting (טעם). Unlike speech, however, ingestion is an internally oriented modality, acquiring information by bringing external objects from the environment into the body through the mouth and throat (Neh 9:20; Ps 78:30; Dan 10:3; see also 1 Sam 14:27, where putting the hand to the mouth is equivalent to ingesting) (<internal $_{yes}$>). Because the object must enter the perceiver, ingestion requires direct, close contact between the perceiver and the object perceived (<contact $_{yes}$>, <closeness $_{yes}$>, <directness $_{yes}$>). Thus David's son Amnon arranges for his sister Tamar to bring food to him so that he may eat it (2 Sam 13:5–6) and God worries that the first human will reach out to the tree of life and bring the fruit close to him in order to eat (Gen 3:22).

Once the object is inside the perceiver's mouth, it immediately comes in contact with the taste buds, "clusters of between 50 and 150 taste receptor cells" that transmit chemical stimuli to the human brain and enable the perceiver to detect and identify with great precision the flavor of the object.[2] Of course, the Hebrew Bible does not refer to these taste buds, yet it recognizes their function, connecting ingestion with the ability to classify objects according to their basic flavors: sweet (מתק, Exod 15:25; Judg 9:11; Ps 19:11; Prov 24:13; 27:7), bitter (מרר/מר, Exod 15:23; Num 5:18–19, 23–24; Prov 27:7), salty (מלח, Exod 30:35; Job 6:6), or tasteless (תפל, Job 6:6).[3] It also recognizes the mouth's capacity to detect the temperature and moisture of an object, for instance, whether an object is cold (קר, Prov 25:25), hot (e.g., עגת רצפים, a "cake of hot coals," 1 Kgs 19:6), or dry (e.g., חרב, Prov 17:1).

---

2. Carolyn Korsmeyer, *Making Sense of Taste: Food and Philosophy* (Ithaca, NY: Cornell University Press, 1999), 73.

3. Four flavors—sweet, bitter, acid, and salt—have frequently been identified across cultures, which has led to their classification as *the* four fundamental flavors. However, the flavors individuals identify vary across cultures. The ancient Greeks, for instance, commonly identified six basic flavors (bitter, sweet, sour, salty, harsh, astringent, and pungent), while sixteenth-century Westerners identified nine basic tastes (sweet, sour, sharp, pungent, harsh, fatty, bitter, insipid, and salty) (ibid., 13–14, 75–76). It is uncertain how many flavors the Israelites identified, although the Hebrew Bible notes at least the four identified here.

7. INGESTING

Through such means, ingestion is capable of identifying objects that enter into the mouth (<detection _{yes}>, <identification _{yes}>). For instance, by ingestion an individual can determine whether a liquid is wine (יין), vinegar (חמץ), strong drink (שכר), water (מים), or grape juice (משרת ענבים) (Num 6:3; Judg 13:4, 7, 14; Ps 69:21).[4] Like touch or hearing, this detection occurs sequentially.[5] The individual puts an object into his or her mouth, tastes it, chews it, and swallows it before the act of ingestion is finally complete. Ezekiel "opens his mouth" (ואפתח את־פי), "eats" (ואכלה) the scroll given to him, and "fills" his stomach with it (ומעיך תמלא את המגלה הזאת) (Ezek 2:8; 3:2–3).[6] The specific act of taste itself is also sequential in that only the part of the object in contact with the taste buds is perceived. To perceive the entire object, one must either rotate it on the tongue or break it into component parts so that the entire object can connect with a taste receptor.[7] Since the taste receptors vary in their sensitivity to tastes—the taste buds on the tip of the tongue, for instance, are more sensitive to sweetness, while those on the back of the tongue are prone to bitterness[8]—the intensity of an object's taste can change, depending upon which taste receptors it is connecting with. Given this sequentially, it is hardly surprisingly that Job 12:11 and 34:3 find taste a dynamic experience, comparing it to a "test" (הלא־אזן מלין תבחן חך אכל יטעם־לו, "does not the ear test words and the palate taste food").[9]

---

4. Numbers 6:3 specifically commands the Nazirite *not* to drink wine, strong drink, or grape juice (see also Judg 13:4, 7, 14). However, the cultural distinctions between these objects in the first place presumably stem from their difference in flavor and not solely on their chemical composition or appearance.

5. Korsmeyer, *Making Sense of Taste*, 82.

6. A scroll is an unusual object to ingest and probably represents the ingestion of the divine word. However, despite its symbolic meaning, within the context of the vision concrete ingestion is clearly intended, indicating that ingestion is not limited to "food" and "water" in the strict sense but includes anything that enters the body through the mouth.

7. In this respect, taste is like touch, a modality upon which it relies.

8. Korsmeyer, *Making Sense of Taste*, 74. This distribution, she argues, likely arose as a biological "safety" mechanism: "Many poisons are intensely bitter. The bitter receptors thus stand guard as the last point where swallowing can be halted."

9. This comparison is the basis for a complex metaphor in which the ear is likened to the palate in its ability to "test" words. Such a complex metaphor assumes, however, that the mouth has the ability to "test" food.

The Hebrew Bible, however, does not often reflect upon this sequentiality, instead presenting ingestion as an instantaneous action ("she ate," Gen 3:6; Ruth 2:14; "he drank," Gen 9:21; Judg 15:19; 1 Kgs 17:6; "they ate and drank," Gen 24:54; 26:30). This is perhaps because ingestion, like touch, creates an impression of simultaneity through its sequence. As modern science suggests, each individual has thousands of taste receptors spread throughout the mouth—in various papillae (the small observable "bumps" on the tongue), on the roof of the mouth, on the cheeks, and on the throat—which makes it possible to connect with multiple parts of the object at once and experience a variety of flavors simultaneously.[10] This lends taste a spatial quality in that concurrent taste sensations are related to each other according to their location on the tongue.[11] Unlike images in a visual field or touch sensations, however, such disparate taste sensations are never completely integrated together. While flavors may blend together or intensify one another, the basic flavors of an object remain distinctive enough that a perceiver can separate the taste of an object into its component parts. To use a modern example, one can discern both the sourness of the lemons and the sweetness of the sugar in a glass of lemonade.[12] The result is what I would call a "composite simultaneity," an impression of an object that is complete, yet composed of distinctive units. By analogy with Jonas, one might therefore argue that ingestion's detection is one of "composite simultaneity through sequence." Because of this complexity, individuals are more likely to describe the taste of an object by comparing it to another object (e.g., כדבש, "like honey," Ezek 3:3; see also Exod 16:31), than to describe it via flavor ("sweet with a touch of bitterness").[13]

On the one hand, this process of detection makes ingestion a fairly dynamic modality and enables the individual consciously to reflect on the process of tasting food (as in Job 12:11; 34:3). On the other hand, ingestion

---

10. Korsmeyer, *Making Sense of Taste*, 72–73; Ibarretxe-Antuñano, "Polysemy and Metaphor in Perception Verbs," 142. In this regard, it is telling that the Hebrew Bible associates taste with a variety of locations in the mouth, not only the פה ("mouth") more generally but also the חך ("roof of mouth, palate"), the לשון ("tongue"), and the גרון ("throat") (Judg 7:5; Job 6:30; 12:11; 34:3; Pss 69:4; 119:103).

11. Paul Breslin and Liquan Huang, "Human Taste: Peripheral Anatomy, Taste Transduction, and Coding," in *Taste and Smell: An Update*, ed. Thomas Hummel and Antje Welge-Lüssen, Advances in Oto-Rhino-Laryngology 63 (Basel: Karger, 2006), 154.

12. Korsmeyer, *Making Sense of Taste*, 77.

13. Ibid., 78.

7. INGESTING

is fairly limited in the scope of its identification. Its concerns are confined to the interior of the body, making the initial location and the limits of the object largely irrelevant.[14] To fill this gap, ingestion is heavily influenced by other modalities: touch, which brings the object into contact with the perceiver; sight, which influences the object's appeal and identification; and smell, which contributes to the perceiver's experience of an object's flavor. Thus Gen 3:6 states that the first humans "took" (לקח) fruit and ate (אכל) it, and Num 11 describes manna not only by its taste ("its taste was like the taste of cake made with oil," 11:8) but also by its color ("its appearance was the appearance of bdellium," 11:7). Moreover, because taste is limited to the confines of the mouth, ingestion is largely incomparable. As Carolyn Korsmeyer explains, the number of papillae in the mouth and the number of taste receptors per papillae varies from person to person.[15] Since the taste receptors vary in their sensitivity to tastes, two people eating the same piece of food can have vastly different responses to it depending upon the predisposition of the taste receptors in their mouth (<subjectivity $_{yes}$>). Despite is subjectivity, ingestion is still capable of evaluating the relative value of an object, whether it is safe to eat or poison (<evaluation $_{yes}$>). Thus a company of prophets determines that a stew is poisonous by eating it (מות בסיר, "there is death in the pot," 2 Kgs 4:40; see also Ps 69:22). That they are able to do so without having long-lasting effects suggests that taste can evaluate the nature of the object quickly (so <briefness $_{yes}$>).

Although a person can be provided food or water by another and be commanded to eat or drink (Gen 24:18, 44, 46; 25:34), the individual chooses whether or not to do so, making ingestion a voluntary modality

---

14. Therefore, although one can detect the relative location of an object within the mouth, the property of <location> itself, in as much as it applies to the relationship of the perceiver to his or her environment, does not apply, nor does the property of <limits>.

15. According to Linda Bartoshuk, "about 20 percent of the population are ... 'supertasters,' people with densely packed papillae who are especially sensitive to flavors (especially to sweet and sour). Another 20 percent have relatively few taste buds and dull taste perception. Most of us fall in between" (cited in Korsmeyer, *Making Sense of Taste*, 87). Although there is a universal predisposition for sweet tastes, the amount and distribution of taste receptors is affected by genetics and can vary over a person's lifetime. This is because the taste buds constantly regenerate every ten to fourteen days, but the older one becomes, the number of taste buds that regenerate declines (74, 87–88). In this regard, one might consider 2 Sam 19:35, which notes how the aged Barzillai lost his ability to taste that which he ate.

(<voluntary $_{yes}$>). Abraham's servant waits until speaking his message before eating the food that Laban lays before him (Gen 24:33–54), and Moses does not eat bread or drink water for forty days (Exod 34:28; Deut 9:9, 18). One can also choose what to eat, and the choice has direct effect on the perceiver and the object perceived (<effects $_{yes}$> $^{PR \rightarrow P}$, <effects $_{yes}$> $^{OP \rightarrow P}$). Eating and drinking, for instance, clearly provides nourishment for the individual. Lack of food or water causes "faintness" (עיף; 1 Sam 14:28; 2 Sam 16:2; 17:29; Isa 29:8; 44:12) and "lack of strength" (כח לא־היה בו, 1 Sam 28:20; see also 1 Sam 28:22; 30:12; Isa 44:12), while adequate food or water provides nourishment (e.g., 1 Sam 30:12; 1 Kgs 19:7–8; Qoh 10:17; Neh 5:2) and "satisfies" (שבע) any sensations of "thirst" (צמא) or "hunger" (רעב) that an individual might have (e.g., Deut 8:3; 2 Sam 17:29; Ruth 2:9; Prov 25:21; see also the combination אכל ושבע, "eat and be satisfied," in Deut 8:10, 12; 11:15). Ingestion can also alter the disposition of an individual, causing contentedness (וייטב לבו, Ruth 3:7), happiness (שמח, 1 Kgs 4:20; Qoh 10:19), or drunkenness (שכר, Gen 9:21; 43:34; 2 Sam 11:13; 1 Kgs 16:9; 20:16).

Moreover, as food or water is broken down and absorbed into the body, ingestion can transfer the inherent qualities from the object to the perceiver. For instance, the one who eats "holy" (קדש) food is endowed with "holiness" (לקדש, Exod 29:33), and the one who eats "unclean" (טמא) or "detestable" (שקץ) animals becomes "unclean" (תטמאו, Lev 11:2–24a, 40–43). To prevent unintended contagion, the Hebrew Bible contains a plethora of commands regulating the consumption of food, some of which identify the intended effect (e.g., removal of guilt, Lev 10:17; avoidance of uncleanliness, Lev 11; 22:8; Deut 14:3–21) and others of which do not (Gen 32:33; Exod 12:9; 21:28). Still, the individual maintains the freedom to choose when and what to eat. Although God commands them not to eat from the tree of the knowledge of good and evil, the first humans choose to eat from the forbidden tree and are punished for it (Gen 2:16–17; 3:1–22).

The properties of ingestion can be summarized as follows:[16]

---

16. As mentioned above, <location> and <limits> are not properties associated with taste. <Correction of hypothesis> may be a property (although Ibarretxe-Antuñano does not believe so; see "Polysemy and Metaphor in Perception Verbs," 153–55) in that the perceiver forms a hypothesis about the identification of an object when he or she tastes it, which may or may not be accurate. However, the Hebrew Bible does not seem to reflect on this aspect, so I have no assigned this property to the biblical typology.

Table 7.1. Biblical Typology of Ingestion

<contact ᵧₑₛ>   <directness ᵧₑₛ>

<closeness ᵧₑₛ>   <effects ᵧₑₛ> ᴾᴿ → ᴾ

<internal ᵧₑₛ>   <subjectivity ᵧₑₛ>

<detection ᵧₑₛ> composite simultaneity through sequence   <effects ᵧₑₛ> ᴼᴾ → ᴾ

<identification ᵧₑₛ>   <evaluation ᵧₑₛ>

<voluntary ᵧₑₛ>   <briefness ᵧₑₛ>

7.2. COGNITION IS INGESTING

Ancient wisdom literature rarely connects ingestion to an individual's knowledge of a situation apart from his or her capacity to pass moral judgment.[17] This is perhaps due to the subjective nature of taste. Even more so than seeing, touching, or hearing/speaking, which can be experienced to

---

17. Possible exceptions in Egyptian are the verbs ʿm ("to know") and s33 ("to be wise"), which Shupak argues is connected to their hononymous lexemes ʿm ("to swallow") and s33 ("to be satisfied, sated with"). He thus argues that each can be used metaphorically to equate learning to an act of eating. However, Shupak (*Where Can Wisdom Be Found?*, 65–66, 222) lists only a few possible occurrences of this connotation (e.g., P.Anastasi 4.4, 11; P.Sallier 1.4, 5–6; P.Lansing 13b, 9; Instruction of Amennakht 8), and each occurs in a situation in which the individual is also making a personal evaluation of a situation. Avrahami (*Senses of Scripture*, 162) notes two possible exceptions in the Hebrew Bible, Ps 34:9 and Qoh 2:25. Qoheleth refers to a concrete experience and thus does not affect our discussion of cognitive metaphors here. Psalm 34:9, on the other hand, may be a good example of טעם being used to indicate thinking: the individual is commanded to "taste [טעמו] and see that the Lord is good," that is, to *consider* the saving power of God in order that to *conclude* that God is good. However, since ingestion rarely expresses thought apart from moral evaluation, טעם may have been chosen here in order to fulfill the need of the poem's acrostic structure, *tet* being a difficult Hebrew letter to find a suitable term to use in a psalm of thanksgiving. If so, then the use of טעם here is again probably an imaginative extension of one of טעם's usual judgmental metaphors (see JUDGING IS TASTING below) rather than reflective of a primary metaphorical usage of the term. This suggestion is supported by the fact that, even here, the final result of cognitive "tasting" is a moral judgment about God. Avrahami herself recognizes this connection, since she also includes this verse in her discussion of other judgment metaphors (170). Alternatively, Avrahami suggests that this verse could indicate "being satisfied through faith" (98), in which

varying degrees by different people and compared, ingestion is a personal experience limited to the inside of the mouth and thus largely incomparable. It is thus better suited as a source domain for personal evaluations of situations than simple mental contemplation of them. In the Hebrew Bible, this is exactly what we find, with ingestion serving as a frequent source domain for cognitive experience that is emotive and evaluative.

7.2.1. Emotion Metaphors

Ingestion is commonly associated with the subjective experience of emotion. Desire, for instance, is described as a hunger or thirst (DESIRE IS HUNGER, DESIRE IS THIRST). In Egyptian wisdom literature desire is described as an uncontrollable hunger [*3f'* or *skn*] for food (Instruction of Ani 8.6–7; see also the Instructions of Kagemni 1.9), wealth (Instruction of Amenemope 15.9; 18.8; see also 7.14), or even women (e.g., Instruction of Ptahhotep 277–297). It is, in other words, a negative trait that leads to ruin.[18] The clearest example of this metaphor in the Hebrew Bible occurs in nonsapiential psalms, which describe the psalmist's longing for God as an insatiable "thirst":

> Ps 63:2   My God, you are my God. I seek you; my נפש *thirsts* [צמאה] for you; my flesh is *faint* [כמה] for you in a dry and weary land without water.

Like a person who cannot find water to drink in a dry land, the psalmist *desires* (צמא) God's saving presence (see also Ps 42:3). Unlike its Egyptian counterpart, the desire mentioned here is not negative; it is a positive sign of devotion. Similar longings appear in Israelite and early Jewish wisdom literature, where the desires of individuals are described as hungers and thirsts:

> Prov 10:3   The Lord does not let the righteous נפש *hunger* [ירעיב], but he drives away the desire[19] of the wicked.

---

case the emotional effect of taste, rather than the evaluative property, would be the governing property.

18. Shupak, *Where Can Wisdom Be Found?*, 108.

19. הוה. As Michael V. Fox argues (*Proverbs 10–31: A New Introduction and Commentary*, AYB 18B [New Haven: Yale University Press], 512), הוה ("destruction") should probably be emended to חיה ("living thing") and functions here as a synonym

Job 5:5　The *hungry* [רעב] *eat* [יאכל] [the fool's] harvest…, and the *thirsty* [צמים] *pant* [ושאף][20] after their wealth.

Job 20:20　For [the wicked] did not know rest *in his belly* [בבטנו]; in his desire [בחמודו], he let nothing escape.

On the one hand, Prov 10:3 clearly refers to the concrete experience of food consumption: the righteous *eat*; the wicked *go hungry*. Yet as Fox notes, this proverb can easily apply to any number of desires (e.g., for wealth, for knowledge, for vindication).[21] Indeed, unlike their Egyptian counterparts, whose discussions of desire are limited to material goods, Israelite sages were comfortable applying the metaphor to material goods or intangible concepts.[22] Thus in Job 5:5b one "thirsts" for the fool's חיל. Since the noun חיל does not refer only to a fool's water but to all of his wealth, the "thirst" described here is clearly metaphorical.[23] Similarly, the "hunger" described in Job 20:20 is not for physical food and water but material possessions more generally (see 20:18–19). Through the conceptual metaphor DESIRE IS HUNGER, a similar generic lesson can be extracted from Prov 10:3, namely, that "God fulfills the desires of the righteous but thwarts the wishes of the wicked." Indeed, the value of Prov 10:3 as a piece of communal knowledge lies in the fact that it can be applied to

---

for "desire" or "appetite" (see Job 33:20 and 38:39 for concrete examples of חיה with this meaning).

20. Although שאף could refer to the act of "gasping" for air (e.g., Ps 119:131; Isa 42:14), here it parallels eating and is thus clearly connected to thirst.

21. Fox, *Proverbs 10–31*, 512.

22. Shupak, *Where Can Wisdom Be Found?*, 112.

23. As Habel notes (*Book of Job*, 131, 117), the "hungry" (רעב) and "thirsty" (צמים) in this passage could be mythological references to supernatural forces of destruction, the "Hungry One" and the "Thirsty Ones." Yet, whether referring the human poor or supernatural agents of death, the basic metaphor here is the same, those without wealth desire it and consume their ill-begotten goods. Note that, while "thirsting" is connected to desire here, "eating" is not. Unlike Job 20:20, "eating" here refers to the physical consumption of food, represented by the "harvest." It is thus a physical image. Like Prov 10:3, the combination of concrete consumption and metaphorical thirst here highlights once again the close connection between physical action and metaphorical meaning and effectively demonstrates how authors can use this connection to advance their rhetoric.

any number of situations and is not limited to the material surfeit of the righteous and wicked.

The fulfillment of such desires is depicted as a state of "fatness" or "satiety," while its obverse is a state of "emptiness" (SATISFACTION IS FULLNESS, DISSATISFACTION IS EMPTINESS):

Prov 13:4   The נפש of the lazy desires but has not, but the נפש of the diligent is *fattened* [תדשן].

Prov 13:25   The righteous *eats* [אכל] to the *satisfaction* [לשבע] of his נפש, but the *belly* [בטן] of the wicked is *empty* [תחסר].

Qoh 5:9   The lover of money is not *satisfied* [ישבע] with silver, nor the one who loves with produce. This, too, is vanity.

Qoh 6:2   There is one to whom God gives wealth and riches and honor,[24] so that he does not lack according to all that his נפש desires, yet God does not empower him to *eat* [לאכל] from them, but a stranger *eats* [יאכלנו] them. This is vanity and a great ill.

Qoh 6:3   If a man begets a hundred [children] and lives many years, but complains that his days of his years will come to pass,[25] and his נפש is not *satiated* [לא־תשבע] from the good....

As with Prov 10:3, the desires referred to in Prov 13:4 and 25 could be for actual food, but these passages can also be applied to intangible desires, in which case the resulting "empty belly" (בטן ... חסר) or "fattened" (דשן) נפש refers not only to a physical state but also to a state of emotional satiety. Similarly, Qoh 6:2 connects one's satisfaction to one's ability to *eat* (אכל). Here, despite having everything provided, the individual described

---

24. Seow (*Ecclesiastes*, 210) argues that "honor" is not an appropriate translation for כבוד, since one must be able to "partake" of these things (he prefers the translation "abundance" or "plenty"). However, as the discussion throughout this monograph demonstrates, conceptual metaphors function by mapping concrete activities onto abstract concepts, like honor. There is no reason to assume, therefore, that this cannot be the case here as well.

25. So Seow, *Ecclesiastes*, 202, 211.

is not able to "eat" wealth or honor; that is, he is unable to *enjoy* them.²⁶ The root שבע, which is used in the next verse (Qoh 6:3) and in Prov 13:25 to indicate the satisfaction of the נפש, is frequently connected to the physical state of being full of food (Job 27:14; Prov 12:11; 20:13; 25:16; 27:7). Its occurrence in these two passages and in Qoh 5:9 therefore probably relies upon the ingestive domain: the individual is not *satisfied* with wealth (Qoh 5:9; see also Job 20:22) or the "good" (Qoh 6:3), the latter of which is probably a reference back to the wealth and honor mentioned in Qoh 6:2.

It is no coincidence that the נפש figures prominently in these descriptions of intangible desire. Although often translated as "soul," the נפש was intimately connected with the "throat" of the individual and was often referenced as the seat of an individual's physical "appetite" (e.g., Job 6:7; Prov 6:30; 16:26; 27:7). Psalm 63:2, Prov 10:3, 13:25, and Qoh 6:2 explicitly draw upon this connection with the physical appetite, using the biological appetite for food or water as a model for nonphysical desires. Presumably the frequent references to the desires of the נפש throughout this literature also draw upon this connection, even when the domain of ingestion is otherwise specifically referred to.²⁷ For instance:

Prov 21:10   The wicked נפש desires wickedness.

Job 23:13   His נפש desires, and he does it.

Rather than simply stating that the "lazy" (עצל) or the "wicked" (רשע) desire (see, e.g., Prov 21:25), Prov 21:20 and Job 23:13 note that the נפש desires, thereby highlighting the ingestive capability of the human individual. In many cases this נפש seems to function as a metonymy for the entire person.²⁸ Thus the righteous נפש of Prov 10:3 *is* the righteous individual who hungers for various desires (see also Prov 21:10); that is, the *entire*

---

26. As Seow notes, it is unclear why the individual cannot enjoy his material goods. "One can only guess whether the author is thinking of economic, physical, or psychological hardship" (ibid., 225).

27. This is not to say that the connection between the נפש and ingestion is ubiquitous. The נפש is also frequently connected to the "breath" of the individual and through it the domain of speaking or breathing. However, when it desires, the נפש seems to be envisioned as a consuming (ingestive) entity.

28. In this it functions like the לב in the primary iteration of THINKING IS SPEAKING above. That the primary metaphors can occur without reference to the נפש (e.g., Job 5:5; 20:20; Qoh 5:9–10) supports this reading.

person is a consuming נפש craving satisfaction. Other passages, however, seem to presume a bifurcated individual, with the נפש functioning as a separate self within the individual that can direct his or her movements and be filled or fattened (THE SELF IS A PERSON). Thus the righteous eat to satisfy their נפש (Prov 13:25)—that is, the essence of the righteous feeds its self—while an ungrateful man cannot "satiate" his נפש (e.g., Qoh 6:3). Like the visual and tactile THINKING metaphors above, then, these primary metaphors of desire can combine with a SELF metaphor to create the idea that DESIRE IS A HUNGRY SELF/DESIRE IS A THIRSTY SELF (e.g., Ps 63:2; Job 23:13) and SATISFACTION IS A FULL SELF/DISSATISFACTION IS AN EMPTY SELF (e.g., Prov 13:4–5; Qoh 6:2, 3).

In themselves, desire and satisfaction appear to be neutral emotions engaged in by both the righteous and wicked. As in Egyptian literature, however, they can be deemed negative qualities. Thus, according to Prov 19:2 "*desire* [נפש] without knowledge is not good" (see also 12:11, where the opposite of physical satisfaction is חסר־לב, a "lack of heart"). Yet, good or bad, DESIRE IS HUNGER/THIRST and the related metaphors SATISFACTION IS FULLNESS/DISSATISFACTION IS EMPTINESS operate by mapping the properties of ingestion onto the abstract domain of desire, most notably the properties of <contact $_{yes}$>, <internal $_{yes}$>, <directness $_{yes}$>, and <subjectivity $_{yes}$>. Each metaphor presumes a direct connection between the perceiver (or the perceiver's self) and the object of his or her desire, whether that desire be God, wealth, or an abstract quality such as wickedness. For such desire to be fulfilled, the object of the desire must then enter into the perceiver and "fill" his or her body. Here, then, the person is also conceptualized as a container (THE SELF IS A CONTAINER), which can be filled with intangible desires that can be consumed (IDEAS ARE FOOD/LIQUID). Having enough to "eat" leaves one satisfied, while having too little leaves one craving more. Such desires, however, vary from person to person. Wealth seems to have been a popular desire, considering how frequently sapiential literature reflects upon it (e.g., Job 5:5; Qoh 5:9; 6:2–3), but individuals could also desire wickedness (Prov 21:10), honor (Qoh 6:2), or even God (Ps 63:2). In the case of Prov 10:3, 13:4, and 25, the subjectivity of desire enables the application of the proverb to multiple situations that remain unnamed in the text. Still, although the object of desire varies as proverbs are applied to new situations, the metaphorical mapping remains consistent. Desire is a personal, subjective experience.

Emotions are also commonly described as flavors (ENJOYMENT IS SWEET, DISTRESS IS BITTER).

Prov 9:17 Stolen water is *sweet* [ימתקו], and secret bread is pleasant.

Job 9:18 He does allow me to return my breath but *satiates* me [ישבעני] with *bitterness* [ממררים].

Qoh 5:11 *Sweet* [מתוקה] is the sleep of the worker, whether he eats [יאכל] little or much, but the surfeit [והשבע] of the rich does not give rest for him to sleep.

Sleep is *enjoyable* (מתוקה) to the worker because he does not have to worry about material possessions as the rich person does (Qoh 5:11; see also Prov 2:10; 3:24; 13:19; Qoh 11:7), and ill-begotten goods are *pleasant* (מתק) to a person who obtains them (Prov 9:17). On the other hand, a person in sorrow is "full" of bitterness; that is, his entire body tastes sorrow (Job 9:18; compare ושבעתי נדדים, "full of tossing," in 7:4 and ושבע־רגז, "full of trouble," in 14:1). When combined with a SELF metaphor, this last conceptualization creates a compound metaphor in which distress is understood to be a "bitter" נפש (DISTRESS IS A BITTER SELF).[29]

Prov 14:10 The heart knows the *bitterness* [מרת] of its נפש.

Job 21:23–25 This one dies with sound bone, completely secure and at ease, his loins full of milk [מלאו חלב] and the marrow of his bones drunk [ישקה]. But this one dies in a *bitter soul* [בנפש מרה] and does not *eat good* [ולא־אכל בטובה].

Job 27:2 By the living God, who takes away my judgment, and Shaddai, who *makes bitter* [המר] my נפש.

Here bitterness is localized in one part of the individual, the נפש, which is "made bitter" (המר) by God (Job 27:2) or by circumstance (Prov 14:10; Job 21:23–25).[30] According to Prov 14:10, the heart can know the "bitterness" (מרת) of its נפש; that is, one self of the individual can experience the *dis-*

---

29. By the same process, enjoyment could theoretically be conceptualized as a "sweet" נפש (ENJOYMENT IS A SWEET SELF), but this does not seem to be attested.

30. See also Job 3:20 and Prov 31:6, which speak of individual being bitter *of* נפש. Although these could envision the נפש as a metonymy for the person as a whole (as in

tress of another self. The individual can also act "with" or "in" a bitter נפש. Thus, unlike the "sweetness" experience by the sleeping worker in Qoh 5:11, the individual in Job 21:25 dies "in" a bitter נפש (see also Job 7:11; 10:1); that is, he dies without being able to *enjoy* the simple pleasures of life or אכל בטובה ("eat good"). Like the phrase ראה טובה ("see good"), אכל בטובה indicates enjoyment, in this case, the *enjoyment* of health and security ("loins full of milk," עטיניו מלאו חלב; "marrow of his bones drunk," ומח עצמותיו ישקשה; "sound bone," בעצם תמו).[31] אכל בטובה is thus the functional equivalent of מתוק (ENJOYMENT IS TO EAT GOOD). As Malul notes, the root טוב is frequently connected to taste (e.g., good wine, good oil) and may itself be derived from the domain of eating and being satisfied.[32] A "good heart" (לב טוב/טוב לב), for instance, frequently "refers to the state of satisfaction after having eaten and drunk one's fill" (e.g., 1 Kgs 8:66; Esth 1:10; Prov 15:15; Qoh 9:7).[33] Given the prolific use of טוב in the Hebrew Bible as an abstract quality without any connection to eating, I would hesitate to push this etymology too far. However, it does suggest that, like נפש or שבע, טוב is not as divorced from concrete experience as might otherwise be assumed.

Like the DESIRE metaphors, ENJOYMENT IS SWEET and DISTRESS IS BITTER map ingestion's properties of <internal $_{yes}$>, <directness $_{yes}$>, and <subjectivity $_{yes}$> onto the abstract domain of emotional experience, creating an impression of emotion as a personal, subjective experience. They also conceptualize the human body as a container into which emotions can be put (BODY IS A CONTAINER). In these cases, however, "being full" is not necessarily a positive experience; although one can be full of happiness, one can also be full of sorrow and trouble. More important, ENJOYMENT IS SWEET and DISTRESS IS BITTER rely upon ingestion's capacity to identify the flavor of an object, mapping such identification onto the emotions themselves (<identification $_{yes}$>). Positive emotions are deemed

---

the primary DESIRE metaphors above), the use of the construct state in these passages suggest a more localized effect.

31. Each of these phrases evokes metaphors of health and security, that is, metaphors of life. For more on ingestion and metaphors for life, see Avrahami, *Senses of Scripture*, 176, 180–82.

32. Malul, *Knowledge, Control, and Sex*, 132. In making this argument, Malul follows the conclusions of Yochanan Muffs, *Studies in the Aramaic Legal Papyri from Elephantine* (Leiden: Brill), 1969.

33. Malul, *Knowledge, Control, and Sex*, 132.

"sweet" (ערב/מתוק) or "good" (טוב), while negative emotions are "bitter" (מרר/מר). One might therefore collectively conclude that EMOTIONS ARE FLAVORS that the individual can "taste." When the נפש is involved, as in Job 21:23–25 and Prov 14:10, it is probably envisioned as that part of the individual that does the tasting (as opposed to being the object that is tasted).[34] Just as an English speaker might say that a situation left a "sour taste" in his or her mouth to indicate dissatisfaction, Biblical Hebrew states that a person has a מר נפש that can be given ל- ("to," Job 3:20; Prov 31:6) or spoken ב- ("in, with," Job 7:11; 10:1; 21:25).[35] The result is an experience that can only be understood by the one who experiences it.

7.2.2. Judgment Metaphors

As noted above, ingestion is frequently used as a source domain for an individual's moral evaluation of a situation. "Taste," for instance, can indicate an individual's capacity to evaluate a situation (JUDGING IS TASTING).

> Prov 31:18 She *tastes* [טעמה] that her wares are good.

> Job 6:30 Is there any injustice on my tongue? Can my *palate* [חכי] not understand calamity?

The industrious woman of Prov 31 does not physically taste her wares; rather, she *judges* (טעמה) that her wares are good (טוב). Similarly, Job scolds his companions for questioning his ability to *evaluate* (יבין ... חך) the nature and cause of his calamity. Presumably everyone has the capacity to "taste" his or her environment; however, as Job 6:30 implies, not everyone can execute it effectively. Therefore, the noun טעם is used more specifically to indicate a person's ability to *judge wisely*.[36]

---

34. It thus relies upon the same understanding of the SELF AS A PERSON that THINKING IS SPEAKING and THINKING IS TRANSFERRING AN OBJECT TO ONE'S SELF do above.

35. See also Prov 14:10, where the "לב" knows the bitterness [מרת] of its "נפש" (no preposition included), and Job 27:2, where the נפש is "made bitter" (המר).

36. The Hebrew Bible rarely specifies that this judgment is טוב (e.g., Ps 119:66), but the adjective is clearly implied in these passages.

Prov 11:22   A ring of gold in the nose of a swine is the woman beautiful but without *taste* [טעם].

Prov 26:16   The lazy person is wiser in his eyes than seven who bring back *taste* [טעם].

Job 12:20   He removes the speech of those who are trusted and takes away the *taste* [וטעם] of the elders.

The lazy person of Prov 26:16 and the beautiful woman of 11:22 are incapable of *judging wisely* (טעם), while the "elders" of Job 12:20, who are listed elsewhere in the Hebrew Bible as leaders of the community (e.g., Num 11:16; Deut 19:12; 21:2–4; 22:15–18; Ruth 4:2–11) and therefore presumably need this ability to fulfill their official duties, have this capacity taken away from them.[37]

By extension, flavors are used to express the end result of such evaluation (GOOD IS SWEET/BAD IS BITTER).

Prov 5:4   In the end, she is as *bitter* [מרה] as wormwood.

Prov 27:9   Oil and incense gladdens the heart, but the *sweet* [מתק][38] of a friend [gladdens the heart] more than the counsel of the נפש.

Qoh 7:26   And I found more *bitter* [מר] than death the woman, for she is a snare.

Similar to emotional metaphors, "sweet" (מתק) indicates a positive evaluation, while "bitter" indicates a negative evaluation.[39] Here, however, the "sweetness" (מתק) of a friend's counsel lies not in its capacity to elicit an

---

37. Compare this to superscription Ps 34:1 (and the corresponding story of David's "madness" in 1 Sam 21:13), where the choice to "change one's taste" (שנה ... טעם) does not indicate a true loss of judgment but a change in demeanor, a conscious choice to feign madness.

38. Literally sweetness. As Fox (*Proverbs 10–31*, 807) notes, the comparison between מתק and עצה ("counsel") is obscure, yet the structure of the verse suggests that it is the good advice of the friend that is "sweet" here.

39. See also the discussion of the possible ingestive nuances of טוב above.

enjoyable emotional experience but in its evaluation as a word that is beneficial to the individual (Prov 27:9). Similarly, a woman deemed "bitter" (מר) is not sorrowful but one who is harmful to an individual (Prov 5:4; Qoh 7:26).

Like desire metaphors, the JUDGING IS TASTING and GOOD IS SWEET/ BAD IS BITTER metaphors function by mapping ingestion's properties of <internal $_{yes}$>, <directness $_{yes}$>, and <subjective $_{yes}$> onto the abstract domain of moral evaluation. Subjectivity is particularly important, since the evaluation of an object as "sweet" or "bitter" depends upon the individual: the unsuspecting individual may think a woman sweet (e.g., Prov 5:3), but the wise know that she is bitter (Prov 5:4; Qoh 7:26). Moreover, in order to come to a conclusion about the relative value of an abstract quality in the first place, these metaphors rely upon the mapping of ingestion's <evaluation $_{yes}$> property. Like a tongue testing food, the individual tests qualities to determine whether or not they are safe for the individual to consume.

Another important ingestive metaphor in sapiential texts is one in which moral identity is equated to the abstract quality an individual consumes (MORAL IDENTITY IS FOOD EATEN).[40]

> Prov 4:17 For [the wicked] *eat* [לחמו] the *bread of wickedness* [לחם רשע] and *drink* [ישתו] the *wine of violence* [יין חמסים].
>
> Prov 15:14 The *mouths* [פה] of fools *feed upon* [ירעה] folly.
>
> Prov 31:27 She guards the way of her house and does not *eat* [תאכל] the *bread of idleness* [לחם עצלות].
>
> Job 15:16 Indeed, he is abhorred and corrupted, the one who *drinks* [שתה] iniquity *like water* [כמים].

In these passages ideas are once again conceived of as consumable objects (IDEAS ARE FOOD/LIQUID). Here, however, as Mary Szlos states, "you are

---

40. Szlos, "Metaphor in Proverbs 31:10–31," 138–39. Szlos labels this metaphor FOOD IS IDENTITY (with the source domain in the position of the target domain?). However, what is at stake here is not simply the physical composition of the individual but his or her moral state. I have thus modified the nomenclature of the metaphor to reflect this.

what you eat"; that is, who a person is can be described by the foods he or she consumes. This is particularly evident in what Szlos calls the "bread of" constructions (לחם + an abstract term) found in Prov 4:17 and 31:27. Here the one who "eats" (לחם) the bread of wickedness (לחם רשע) is wicked, and the one who "eats" (אכל) the bread of idleness (לחם עצלות) is idle.[41] Similarly, the one who "drinks iniquity" (שתה כמים עולה) is corrupt (see also Prov 19:28), and the one who "feeds on" (ירעה) folly is a fool (Prov 15:14).[42] In this last example, the corruption has gone so far that the person is conceptualized as an animal feeding upon wickedness (THE PERSON IS AN ANIMAL). Like the JUDGING IS TASTING metaphor, MORAL IDENTITY IS FOOD EATEN maps ingestion's properties of <internal $_{yes}$>, <directness $_{yes}$>, <subjective $_{yes}$>, and <evaluative $_{yes}$> onto the abstract domain of judgment. It focuses, however, on the effective nature of ingestion (<effects $_{yes}$> $^{PR \rightarrow P}$). Just as concrete food transfers its inherent qualities onto the perceiver as it is broken down and absorbed into the body, moral "food" transfers its essential character onto the one who eats it. Thus the industrious woman of Prov 31 is said to avoid eating the "bread of idleness" (לחם עצלות) lest she become idle.

7.3. SUMMARY

Ingestion, then, serves an important function as a source domain for emotive and evaluative metaphors by mapping ingestion's key properties onto cognition.

---

41. As Szlos (ibid., 138) notes, not all "bread of" constructions indicate moral identity. She distinguishes, for instance, between "bread of + abstract noun constructions" and other "bread of" constructions (e.g., Prov 23:6; 27:27; 30:8). I would add that even "bread of" construction that do include an abstract quality do not necessarily indicate moral identity. For instance the "bread of secrecies" (לחם סתרים) listed in 9:17 and the "bread of deceit" (לחם שקר) in 20:17 indicates ill-gotten bread, not "secret" or "deceitful" individuals. Similarly, the "bread of lies" in 23:3 does not make one a liar but is bread that deceives the individual, because "the pleasure it gives is fleeting" (Fox, *Proverbs 10–31*, 720; see also 897).

42. On the other hand, to "drink down violence" (חמס שתה; Prov 26:6) indicates that the individual is inviting destruction, not that one is violent. For more on the connection between ingestion and metaphors of harm, see Avrahami, *Senses of Scripture*, 146–50.

Table 7.2. Metaphorical Mappings: COGNITION IS INGESTING

DESIRE IS HUNGER/THIRST
    <internal $_{yes}$>, <directness $_{yes}$>, <subjectivity $_{yes}$>
DESIRE IS A HUNGRY/THIRSTY SELF
    <internal $_{yes}$>, <directness $_{yes}$>, <subjectivity $_{yes}$>
SATISFACTION IS FULLNESS/ DISSATISFACTION IS EMPTINESS
    <contact $_{yes}$>, <internal $_{yes}$>, <directness $_{yes}$>, <subjectivity $_{yes}$>
SATISFACTION IS A FULL SELF/ DISSATISFACTION IS AN EMPTY SELF
    <contact $_{yes}$>, <internal $_{yes}$>, <directness $_{yes}$>, <subjectivity $_{yes}$>
ENJOYMENT IS SWEET, DISTRESS IS BITTER
    <internal $_{yes}$>, <directness $_{yes}$>, <subjectivity $_{yes}$>, <identification $_{yes}$>
DISTRESS IS A BITTER SELF
    <internal $_{yes}$>, <directness $_{yes}$>, <subjectivity $_{yes}$>, <identification $_{yes}$>
ENJOYMENT IS TO EAT GOOD
    <internal $_{yes}$>, <directness $_{yes}$>, <subjectivity $_{yes}$>
JUDGING IS TASTING
    <evaluation $_{yes}$>; also <internal $_{yes}$>, <directness $_{yes}$>, and <subjective $_{yes}$>
GOOD IS SWEET/BAD IS BITTER
    <evaluation $_{yes}$>; also <internal $_{yes}$>, <directness $_{yes}$>, and <subjective $_{yes}$>
MORAL IDENTITY IS FOOD EATEN
    <effects $_{yes}$> $^{PR \rightarrow P}$; also: <internal $_{yes}$>, <directness $_{yes}$>, <subjective $_{yes}$>, <evaluative $_{yes}$>

While DESIRE IS HUNGER/THIRST and SATISFACTION IS FULLNESS/DISSATISFACTION IS EMPTINESS focus on whether the individual is "filled" with an abstract quality, the GOOD IS SWEET/BAD IS BITTER metaphors draw heavily upon ingestion's ability to identify objects from the environment. Similarly, evaluative metaphors focus on that aspect of ingestion, although MORAL IDENTITY IS FOOD EATEN also relies upon ingestion's capacity to affect the perceiver. Yet regardless of their individual focus, each ingestive metaphor envisions cognition to be an internal experience, largely incomparable from one individual to another and dependent upon the subjective, personal perspective of the individual involved.

8
Breathing

Like touch and taste, the sense of smell is typically excluded from epistemological discussions due to its seemingly "base" connotations. Thought to be the most primal sense, smell is considered to be too subjective and emotional to aid in epistemological discussions.[1] It does not help that, in the Hebrew Bible at least, references to smell tend to occur in human-divine sacrificial interactions and therefore seem to be of limited value for understanding human epistemological endeavors.[2] Yet like tactility and ingestion, smell—or, more accurately, breathing—provides a distinct mode of acquiring information about the environment and in doing so generates its own cluster of associated epistemological metaphors in which knowledge is conceptualized as an indirect, subjective experience.[3] It is thus helpful to discuss this sense alongside the other senses here.

8.1. Typology of Breathing

As intimated above, the sense of smell is largely indistinguishable from the larger perceptual system to which it belongs, the sense of breathing. Both share the same linguistic root in Biblical Hebrew (רוח) and are conceptualized as part of the same biological process. As Deborah Green puts it,

---

1. See ch. 6 n. 1 above.
2. Hence the initial exclusion of the sense from my original study, Tilford, "Taste and See."
3. In generating indirect and subjective metaphors, the sense of breathing is similar to the sense of ingestion. This is not surprising, considering that the two senses are physiologically connected (the smell of an object affects its taste and vice versa). As shall be discussed here, however, this indirect subjectivity is realized differently in both clusters of metaphors. It is therefore appropriate to treat the two senses separately, even if the conclusions are similar.

"An object emits an odor (ריח) which travels in the air (רוח) and a subject breathes in (הריח) the odor (ריח)."[4] To smell is to breath, and to breath is to smell.

Like other senses, the sense of breathing is closely connected to specific physical apparatuses, in this case the nose (אף, Gen 2:7; Ps 115:6) and the mouth (פה, 1 Kgs 22:23; Pss 33:6; 135:17; Isa 11:4), which together regulate the inhalation and exhalation of air. Through inhalation, the nose can detect and identify the scent of an object (<detection $_{yes}$>; <identification $_{yes}$>): the smell of burning incense (קטרת, Exod 30:1; Num 4:16; 1 Sam 2:28), sweet oil (שמן, Exod 30:25; Lev 6:14; Prov 27:9), or a fragrant tree (Song 2:13). However, breathing's ability to identify is less exact than vision or tactility and limited in scope (<correctness of hypothesis $_{yes/no}$>, <location $_{no}$>). When the blind Isaac "breathes in" (וירח) the "odor" (ריח) of Jacob's garment, for instance, he is able to detect that an individual stands before him and identify that his garments have been in the fields; however, without his eyesight, Isaac mistakenly believes that that the garment belongs to his son Esau (Gen 27:27).

Not surprisingly, the Hebrew Bible does not say much about the physical processes by which this identification occurs. Modern science suggests that, when an individual inhales air, "the odor molecules float back into the nasal cavity behind the bridge of the nose, where they are absorbed by the mucosa containing receptor cells bearing microscopic hairs called cilia." When activated, "five million of these cells fire impulses to the brain's olfactory bulb or smell center," thereby allowing the brain to detect and identify the odor it encounters.[5] This process is nearly instantaneous, taking only as long as required for the odor to reach the individual and filter through the nose cavity. By analogy with sight, I would call this a "delayed simultaneity."

Biblical authors are, of course, unaware of these details. They do, however, recognize breathing as a largely internal sense (<internal $_{yes}$>), with the breath entering the body through the nostrils (Gen 7:22; see also Lev 26:31). Because of this, smell is incomparable and therefore largely subjective (<subjectivity $_{yes}$>). Individuals respond to odors differently, and

---

4. Deborah Green, "Soothing Odors: The Transformation of Scent in Ancient Israelite and Ancient Jewish Literature" (PhD diss., University of Chicago, 2003), 81. See also Avrahami, *Senses of Scripture*, 125–26.

5. Diane Ackerman, *A Natural History of the Senses* (New York: Vintage Books, 1990), 10; quoted in Green, "Soothing Odors," 7.

descriptions are often vague (e.g., perfumed, aromatic) or formed by analogy with other senses (e.g., ingestion: sweet, sour; tactility: sharp, damp). Indeed, in the Hebrew Bible, smells are most frequently described by comparable objects. Jacob's garments, for instance, smell like "fields" (שדה, Gen 27:27), and the lover's breath smells like "apples" (תפוח, Song 7:9).

Like hearing, such detection is indirect (<direct $_{no}$>). That which is detected through smell is not an object or a person but the odor emitted from the object or person, the ריח. As such, breathing does not require direct contact (<contact $_{no}$>) nor does it require the perceiver to be close to the object emitting the odor (<closeness $_{no}$>). Although it helps that Jacob comes near Isaac before the latter can smell him (Gen 27:27), the stench of a battle can be detected from a great distance (Job 39:25), and the sweet perfumes of a garden can be carried upon the wind (Song 4:16). As such, scents can last some time (<briefness $_{no}$>).

Perhaps most important, the Hebrew Bible recognizes breathing's ability to affect the perceiver (<effects $_{yes}$> $^{OP \rightarrow P}$). Breathing itself is a prerequisite for living. The one who breathes or has breath inside is alive (Gen 6:3; 7:15; Job 7:7; 12:10; Qoh 12:7); the one who does not breathe is dead (Job 17:1). It is thus an involuntary sense (<voluntary $_{no}$>). Although God can refuse to smell sacrifices (Lev 26:31) and an individual can hold his or her breath for a short time, individuals cannot choose to stop breathing altogether. Thus it is not surprising that the "breath" (רוח) is equated to the innermost essence of an individual.[6]

Breathing, however, not only provides life to the individual; it also allows the individual to smell and be smelled by others. Smell can affect an individual's mood, either calming an individual or eliciting sexual desire. Proverbs 27:9 notes, for instance, that "[scented] oil and incense gladden the heart," and Gen 8:21 describes how God's anger abates when smells the "soothing odor" (ריח הניחח) of Noah's sacrifice (see also the frequent references to "soothing odors" in the sacrificial literature of Leviticus and Numbers).On the other hand, when the lovers of Song of Songs smell the sweet oils of a beloved, they become aroused (Song 1:3–4, 4:10–11); similarly, the highly metaphorical Strange Woman of Proverbs purposefully uses smell to entice the unwary student into an illicit sexual encounter (Prov 7:17). Inhalation can also negatively impact an individual's mood. The stench of decaying animals polluted the land of Egypt and prevented

---

6. See §1.1 above.

people from drinking from its rivers (Exod 7:21; 8:14). Similarly, the foul stench of Job's breath repulsed his wife (Job 19:17), leaving him rejected and alone. In other words, individuals evaluate the relative value of an object based on the effect its odor has on them (<evaluation $_{yes}$>).

In some cases exhalation can also affect the environment (<effects $_{yes}$> $^{PR \rightarrow OP}$), at which point it also becomes an external sense (<internal $_{no}$>). In the examples above, for instance, the exhalation of Job's foul breath and the lover's sweet breath affects their repective partner's mood when they subsequently inhale it. On an even more basic level, however, exhalation changes the physical properties of the air around an individual. When an individual breathes out, he or she emits carbon dioxide and heat. Although such changes are minor and of limited consequence in the human sphere, they can have a great impact when projected onto the divine sphere. By simply exhaling, God can create the world (Gen 1:2; Ps 33:6) or destroy it (Exod 10:13; 2 Sam 22:16; Ps 18:16). Like hearing and speech, in other words, the inhalation and exhalation of breath act as two sides of the same coin, affecting the perceiver who breathes in the air and allowing the perceiver who exhales the air to affect the surrounding environment.

The following typology of breathing emerges:[7]

Table 8.1. Biblical Typology of Breathing

<contact $_{no}$>	<directness $_{no}$>
<closeness $_{no}$>	<effects $_{yes}$> $^{PR \rightarrow P}$
<internal $_{yes/no}$>	<correction of hypothesis $_{yes/no}$>
<location $_{no}$>	<subjectivity $_{yes}$>
<detection $_{yes}$> $^{delayed\ simultaneity}$	<effects $_{yes}$> $^{OP \rightarrow P}$
<identification $_{yes}$>	<evaluation $_{yes}$>
<voluntary $_{no}$>	<briefness $_{no}$>

---

7. Again, <limits> does not seem applicable.

8.2. COGNITION IS BREATHING

The sense of smell is rarely connected to knowledge in biblical wisdom literature, perhaps because its sacrificial connotations are of little concern to the writers of wisdom literature. There are, however, echoes of this sense in the epistemological and emotional metaphors found in this literature, especially when one broadens the discussion to include breathing more generally.[8]

8.2.1. Knowledge Metaphors

As noted at §5.2.1, words can indicate the knowledge of an individual (KNOWLEDGE IS A WORD). By the same token, the breath that carries those words can indicate the knowledge of an individual (KNOWLEDGE IS A BREATH).

> Prov 1:23 Turn to my reproof. I will pour out my *breath* [רוחי] to you. I will make known my words to you.

When the wise speaker breathes, she transfers her knowledge to those who would hear her (Prov 1:23). In the book of Job, however, breath signals a lack of knowledge (IGNORANCE IS A BREATH).

> Job 8:2 How long will you speak these things and the words of your mouth be a great *breath* [רוח]?

> Job 15:2 Will the wise man answer with the knowledge of *breath* [רוח] and fill his belly with the *east wind* [קדים]?

> Job 16:3 Is there no end to words of *breath* [רוח]? What vexes you that you talk?

---

8. Perhaps the most famous breath metaphor in the Hebrew Bible is that which is found in Qoheleth: "all is vanity and a chasing after breath" (e.g., Qoh 1:14, 17; 2:11, 17, 26; 4:4, 6, 16; 5:16; 6:9). This metaphor, whatever its origin and exact nuance, reflects upon the futility of life and human activity. As such, it is not a cognitive metaphor like those discussed in this study and shall thus not detain us here.

Job and his friends accuse each other of breathing without substance. They fill their bellies with air (רוח, קדים) and exhale empty words (רוח ... אמרי, Job 8:2; דעת רוח, 15:2; דברי־רוח, 16:3). In such cases the breath is conceptualized as a container for words (BREATH IS A CONTAINER). When full, the breath carries knowledge to those who need it. When empty or filled with useless words, the breath conveys the ignorance of the speaker. Breathing is thus the functional equivalent of speaking and carries the same cognitive connotations (<internal $_{no}$>, <voluntary $_{yes}$>).[9] Yet it also maintains the involuntary nature of breathing (<voluntary $_{no}$>). Although a speaker can hold his or her breath for a time and choose when to release it, eventually the speaker must breathe out. As Elihu states, "I am full of words; the *breath* [רוח] within my belly constrains me" to talk (Job 32:18). He must let the air out. When he does, his wisdom or lack thereof will be displayed whether he wishes it to be or not.

8.2.2. Emotion Metaphors

Even more so than knowledge, breathing is associated with subjective, emotional experience. In this regard, one immediately recalls the olfactory experiences in the Song of Songs, with its aromatic plants (2:1, 12–13; 4:16; 5:1; 7:8), fragrant oils (1:3; 4:10), and perfumed spices (3:6; 4:6, 14; 5:5, 13). The rich images found within the Songs are certainly intended to elicit an emotional reaction. However, they do not refer to that emotional experience itself. The scent of apples in Song 7:8, for instance, is intended to elicit desire, but it is not itself a conceptual metaphor for desire. As such, an analysis of the olfactory images of the Song of Songs falls outside the scope of the present study.

More relevant for the present discussion are those instances where the breath can take on a variety of physical properties, each of which indicates a different emotional state. A long or short breath indicates one's patience or lack thereof (PATIENCE IS A LONG BREATH; IMPATIENCE IS A SHORT BREATH), while a high or low breath indicates pride or humility (HUMILITY IS A LOW BREATH; PRIDE IS A HIGH BREATH).

---

9. See §5.1 above. That an individual can hold his or her breath for a time no doubt facilitates the confluence, as it provides the impression that an individual can control his or her breathing.

8. BREATHING

Job 21:4 Is my complaint to humans? Why should my *breath* [רוחי] not be *short* [תקצר]?

Qoh 7:8 The one with *long breath* [ארך רוח] is better than the one with *high breath* [מגבה רוח].

Prov 16:18 Pride is before a fall, and a *high breath* [גבה רוח] is before a stumbling.

Prov 29:23 The pride of a man will be brought low [תשפילנו], while the *low of breath* [שפל רוח] will gain honor.

When Job grows impatient with his friends, he speaks with a short breath (קצר רוח, Job 21:4; see also Prov 14:29).[10] Conversely, when the Teacher counsels patience, he advises a long breath (ארך רוח, Qoh 7:8). Similarly, the proud individual has a high breath (גבה רוח, Prov 16:18; Qoh 7:8), while the humble individual has a low breath (שפל רוח, Prov 29:23). As with many uses of the term, רוח in these passages may have lost some of its physical connotations and instead refer more abstractly to the "spirit" or essence of the individual. Yet the fact that רוח appears in Job 21:4 in connection to Job's request to speak suggests that the physiological experience of breathing has not been completely lost in the metaphorical utterances. Just as the one who is impatient breathes and speaks quickly, the one who is impatient is metaphorically short of breath. In either case, these metaphors convey breathing's internal, subjective nature (<internal $_{yes}$>, <subjectivity $_{yes}$>).[11] Pride, patience, humility—although others can see the effect of such behaviors, the experience of these emotions remains internal and unique to the one experiencing them.

Anger, on the other hand, is expressed using the more outwardly directed nuances of breathing (ANGER IS A HOT NOSE, CALM IS A COOL BREATH).

Prov 15:1 A soft answer will turn *wrath* [המה], but a harsh word will raise *anger* [אף].

---

10. See also Job 7:11, where a "tight breath" (צר רוח) indicates emotional distress.

11. These metaphors also rely on proprioceptive adjectives—short, long, high, low—and as such carry with them proprioceptive connotations as well, specifically, proprioceptive's <location $_{yes}$> and <detection $_{yes}$>^{amplitudinal} properties. For more on these proprioceptive nuances, see §9.2.3 below.

Job 32:2   Elihu ... *heated his nose* [חרה אפו] because he [Job] justified himself over God.

Prov 17:27   One who withholds words knows knowledge; one who is *cool of breath* [קר רוח] has understanding.

As elsewhere in the Hebrew Bible, the word most commonly used for "anger" in the Hebrew Bible is אף (lit. "nose"). A harsh word will kindle אף (Prov 15:1; see also 21:14; 22:24; 27:4; 29:8, 22; 30:33); Elihu kindles his אף (Job 32:2; see also 18:4; 32:3, 5; 36:13).[12] Conversely, the one who is calm breathes cool air (קר רוח, Prov 17:27). The use of the nose and its breath to indicate intense emotions likely reflects a physiological reality: when an individual is calm, his or her breath remains cooll when the individual becomes angry, the innards seem to boil, the breath quickens, and the air that comes out of the nose heats up.[13] Thus, not surprisingly, anger can be referred to simply as heat (חמה: Prov 15:1; see also Job 19:29; 36:18). Whatever the physiological origin, the metaphorical nuances are clear. One breathes anger.

In making these connections, ANGER IS A HOT NOSE relies upon breathing's dual affective nature (<internal $_{yes/no}$>, <effects $_{yes}$> $^{OP \rightarrow P}$, <effects $_{yes}$> $^{PR \rightarrow P}$). Like air that first enters the body and then leaves it again, anger forms within the body and then causes the individual to act out. Thus Elihu's anger is kindled by the words of his companions, and he subsequently lashes out against them. Similarly when Bildad accuses Job:

Job 18:4   You who tear yourself in your *anger* [אפו]—shall the earth be forsaken because of you, or the rock be removed out of its place?

Here Job becomes angry due to external circumstances (i.e., his illness), yet he does not simply become angry. His anger causes him to act out and rend his garments. Elihu's and Job's anger are deeply personal, subjective experiences. However, there are also external side effects of those experiences.

This comes to the foreground most clearly in metaphors about God's anger.

---

12. See also Qoh 10:4, where רוח by itself seems to indicate anger.
13. Grady, "Primary Metaphors as Inputs," 1600.

Job 16:9 His *anger* [אף] tears me. He bears a grudge. He gnashes his teeth at me. My foe sharpens his eyes against me.

Job 20:28 The produce of his house will be carried away, stolen away in the day of God's *anger* [אפו]

Like human anger, God's anger is described as the inhalation and exhalation of hot air through the אף (nose). God becomes אף when he sees iniquity; in his אף, God lashes out (Job 16:9; 20:28; see also 9:13; 21:17; 35:15; 36:33). God's anger is a violent, internal emotion with external consequences. God becomes angry inside after seeing the activities of the wicked and violently lashes out because of it. Yet the exhaled heat of God's angry breath is even more powerful than that of humans. "By the *breath* [מנשמת] of God [humans] perish; from the *breath* [מרוח] of his nose [אפו] they are finished" (Job 4:9). God's anger "burns" so hot that it "overturns" mountains and seers the belly of the wicked from within (see Job 9:5; 19:11; 20:23; 42:7). Like human anger, it has external effects.[14]

8.2.3. Judgment Metaphors

Elsewhere in the Hebrew Bible the breath of an individual is used to describe his or her moral character. Thus various individuals are said to possess the רוח אלהים ("breath of God"). This does not necessarily mean that the individual is pure. Sometimes having the breath of God implies bravery (Judg 11:29; 13:25) or a blood-thirsty temperament (14:6, 19). Elsewhere it implies sound judgment (Gen 41:38; Exod 31:3; 35:31). It is this latter connotation that one finds in the book of Job.

Job 32:8 Truly. It is the *breath* [רוח] in a person—the breath [נשמת] of the Almighty—that understands.

According to Elihu, long life and grey hairs do not make a person wise. Rather, wisdom comes from God.

In each of these cases, however, רוח seems to refer to an external quality that is endowed by God for an unspecified length of time. Thus

---

14. For more on the differences between human and divine metaphors, see my discussion in Nicole L. Tilford, "When People Have Gods: Sensory Mimicry and Divine Agency in the Book of Job," *HeBAI* 5 (2016): 42–58.

Samson is temporarily crazed (Judg 14:6), and Jephthah is made brave for the duration of his battle with the Ammonites (Judg 11:29), much like individuals are filled with a prophetic ecstasy for a short period of time (e.g., 1 Sam 10:6, 10) and Saul is temporarily driven mad by an evil spirit (1 Sam 16:14-16, 23; 18:10; 19:9). In other words, these usages of רוח appear to be a theological proposition, and it is likely that statements such as those found in Gen 41:38, Exod 31:3, 35:31, and Job 32:8 function in a similar way. That is, they are theological statements about the origin of knowledge. Although in later reception history "spirit of God" became a metaphor by which one judged an individual (e.g., as pure or loving), in the Hebrew Bible breathing more generally does not seem to carry judgmental connotations.

Smelling more specifically, however, does. One person can "stink" (באש) to another. Thus Jacob complains that he and his sons "stink" to the Canannites (Gen 34:40), and the Israelites complain that they "stink" to pharaoh (Exod 5:21).[15] In such cases physical stench is not envisioned. Rather, באש indicates a negative judgement: the Canaanites and Pharaoh dislike Jacob and the Israelites. This meaning is not prevalent in biblical wisdom literature, although one finds echoes of it in Proverbs (TO BE DISLIKED IS TO STINK).

> Prov 13:5 The righteous hates a word of deception. A wicked act *stinks* [יבאיש] and is shameful.

As with Jacob and the Israelites, wickedness does not emit a foul odor. Rather, it is evaluated disapprovingly by those who should know better, the righteous. In such cases the properties of <effects $_{yes}$> ^{OP} → ^{P} and <evaluation $_{yes}$> dominate the mapping. The metaphorical smell of wickedness adversely affects the righteous and leads them to evaluate the act with disapproval.

8.3. Summary

Although not as prominent as other senses, breathing does provide a source domain for epistemological and emotional metaphors in biblical wisdom literature.

---

15. See also 1 Sam 13:4; 27:12; 2 Sam 10:6; 16:21.

Table 8.2. Metaphorical Mappings: COGNITION IS BREATHING

KNOWLEDGE IS BREATH
    <internal $_{no}$>, <voluntary $_{yes/no}$>
IGNORANCE IS BREATH
    <internal $_{no}$>, <voluntary $_{yes/no}$>
PATIENCE IS A LONG BREATH
    <internal $_{yes}$>, <subjective $_{yes}$>
IMPATIENCE IS A SHORT BREATH
    <internal $_{yes}$>, <subjective $_{yes}$>
HUMILITY IS A LOW BREATH
    <internal $_{yes}$>, <subjective $_{yes}$>
PRIDE IS A HIGH BREATH
    <internal $_{yes}$>, <subjective $_{yes}$>
ANGER IS A HOT NOSE
    <internal $_{yes/no}$>, <subjective $_{yes}$>, <effects $_{yes}$> $^{OP \to P}$, <effects $_{yes}$> $^{PR \to P}$
CALM IS A COOL BREATH
    <internal $_{yes/no}$>, <subjective $_{yes}$>, <effects $_{yes}$> $^{OP \to P}$, <effects $_{yes}$> $^{PR \to P}$
TO BE DISLIKED IS TO STINK
    <effects $_{yes}$> $^{OP \to P}$, <evaluation $_{yes}$>

Knowledge metaphors, conflating with speech metaphors, focus on the external nature of breathing and its seemingly voluntary nature. Emotional metaphors, drawing largely on proprioceptive qualities, focus largely on the internal nature of breathing and its subjective effect on the individual, although ANGER IS A HOT NOSE deviates from this by reflecting on the external effects of anger as well. As a whole, however, breathing metaphors move beyond the simple experience of scent to portray a cognitive experience that is emotional, subjective, and affective.

9
Moving

Although sight and sound are generally considered to be the primary modalities by which individuals gain knowledge of their environment, Maxine Sheets-Johnstone has convincingly argued that movement is foundational for nearly all of our experience with the world. As she states, from the beginning we "are simply infused with movement—not merely the *propensity* to move, but with the real thing." We are either "still-born" or "movement-born."[1] We walk, squirm, move our arms and legs, open and close our eyes, and swing our head from side to side. Air enters into our body and expands our lungs; blood courses through our veins and establishes our pulse. It is by movement that we know ourselves to be alive, and it is by lack of movement that we classify other entities as inanimate or even dead.[2] Movement, then, is a very real mode of perception, and it governs all other modalities.[3] Movement also offers a distinct way of engaging the world and serves as a frequent source domain for metaphors of cognition. Like other modalities, such kinesthetic metaphors reflect a particular conception of cognition, in this case one in which cognition is conceived of as a continual, self-perpetuated process.

---

1. Maxine Sheets-Johnstone, *The Primacy of Movement*, Advances in Consciousness Research 14 (Amsterdam: Benjamins, 1999), 136, 232.
2. Ibid., 135–36.
3. For instance, it is by movement that the eyes track objects (sight), food is put into the mouth (ingestion), and objects are moved from one location to another (touch). Movement is not, however, simply a prerequisite to other modalities. As Sheets-Johnstone (ibid., 139) argues, sensations of movement are "in their own right, *perceptual experiences*, the most fundamental of perceptual experiences."

9.1. Typology of Movement

Like touch or ingestion, movement belongs to a more complex system of bodily functions, in this case the system of proprioception ("perception of one's self"), that is, the system of mechanisms by which individuals perceive their bodily movement (kinesthesia) and their bodily position (statesthetesis).[4] While there are many types of kinesthesia, the most important for the construction of Israelite epistemology is locomotion, which is reflected in various Hebrew terms for "walking" (הלך, בוא, נגש, קרב, ירד, אשר, שוט) and which, although experienced by the entire body, is commonly grounded in the "foot" (רגל; e.g., + דרך, "walk the foot," Deut 11:24; Josh 1:3; + בוא, "come by foot," 2 Sam 15:18; 1 Kgs 14:12; Isa 41:3; + יצא, "go out by foot," 2 Sam 15:16–17; + נשא, as in "to lift the foot," Gen 29:1; + עבר, "cross over by foot," Num 20:19; Deut 2:28; Ps 66:6). Statesthetesis is more difficult to pin down, referring as it does to the position of the entire body. However, since it is often realized through vertical motion or the minute sensations of the stationary body, it is best reflected by Hebrew verbs of "standing" (עמד, קום, יצב), "sitting" (ישב), "lying down" (שכב), and "being still/at rest" (נוח). While statesthetesis can also be represented by the foot (e.g., Josh 3:13; Pss 26:12; 122:2; Ezek 2:2), its location in the body is often left unspecified. One simply "stands" (e.g., Gen 18:8; 19:27; 41:17), "sits" (e.g., Exod 2:15; Isa 47:1; Ezek 26:16), or "lies down" (e.g., Gen 19:4; Josh 2:8; 1 Sam 3:2).

---

4. Olivier Gapenne, "Kinesthesia and the Construction of Perceptual Objects," in *Enaction: Toward a New Paradigm for Cognitive Science*, ed. John Robert Stewart, Olivier Gapenne, and Ezequiel A. Di Paolo (Cambridge: MIT Press, 2010), 186. The relationship between kinesthesia and proprioception is debated. Some scholars use the two terms synonymously to refer to the same modality, while others argue that they are two separate modalities capable of being distinguished based on the presence or absence of equilibratory sensations (proprioception being connected to equilibrium, kinesthesia not). Sheets-Johnstone (*Primacy of Movement*, passim), for instance, does not distinguish between the two, preferring to use the terms "self-movement" or "movement" to refer to the entire phenomenon of bodily movement. Malul (*Knowledge, Control, and Sex*, 102 n. 3, 127), on the other hand, distinguishes between "motion" (e.g., walking, digging, separating) and "equilibratory sensations" (e.g., standing), both of which he groups under the general heading "kinesthesis." He argues, however, that in Biblical Hebrew the two sensations are inexorably linked. Here I follow Gapenne in regarding proprioception as a generic term used to refer to a variety of sensations, including kinesthesia, equilibrium, and statesthetesis.

Like other modalities, proprioception is capable of detecting its object and identifying its current status, for example, whether the body is standing, walking, or lying down (<detection $_{yes}$>, <identification $_{yes}$>). Unlike other modalities, however, the object of proprioception is not distinct from the individual who experiences it. As the name suggests, in proprioception there is nothing external to the body to detect or identify, nothing tangible, audible, or visual to inspect. Rather, as Sheets-Johnstone states, "*what is created and what is constituted are one and the same*"; that is, the perceiver *is* the object perceived (PR = OP).[5] This creates a more intimate connection between proprioception and the individual's sense of corporeal being than any other perceptual modality enjoys.[6] The Hebrew Bible recognizes this when it speaks of movement as a prerequisite of life. Qoheleth, for instance, speaks of the living as "the ones who *walk* [המלכים] under the sun" (4:15), and 2 Kings describes them as those "*rising* [קום] upon the *feet* [רגליו]" (13:21; see also Ezek 3:24; 37:10; Zech 14:12).[7] As Brenda Farnell would say, "I move, therefore I am."[8]

On a practical level, this convergence between object and perceiver means that many of the properties identified by Ibarretxe-Antuñano are irrelevant to proprioception, particularly those of the PR → OP category (<contact>, <closeness>, <internal>, <limits>).[9] More importantly, this intimate connection between perceiver and object makes proprioception difficult to analyze. As modern researchers have argued, proprioception is both subjective and indeterminate. Although others can see an individual move, the actual experience of movement is experienced in and determined by the body of the individual (<subjective $_{yes}$>). Job knows when he is "standing" (עמד, Job 30:20) and when he is "lying down" (שכב, 7:4), not because he has seen it or someone has told him, but because he has detected movement in his body and identified its position. Similarly, the psalmists knows themselves to be "sitting" (ישב, e.g., Ps

---

5. Sheets-Johnstone, *Primacy of Movement*, 153–54, emphasis original.

6. Ibid, 139.

7. Avrahami, *Senses of Scripture*, 181.

8. Brenda Farnell, *Dynamic Embodiment for Social Theory: "I Move Therefore I Am"* (New York: Routledge, 2012). In titling her book as she does, Farnell is playing on the famous phrase of Descartes, "I think, therefore I am."

9. Also irrelevant are the properties of <directness>, <correction of the hypothesis>, and <evaluation>. However, as will be discussed below, <location> (which is from PR → OP) is still highly relevant.

137:1), "standing" (ישב, 122:2), or "lying down" (שכב, 3:6; 4:9) because they have experienced it for themselves. Proprioception is also indeterminate in that, although one can choose when to walk and when to stand (Gen 24:58; 33:14; Exod 9:29; Neh 2:12; Hab 2:1) (<voluntary $_{yes}$>), bodily movements and positions are so ingrained in us that individuals are not typically conscious of their operation except when they deviate from the habitual norms (e.g., the individual כשל, "stumbles," 2 Chr 28:15; Job 4:4; Isa 40:30; Lam 5:13; צלע, "limps," Gen 32:32; or is פִּסֵּחַ, "lame," Lev 21:18; 2 Sam 9:13; 19:27).[10] Consequently, although movement is commonly described in the Hebrew Bible, it is rarely reflected upon. Individuals "walk," "lie down," or "take their stance"; they do not pause to consider the nature or import of their actions.

Yet as Sheets-Johnstone has demonstrated, it is precisely through such routine activities that the individual detects his or her body and establishes a sense of self. By moving in the world, people discover what they can and cannot do, who and what they are, and how they relate to others.[11] For instance, movement reveals what Sheets-Johnstone calls the "amplitudinal quality" of the body, that is, the "expansiveness or contractiveness of [the] moving body and the spatial expansiveness or contractedness of [its] movement."[12] Statesthetesis, for example, detects the amplitude of the stationary body, whether it is contracted (ישב, "sitting," Gen 31:34; Exod 17:12; 1 Sam 20:25; שחה, "bowed down," Gen 18:2; 19:1; 24:52; ברע, "kneeling," Judg 7:5–6; 2 Kgs 1:13) or stretched out (vertically, e.g., עמד, "standing," Job 29:8; Ezek 2:1; 37:10; horizontally, e.g., שכב, "lying down," Gen 28:11; Judg 5:27; 1 Sam 3:5). Generally the individual can affect this amplitude (<effects $_{yes}$>[13]). Samuel can choose to stand (קום, 1 Sam 3:6); Abraham can choose to bow down (שחה, Gen 18:3). Yet this ability can be hampered by age, natural deformity, or circumstance. Thus Laban accepts Rachel's explanation that she is unable to stand because of her menses (Gen 31:35), and the law prescribes restitution for the person who is forced to lie down (נפל למשכב, "fall to a bed") because of an injury (Exod 21:18).

Locomotion, on the other hand, creates a sense of contracted or expansive space. As Sheets-Johnstone states, "it is erroneous to think that

---

10. Sheets-Johnstone, *Primacy of Movement*, 142–44.
11. Ibid., 135–38.
12. Ibid., 143.
13. Since the perceiver and the object are the same, there is no need to distinguish between <effects> PR → P and <effects> OP → P.

movement simply takes place *in* space.... On the contrary, we formally create space in the process of moving; we qualitatively create a certain spatial character by the very nature of our movement—a large, open space, or a tight, resistant space, for example."[14] Thus the Hebrew Bible classifies some spaces as "broad" (רחב, Exod 3:8; Judg 18:10; 1 Kgs 6:2; see also the nominal form רחוב, a "broad place," Gen 19:2; Judg 19:17; 2 Sam 21:12) and other spaces as "narrow" (משעול, Num 22:24; צר, Num 22:26; 2 Kgs 6:1; Isa 49:20), classifications deduced by how an individual might move through them (2 Sam 22:37). When combined with other modalities, especially visual observation and haptic exploration, such motion enables one to detect information about the external world. According to Gen 13, Abram is able to learn about the land he is to inherit by looking (ראה) at it from afar (13:14) and walking (התהלך) its length and breadth (13:17) (see also Josh 1:3). Similarly, when the satan "walks about" the earth (שוט/הלך, Job 1:7; 2:2) or individuals "foot about" the land (רָגַל, e.g., Num 21:32; Deut 1:24; Josh 2:1; 6:25; 7:2), they do so not simply for the pleasure of walking or to reach a destination but in order to acquire information about their surroundings.[15]

Proprioception also reveals the "linear quality" of the body and its movement. Physically a body can be vertically or horizontally "straight" (ישר; see, e.g., the description of the legs and wings of the creatures on the divine chariot in Ezek 1:7, 23)[16] or "curved" (גהר, "bent over," 1 Kgs 18:42;

---

14. Sheets-Johnstone, *Primacy of Movement*, 143–44; see also Gapenne, "Kinesthesia and the Construction of Perceptual Objects," 200–208.

15. Hence the common translation of the verb רגל as "to spy" (NRSV). See also the verbs שוט ("to roam") and תור ("to walk about, scout"), each of which expresses locomotion that has as its goal the acquisition of knowledge (Malul, *Knowledge, Control, and Sex*, 141–43; Avrahami, *Senses of Scripture*, 160–62). בקש ("searching, seeking") may also carry kinesthetic connotations, yet as Malul (*Knowledge, Control, Sex*, 105 n. 14) points out, the etymology and thus modal domain is unclear (he, for instance, tentatively places בקש with oral terms).

16. Although there are no clear concrete examples of a human body being "straight," it is the linear quality of the body (as opposed to its movements) that seems to be of concern in metaphorical extensions of the term, ישר being the opposite of a "bent" or "crooked" body. Given that cross-culturally *up* is typically associated with *good* (GOOD IS UP), vertical straightness is probably envisioned (see discussion of RIGHTEOUS PERSON IS A STRAIGHT PERSON below). Hence many scholars translate ישר as "upright" when it refers metaphorically to the human person, thereby preserving the term's vertical linearity.

2 Kgs 4:34–35; עוּת, "bent," Qoh 12:3). Kinesthetically a person can move forward (נגד, Josh 6:5, 20; Amos 4:3; Neh 12:37; קדם, Job 23:8), backward (אחרנית, Gen 9:23; אחור, Job 23:8), in a straight line (ישׁר, 1 Sam 6:12; Jer 31:9; Ps 107:7; Prov 9:15; Isa 40:3; נכח, Ezek 46:9), circuitously (סבב, Josh 6:3–4, 7, 14–15), or aimlessly (תעה, Gen 21:14; 37:15; Ps 107:4).[17] Such routine linear motion creates what Johnson calls a source-path-goal schema, an expectation that every movement has a beginning point, an end, and a trajectory that takes a person between the two.[18] In the Hebrew Bible the point of origin and the destination can be a specific location or a broader geographical region. Thus Isaac "walks" (הלך) to Gerar (Gen 26:1), and Jacob "goes out" (יצא) from Beer-sheba and "walks" (הלך) to Haran (28:10; see also 29:1; 36:6). Although deviations from the path are possible (the individual can "turn to the left or to the right," סור ימין ושמאול, Deut 2:27; 2 Sam 2:21; see also Num 22:26), the perceiver expects movement to have a point of origin, a path, and a destination. Thus it is noteworthy when someone "wanders about" (תעה) without a defined path or destination (e.g., Gen 21:14; 37:15).

Because proprioception creates a sense of space, linear movements enable the perceiver to determine his or her relative location vis-à-vis other bodies in the environment (<location $_{yes}$>).[19] Lot can sit *in* (ישׁב ב־) the gateway of Sodom (Gen 19:1; see also 18:1; 2 Sam 23:12 // 1 Chr 11:14); Hagar can walk away and sit *in front of* (ישׁב מנגד) of her son (Gen 21:16). Each is aware of his or her own relative location. Similarly, when biblical texts classify some objects as "near" (קרוב, Gen 19:20; Exod 13:17; אצל, 1 Sam 5:2; 20:19) and others as "distant" (מרחק, e.g., Gen 22:4; 37:18; Exod 2:4), they do so based upon kinesthetic appreciation of the environment. Unlike sight or touch, however, proprioception does not present a static spatial body. The body is not simply an object *in* space; it is an object *moving through* space. Even a seemingly stationary body, standing still or resting, exhibits subtle movement (e.g., the tightening of muscles, minute changes in position) and contains within it the potential for still greater

---

17. Again, the individual can typically affect the quality of his or her movement, save when one's ability has been hampered by nature or circumstance (e.g., when Jacob is struck on the thigh by a divine man in Gen 32:22–32, he is unable to walk properly).

18. Johnson, *Meaning of the Body*, 138–39.

19. Frédérique de Vignemont, "Bodily Awareness," in *The Standford Encyclopedia of Philosophy*, ed. Edward Zalta, http://tinyurl.com/SBL2634b.

movement (e.g., to stand up, to start walking).[20] Thus in one fluid motion Esau "arises" (קום) and "walks" (הלך); that is, his stationary body transitions smoothly into an ambulatory one (Gen 25:34). The question, then, is not whether movement is present or absent but the degree of force that the individual exerts.

Proprioception can detect this as well. As Sheets-Johnstone argues, through proprioception the individual can detect the "tensional" and "projectional" qualities of movement, that is, the sense of how much effort or force is exerted by the body.[21] Movement can be fast (רוץ, Gen 18:2, 7; 24:17; מהר, 18:6; 27:20; 43:30) or slow (לאטי לרגל, "by gentle foot," Gen 33:14; מהה, lit. "linger, delay," Gen 19:16; Exod 12:39; Judg 3:26), easy (e.g., one can "stand firmly," Josh 3:17; 4:3; see also the vast majority of cases where movement is performed without conscious thought or qualification) or difficult (e.g., "one stumbles," כשל, Lev 26:37; 2 Chr 28:15). For this reason descriptions of terrain as "level" (מישור, e.g., Deut 3:10; Josh 13:16; Ps 26:12) or "uneven" (עָקֹב, "hilly," and רְכָס, "rough," Isa 40:4) are instructive, not because of their aesthetic value, but because they reflect the relative effort the individual perceives that it would take to traverse them.

Like speech or hearing, then, proprioception is a temporal modality. It does not present a static spatiality of the body but the body's "unfolding kinetic dynamic," the quality and manner of its constant changes.[22] Unlike hearing or speech, however, this temporality is not sequential. There is not a sense of "befores, nows, or afters" but rather one continuous "streaming present" in which actions and consequences fluctuate and unfold in a dynamic pattern.[23] Movement is a process that begins with birth and ends with death; although the quality of it and the degree of the perceiver's awareness of it may change, its presence remains constant (so <briefness $_{no}$>). In this respect, it is hardly surprising that in the Hebrew Bible the classic verb of "walking" (הלך) comes to mean "continually" when it is paired with another verb. Thus Tamar walks away, "crying continually" (הלוך וזעקה, 2 Sam 13:19; see also Gen 8:3, 5; 12:9; 15:2). By

---

20. As Gapenne states, "except when dead, the body is never really static" ("Kinesthesia and the Construction of Perceptual Objects," 185).
21. Sheets-Johnstone, *Primacy of Movement*, 143.
22. Ibid., 142, 160.
23. Ibid., 151–54.

analogy with the other modalities, one might call this type of detection one of "dynamic continuity."

The properties of proprioception can be summarized as follows:[24]

Table 9.1. Biblical Typology of Movement

<location $_{yes}$>	<effects $_{yes}$>
<detection $_{yes}$> dynamic continuity	<subjectivity $_{yes}$>
<identification $_{yes}$>	<briefness $_{no}$>
<voluntary $_{yes}$>	

9.2. COGNITION IS MOVING

As with other modalities, proprioception serves as a natural source domain for metaphors of cognition. Sapiential texts frequently conceptualize cognition as horizontal motions, vertical positions, or directional orientations of the body, thereby drawing upon both locomotion and statesthetesis to structure the cognitive experience. Movement also serves as a source domain for human behaviors. Although not technically cognitive metaphors, these behavior metaphors greatly influence the development of complex metaphors for wisdom and thus also warrant consideration here.[25]

9.2.1. Knowledge Metaphors

Since movement is a common means of acquiring information about the environment, it naturally becomes a source domain for cognition. In Egyptian wisdom literature, for instance, learning is conceptualized as an act of "entering" into the instruction of one's teacher: "Be proficient in the writings; *go into the writings* [*ʿḳ m sš.w*]; give them in your heart" (Instruction of Ani; see also P.Anastasi 5.23, 5–6; P.Chester Beatty 4, pl. 19, verso 4, 6). Conversely, ignoring the instruction of one's teacher or failing to imi-

---

24. For <effects $_{yes}$>, see n. 13 above.
25. Although they carry certain cognitive connotations, these behavior metaphors are more appropriately classified as life metaphors. See Avrahami, *Senses of Scripture*, 179–80.

tate him precisely is an act of "going past" (*wni* or *sni*) his words: "Do not go beyond [*sni*] my example; do not go past [*wni*] my words (Instruction of Sehetep-ib-Ra 7, 6; see also Instruction of Amennakht 4; Instruction of Ptahhotep 151; Instruction by a Man for His Son 1.3; Instruction of Kagemni 2.5).[26] Similarly, in ancient Israel thinking can be described as an act of moving toward an abstract concept (THINKING IS WALKING):

Prov 6:6   *Go* [לך] to the ant, you lazy one; see its ways [דרכיה] and be wise.

Qoh 2:1   I said, I in my heart, "Let us *go* [לכה־נא]; let us test joy and see good. But indeed, this, too, vanity."

Qoh 2:3   I *scouted about* [תרתי] with my לב [how] to induce[27] my flesh with wine—and my לב was leading [נהג] me with wisdom—and [how] to seize folly.

Like the imperative of ראה, the command to "go" challenges the listener to *consider* the subject at hand. The command to go to the ant is not a request to physically walk to an ant but rather an injunction to *contemplate* the nature of ants (Prov 6:6).[28] Similarly, the Teacher's attempt to "scout out" (תור) the nature of pleasure does not indicate physical walking but cognitive exploration (Qoh 2:3; see also 1:13; 7:25).[29] The Teacher's command

---

26. Shupak, *Where Can Wisdom Be Found?*, 79–81. The translations here follow those of Shupak with slight modifications to highlight the kinesthetic dimensions of the passage.

27. So Seow, *Ecclesiastes*, 127. For the debate surrounding the translation of this term, see therein.

28. In his essay on the empiricism of Proverbs, Fox implies that the lazy person is commanded to physically *go* to the ant in order to consider it (*Proverbs 10–31*, 216); however, as he states in his comment on the verse, the main point of the passage is that "the sluggard is directed to *consider* the ant as a paragon of enterprise" (Fox, *Proverbs 1–9*, 216, emphasis added).

29. Comparing Qoh 2:3 with Num 15:39 (תתרו אחרי לבבכם, "to follow the heart") and Qoh 11:9 (והלך בדרכי לבך, "to walk in the ways of the heart"), Seow (*Ecclesiastes*, 126–27) suggests that "to go about with the heart" (תור לב) here indicates an emotional experience, not an intellectual one. By this reading, the Teacher actually *enjoys* wine; he does not contemplate *how* to do so. Yet as Seow points out, all of the ancient versions of this passage understand תור here to indicate an intellectual activ-

to his self in Qoh 2:1 to "go" (לכה) is likewise a command to *consider* the nature of pleasure. In these latter two examples the self is conceptualized as a person (THE SELF IS A PERSON) who can accompany the essence of the speaker on his cognitive journey.[30] In Qoh 2:3 the לב even "guides" (נהג) the cognitive expedition. The root metaphor itself, however, assumes that the concept under consideration—the ant's behavior, the nature of pleasure—is a location to which one can go (IDEAS ARE LOCATIONS). In doing so, it relies upon proprioception's ability to detect the movement of the body and its intended goal (<detection $_{yes}$>). Because it specifies thought as an act of walking, there is a projectional quality to cognition; it progresses in a sustained manner at a regular speed. There is also, however, a certain linear quality to thought; it has a beginning, middle, and an end, although here only the latter is clearly defined. Unlike visual metaphors in which conclusions appear to the individual instantaneously and seemingly without effort, the THINKING IS WALKING metaphor conceptualizes thought as an ongoing process that takes times and effort. Like one walking to a location, one must first *go* to the ant; only then can one *see* it. Moreover, like physical motion, such cognitive motion is voluntary (<voluntary $_{yes}$>). Although presumably thought is always present, one chooses when to begin a particular line of reasoning.

Thinking can also be described as a bodily position. For instance, one can "stand" to consider an idea (THINKING IS STANDING).

> Job 37:14   Give ear to this, Job. *Stand* [עמד] and understand the wonders of God.

As Malul argues, the parallel between עמד and the verb בין ("understand") suggests that, as with ראה, the bodily position of standing carried an

---

ity. The LXX, for instance, reads κατεσκεψάμην ("I examined"); Aquila and Symmachus, ἐνοήθην ("I considered"); Theodotion, διανοήθην ("I purposed"); and the Vulgate, *cogitavi* ("I thought") (Seow, *Ecclesiastes*, 127). Given the similar usages of תור in Qoh 1:13 and 7:25, the intellectual connotation seems to make sense here. Although there may be emotional ramifications to the Teacher's cognitive exploration, the act itself is an intellectual activity.

30. For a discussion of the relationship between the essence of the individual and his or her various selves, see KNOWING IS HEARING/SPEAKING above. Here, however, the presence of the לב does not affect the primary metaphor, which still envisions the action of the walking being done by the person as a whole. In other words, these passages here do not witness a significant extension of this primary metaphor.

epistemological nuance.[31] Physically, standing is a stationary position, reflecting a temporary cessation of horizontal motion; metaphorically, the individual is commanded to cease all other motion—all other activity and thought—in order to contemplate the matter at hand, the wonders of God. One can also "turn" toward an abstract concept (THINKING IS TURNING).

> Qoh 2:12   And I *turned* [ופניתי] to see wisdom, madness, and folly.
>
> Qoh 7:25   I *turned around* [סבותי], I and my heart, to know and to spy out and to seek wisdom and the accounting of things and to know wickedness and foolishness and folly and madness.
>
> Qoh 9:11   I *turned again* [שבתי] and saw under the sun that the race was not to the swift.

Like a body turning toward or away from a particular object or destination, the individual "turns" toward or away from a specific abstract concept. In Egyptian wisdom literature the act of turning frequently indicates cognitive inattention: "Do not *turn* the head [*mkḥ3*] away from my excellent sayings" (Instruction of Amennakht 9; see also P.Lansing 3, 5; P.Anastasi 5.17, 3).[32] In biblical literature it indicates cognitive attention.[33] The Teacher turns toward wisdom (Qoh 2:12; 7:25), folly (2:12), and the like (see, e.g., בכל־מעשי שעשו ידי, "all the doings that are done by my hands," in 2:11). Qoheleth 9:11's use of שוב also connotes a cognitive turn. Although often translated as "again" (e.g., NRSV) or "further" (e.g., Seow),[34] שוב itself connotes a kinesthetic turn toward or a return to a pre-

---

31. Malul, *Knowledge, Control, and Sex*, 141. Malul compares the usage here to similar constructions in Exod 9:16; 1 Sam 9:27; 2 Chr 20:17; Song 2:9; Jer 6:16; 48:19; Hab 2:1, each of which connect עמד to obtaining knowledge, either metaphorically or concretely.

32. Shupak, *Where Can Wisdom Be Found?*, 80.

33. For the Israelite connotations of "turning away" from something, see the discussion of ACTING IS TURNING below.

34. Seow, *Ecclesiastes*, 177. These translations thus treat שוב as an auxiliary verb. Although שוב, like הלך, does indicate repeated action when paired with another verb (see, e.g., Exod 32:27; Ezek 35:7; Dan 11:10; Zech 7:14; 9:8), the kinesthetic value of שוב should not be lost.

viously held position or locale (see, e.g., Gen 14:7; Num 33:7; Judg 8:13). Here the Teacher "turns again" to contemplate a matter, in this case the equal fate destined for all (Qoh 9:11; see also 4:1, 7). As with the oral, tactile, and ingestive metaphors above, THINKING IS TURNING can combine with a SELF metaphor (THINKING IS TURNING ONE'S SELF).

> Prov 2:2 To make your ear attentive to wisdom and to *turn* your heart [תטה לבך] to understanding.

In Prov 2:2 the sage commands his student to נטה his self toward understanding. While נטה can be used to signify the extension of an object to someone (e.g., "stretch out one's hand," Exod 7:19; 8:1, 2; "extend a sword," Josh 8:18, 26; Ezek 30:25), it often connotes a person's change in direction toward or away from something (e.g., Gen 38:16; Num 20:17; 21:22; 22:23).[35] This latter connotation seems to be the nuance in Prov 2:2, where the act of turning reflects a distinct change in the position of the self, which is conceptualized as a person (THE SELF IS A PERSON). In any case, as Fox notes, this cognitive turn does not "demand understanding," only a "receptivity" toward it;[36] that is, the change in position represents a preliminary stage toward understanding, not the actual arrival at it.

As with the THINKING IS WALKING metaphor, THINKING IS STANDING and THINKING IS TURNING rely upon proprioception's ability to detect the motion of the body (<detection $_{yes}$>). In these metaphors, however, it is the motion of the stationary body that is under examination. As with physical statesthetesis, the concern of THINKING IS STANDING is with the tensional quality of motion, the degree of force that the individual exerts in the cognitive act, in this case relatively little. Thus when one "stops" to consider a particular matter (as in Job 37:14), there is a temporary decrease in the amount of force exerted in other activities in order to focus on the contemplation at hand. THINKING IS TURNING, on the other hand, relies on proprioception's ability to detect the directional orientation of the body,

---

35. Helmer Ringgren, "נטה," *TDOT* 9:381–83. The reading of נטה as "stretch out" or "extend" still connotes kinesthesia, although of a different sort: that of movement that is localized in the arm or hand rather than distributed throughout the entire body. Such cases describe how the person manipulates objects, and any metaphors based on them therefore belong to the tactile domain.

36. Fox, *Proverbs 1–9*, 109. Fox is speaking specifically about the directive in Prov 2:2, but the sentiment is applicable to the entire conceptual metaphor.

whether one faces toward one concept or another. Yet as with THINKING IS WALKING, both of these metaphors assume that the cognitive act is voluntary and continuous (<voluntary ~yes~>). The individual chooses when to stand and when to turn (e.g., Qoh 2:12; 7:25; 9:11) and often must be cajoled into doing so (e.g., Job 37:14; Prov 2:2), but the movement itself is part of a larger cognitive motion, either a cessation of motion that has gone before (as in THINKING IS STANDING) or a preparatory stage for motion that is to come (as in THINKING IS TURNING).

If contemplating a matter is going *to* or turning *toward* it, than understanding a matter is arriving *at* it (UNDERSTANDING IS ARRIVING AT A LOCATION).[37]

> Job 28:12 Where shall wisdom be found? And where is the *place* [מקום] of understanding?

> Job 38:16 Have you *come* [הבאת] to the depths of the sea or *walked about* [התהלכת] the hidden places of the deeps?

> Job 41:5 Who can uncover the front of its garments? Who can *come* [יבוא] into his double coat of mail?[38]

> Qoh 3:22 I saw that there is nothing better than that an individual enjoy his work, for it is his lot. But who can *bring* him [יביאנו] to see what will be after him?[39]

In Job 38:16, God questions Job about his ability to "come" to the otherwise inaccessible locales of creation, the sea and the deep (see also Job

---

37. A similar concept may be present in Egyptian literature in that the term ꜥrk ("to be clever") may be related to its homonym ꜥrk ("to be complete"). Thus Shupak argues that to be "clever" is to "comprehend to the end": "My master, clever [ꜥrk, lit. "completed"] in the image of Sia, a teacher who penetrates hearts" (Shupak, *Where Can Wisdom Be Found?*, 63).

38. As Habel (*Book of Job*, 555) notes, רסנו normally means "halter," but the LXX translates it as θώραξ ("coat of mail)," which seems to fit the context here.

39. אחריו ("after him") is also a kinesthetically derived expression, referring here to the passage of time. The past is conceptualized spatially as that which comes "before" a person while the future is that which comes "after" (PAST IS BEFORE, FUTURE IS AFTER). See, for instance, Qoh 1:10, 11, 16; 2:7, 9, 16, 18. Such time metaphors belong to the semantic domain of life.

38:22; Prov 30:4). That the same action can be done of Leviathan's mouth (Job 41:5), a destination one would not physically want to walk, suggests that a physical journey through the heavens à la Enoch is not intended here but rather a cognitive one.[40] The point of these Job passages is that humans are not God. They cannot *comprehend* such matters; they cannot come to the "place" (מקום) of understanding (Job 28:12; see also 28:20). Likewise, the Teacher reflects upon the impossibility of "bringing" (יביאנו) others to understand their fate. By the same token, that which is unknown remains "far" away (LACK OF UNDERSTANDING IS FAR).

> Qoh 7:23-24   All of this I have tested by wisdom; I said, "I will be wise," but it was *far* [רחוקה] from me. That which is, is *far* [רחוק], and that which is exceedingly deep, who can find it?

Just as he laments of "bringing" others to understanding, the Teacher despairs of ever obtaining knowledge himself, stating that it remains "far" (רחוק) from him (Qoh 7:23-24). These two metaphors focus on proprioception's locative and amplitudinal detective capabilities (<location $_{yes}$>, <detection $_{yes}$>). An individual can detect his or her relative position vis-à-vis knowledge and how much distance lies between. These metaphors also, in many respects, reflect the final stage of the previous cognitive motions. The process that began with stopping, turning, and moving toward a concept culminates when one finally arrives *at* it.

9.2.2. Emotion Metaphors

Proprioception also serves as a source domain for emotional experience. Pride, for instance, is described as having an elevated character (ARROGANCE IS BEING HIGH, HUMILITY IS BEING LOW).

> Prov 3:35   The wise will possess honor, but *high* [מרים] fools [will inherit] dishonor.

---

40. Enoch, the ancestor of Abraham who is said to have "walked with God" (ויתהלך חנוך את־האלהים) in Gen 5:22. In Genesis "walking with God" is probably a metaphor for death (TO DIE IS TO WALK WITH GOD), but early Jews took this as a reference to a literal journey through the cosmos (see, for instance, 1 Enoch).

9. MOVING

Prov 21:4   *High* eyes [רָם־עֵינַיִם] and a *broad* heart [וּרְחַב־לֵב], the lamp of the wicked are sin.

Prov 30:32   If you have been foolish, *lifting yourself* [בְהִתְנַשֵּׂא], or if you have schemed [with] hand to mouth…

Job 22:29   When [others] are humiliated, then you will say, "It is pride; the *lowly of eyes* [וְשַׁח עֵינַיִם] are saved."

In general, to be "lifted up" is a sign of honor. Thus a city is "lifted up" (רוֹם) through the blessing of the upright (Prov 11:11; see also Job 24:24), and a nation is "lifted" (רָמַם) through it righteousness (Prov 14:34; see also 4:8). However, being inappropriately "high" is condemned. Thus the fool who is "high" (רוֹם, Prov 3:35) or who has "lifted himself up" (30:32) is inappropriately prideful and will come to disgrace. Similarly, having "raised" eyes (רָם־עֵינַיִם) is a characteristic of the proud and therefore condemned as a sin (Prov 21:4, see also 6:17; 30:13), while having "lowered" eyes (שַׁח עֵינַיִם) is a sign of humility and is praised (Job 22:29). As Prov 21:4 illustrates, a wicked person is also distinguished by the "broadness" of the self (רְחַב־לֵב). Although elsewhere having a "broad לֵב" is a sign of intellectual aptitude (see, e.g., 1 Kgs 4:29; Ps 119:32; HAVING KNOWLEDGE IS HAVING A BROAD HEART), here it is condemned as a negative quality. Like "high eyes," a "broad" self belongs to someone who over exaggerates his or her own worth (ARROGANCE IS A BROAD SELF).[41] A similar negativity is found in Prov 28:25, where a "broad" self indicates greed (GREED IS A BROAD SELF):

Prov 28:25   A *broad* [רְחַב] נֶפֶשׁ stirs up strife, but whoever trusts in the LORD will be fattened.

As noted in the discussion of DESIRE IS HUNGER above, the נֶפֶשׁ is frequently connected to physical appetite. Here, like a mouth wide open to

---

41. For the reading of "broad לֵב" as an indicator of arrogance, see Fox, *Proverbs 10–31*, 680. Alternatively, the phrase could indicate "greed," as a "broad נֶפֶשׁ" does in Prov 28:25 (see GREED IS A BROAD SELF below). Yet as Fox points out, while the נֶפֶשׁ is clearly connected to appetite elsewhere in the Hebrew Bible, the לֵב is not. Given the connection of רְחַב־לֵב with haughty eyes here and in Ps 101:5, "arrogance" seems to be a more appropriate nuance for this construction.

receive food, the נפש is a broad cavity waiting to be filled. In each case these spatial metaphors map proprioception's detective ability onto the emotional experience. In ARROGANCE IS BEING HIGH and HUMILITY IS BEING LOW, the emphasis is on the locative dimension of proprioception, that is, where the body is in relation to other bodies (<location ᵧₑₛ>). Pride and humility are characterized as the location at which one is situated (EMOTIONS ARE LOCATIONS). ARROGANCE IS A BROAD SELF and GREED IS A BROAD SELF, on the other hand, emphasize the amplitudinal qualities of proprioception, conceptualizing the self as a space with width and breadth (THE SELF IS A SPACE) (<detection ᵧₑₛ> amplitudinal).[42]

9.2.3. Behavior Metaphors

Like thinking metaphors, specific actions can be conceptualized as either horizontal motions or changes in bodily position. In Egyptian wisdom literature, a moral transgression can be described as an act of "going past" a place: "Woe to him who would *walk past* [*thi*] this" (Instruction of Ptahhotep 50).[43] Similarly, in biblical wisdom literature, a single action can be described as an act of "walking" (ACTING IS WALKING).

> Prov 12:11   The one who works the land will have enough food,
> but the one who *pursues* [ומרדף] empty things will lack heart.
>
> Prov 20:19   The one who reveals secrets *walks* [הולך] slander.
>
> Job 31:5   If I have *walked* [הלכתי] with falsehood or my *foot* [רגלי] has *hurried* [ותחש] to deceit...

Fools "pursue" worthless goals (מרדף ריקים, Prov 12:11; see also 11:19; 15:9; 21:21; 28:19), gossips "walk" slander (הולך רכיל, Prov 20:19; see also 11:13), and individuals "walk" with falsehood (הלכתי עם־שוא; Job 31:5). The goal of the actions determines the direction in which one moves. In Prov 12:11, the goal seems to be a person whom the individual chases (A

---

42. By analogy with other cognitive metaphors, one would assume that these two "broad self" metaphors arise when a primary metaphor (ARROGANCE IS BROADNESS or GREED IS BROADNESS) is combined with a SELF metaphor (THE SELF IS A SPACE). The primary metaphors themselves, however, do not seem to be reflected in the literature.

43. Shupak, *Where Can Wisdom Be Found?*, 82

purpose is a person); in Prov 20:19 and Job 31:5 the form of the goal is not specified. However, in each case the root metaphor clearly conceptualizes behavior as a horizontal motion moving purposefully through space. Like the thinking is walking metaphor, acting is walking maps proprioception's capability to detect motion onto an abstract domain, in this case that of human behavior. In particular, it conceptualizes behavior as a progressive, linear motion with a beginning, middle, and end (<detection $_{yes}$> $^{projectional/linear}$). Again, the destination of this motion is of primary importance, whether one moves toward evil (Prov 1:16; Job 31:5) or worthless pursuits (Prov 12:11). acting is walking also presumes that such activity is voluntary (<voluntary $_{yes}$>).

Action can also be described as a change in bodily posture, a turning *toward* or *away from* a behavior. Thus, echoing the Instruction of Ptahhotep, the Egyptian Instruction of Amenemope declares, "Woe to him who *turns* [*wni*] from them" (3.12).[44] Similarly, in the Hebrew Bible, an action can be described as an act of turning (acting is turning).

Job 36:21   Take care; do not *turn* [אל־תפן] to iniquity.

Prov 3:7   Do not be wise in your eyes; fear the Lord and *turn* [וסור] from evil.

Job 1:1   There was a man in the land of Uz; his name was Job. That man was perfect and straight [וישר], and he feared God and *turned* [וסר] away from evil.

Job 27:5   Until I die, I will not *turn* [לא־אסיר] integrity from me.

Job 33:17   [God disciplines] in order to *turn* [להסיר] a person from his deeds.

Engaging in a behavior is turning *toward* it. Thus Elihu warns Job not to "turn" (פנה) toward iniquity (Job 36:21). Avoiding behavior, on the other hand, is turning *away* from it. Thus the sage warns his student to "turn" (סור) from evil (Prov 3:7, see also 14:16; 16:6; Job 28:28; and the command to שוב, "turn back," from iniquity in Job 36:10). Job is well known

---

44. Ibid., 83. The translation follows that of Shupak.

for doing just that (Job 1:1; see also 1:8; 2:3); in fact, he insists that he will not *avoid* (סור) behaving with integrity (Job 27:5). As with THINKING IS TURNING, ACTING IS TURNING relies upon proprioception's ability to detect directional orientation of the stationary body (<detection $_{yes}$> directional orientation). The individual can detect the "direction" of behavior, whether one turns toward integrity (Job 27:5), iniquity (36:21) or evil (Prov 3:7; cf. Job 1:1). Moreover, as with THINKING IS TURNING, the choice to behave in a certain manner here is voluntary (thus mapping kinesthesia's <voluntary $_{yes}$> property onto behavior), although another individual can influence this choice. Thus in Job 33:17 God "turns" (סור) the individual away from his actions toward better behavior (see also the negative realization of this in the complex metaphor of Prov 7:21).

Most importantly for sapiential circles, routine behavior is conceptualized as a "path." Thus in Egyptian wisdom literature the one who transgresses a "path" is one who forsakes a certain proscribed behavior: "Knives are sharp against the one who transgresses a path [*mtn*]" (Instruction of Kagemni 1.2–3).[45] Similarly, in the Hebrew Bible, behavior is a path upon which one walks (BEHAVIOR IS A PATH).

> Prov 5:21   For the *ways* [דרכי] of humans are in front of the eyes of the LORD, and he makes level [מפלס][46] all their *tracks* [מעגלתויו].
>
> Prov 6:6   Go [לך] to the ant, you lazy one; see *its ways* [דרכיה] and be wise.
>
> Job 13:15   Indeed, he will kill me, I have no hope; but I will argue my *ways* [דרכי] to his face.
>
> Job 26:14   Indeed, these are the ends [קצות] of [God's] *way* [דרכו],[47] but what a whisper of a word we hear of it!

---

45. The translation here follows that of Shupak, *Where Can Wisdom Be Found?*, 82, with slight modification.

46. For the nuance of this kinesthetic expression, see the discussion of LIVING WELL IS WALKING LEVELLY in Tilford, "Taste and See," 247–50.

47. Thus following the *ketiv*. The *qere* suggests דרכיו ("his ways").

Just as repeatedly walking the same route marks out a path on the ground, routine behavior establishes the path of one's life. Ants, for instance, routinely gather and prepare food in the summer; that is their "way" (דרך) (Prov 6:6; see also 6:8; 30:19, 29). Similarly, people have "ways" (דרכי־איש) that can be observed by others (Prov 5:21). Job's actions conform to certain patterns (Job 13:15; see also 23:10; 31:4–5), as do God's (26:14). According to Norman Habel, God's דרך is the "law or principle of God's cosmic design"; that is, it is not the works of creation themselves but the established principles by which creation is structured.[48] God, like humanity, operates according to consistent patterns. As Fox states, "once a person enters onto [a] path, he is likely to follow it to the end. It becomes his natural course and, in spite of its difficulties, is easier to stay on than to leave."[49] Like physical markings on the terrain, then, such "paths" have an enduring quality; they are imprinted, so to speak, on the landscape of a person's life.

According to Fox, there are two forms of this path metaphor: the MANY PATHS iteration and the TWO PATHS iteration. The MANY PATHS iteration envisions life as a series of paths, some of which lead to life and others of which lead to death. The TWO PATHS iteration narrows these options down, arguing that there are "really only two paths, or types of path, of fatal importance": those of "life" and those of "death."[50] Both metaphors are what Fox calls "ground metaphors"; that is, they "organiz[e] other perceptions and images and conve[y] a way of perceiving the world."[51] They are, in other words, core images in the rhetoric of Proverbs.

While Fox is basically correct, his treatment of these metaphors gives the reader the impression that there is not much difference between the two metaphors. Both metaphors involve many ways of acting—according to Fox, even the TWO PATHS metaphor acknowledges that there are many "paths of life" and "paths of death" (that is, good and bad behaviors) from which a person can choose—and both ultimately classify behaviors according to those that lead to life or those that lead to death. Conceptual metaphor theory, however, can help differentiate between the different BEHAVIOR metaphors and the nuances provided by each.[52] What Fox calls

---

48. Habel, *Book of Job*, 365–66.
49. Fox, *Proverbs 1–9*, 129.
50. Ibid., 128–30.
51. Ibid.
52. Fox is aware of conceptual metaphor theory. In fact, he uses the theories in Lakoff and Johnson's *Metaphors We Live By* to frame his discussion of behavior meta-

the MANY PATHS iteration is, I would argue, the primary metaphor seen here, a conception of human behavior as a plethora of paths from which the individual may choose over his or her lifetime (BEHAVIOR IS A PATH). What Fox calls the TWO PATHS iteration is, on the other hand, a series of complex imaginative extensions based on this primary metaphor, whereby human behavior is restricted to two main courses by which the individual can travel. These two paths are conceptualized by a variety of dichotomies, only some of which distinguish between paths of life and paths of death: GOOD/EVIL BEHAVIOR IS A PATH, RIGHTEOUSNESS/WICKEDNESS IS A PATH, GOOD/EVIL BEHAVIOR IS A PATH OF LIFE/DEATH (see the discussion at §10.1). These extensions are then blended together with other metaphors to create the complicated moral system of Proverbs in which RIGHTEOUSNESS IS A STRAIGHT PATH, WICKEDNESS IS A CROOKED PATH, and WISDOM IS A PATH OF LIFE.[53] In other words, the conception of behavior as two paths derives from the more basic BEHAVIOR IS A PATH metaphor, is more complicated in nuance, and is not equivalent to it in terms of the cognitive processes by which it develops. Recognizing the degree of cognitive sophistication in each metaphor can help us distinguish between the BEHAVIOR metaphors and determine the reason the language user utilizes a given metaphor at any particular moment.

Because it conceptualizes behavior as a path, the more basic BEHAVIOR IS A PATH metaphor draws upon proprioception's expectation that motion has a beginning, a middle, and an end and that the individual can detect these different stages (<detection $_{yes}$> ^{linear}). With this metaphor, however, the focus is on the middle of the motion, the path it takes to get from point A to point B. As such, this metaphor highlights the continual nature of motion. One can change direction or choose a different path, but the movement of life never ceases. Moreover, like ACTING IS WALKING, BEHAVIOR IS A PATH assumes that there are many paths one can choose from and that the individual has the choice of which path to follow (<voluntary $_{yes}$>). Thus the student must be warned:

---

phors (see Fox, *Proverbs 1–9*, 128 n. 113). However, as mentioned in ch. 1 n. 69 above, the conceptual metaphor theory in contemporary scholarship is more complicated than the original theory put forth by Lakoff and Johnson, especially with respect to the distinction between the different degrees of metaphorical complexity and the processes by which they develop. Drawing upon this theoretical advances here can help nuance Fox's basic argument about the path metaphors of Proverbs.

53. For a discussion of these complex blends, see Tilford, "Taste and See," 261–62.

Prov 1:15 My son, do not *walk* [אל־תלך] in their *way* [בדרך]; withhold your *feet* [רגלך] from their *tracks* [מנתיבתם].

The student is not to "walk" on the "path" (דרך, נתיבה) of robbers; that is, he is not to *mimic* their behavior (see also Prov 3:31; 16:29). Such a warning presumes that the student can choose the path upon which he walks and must therefore be instructed about proper behavior.

Like the OBEYING IS HEARING metaphor discussed above, these behavior metaphors assume that more is going on than simple bodily activity; conscious choices are being made. Job, for instance, can choose to "turn" from evil (Job 1:1), just as the student can choose to disregard the "path" of robbers (Prov 1:15). What is at stake is not simply the behavior of the individual but the mindset that such behavior represents. There is, then, a certain inherent overlap between the semantic domains of cognition and these behavior metaphors. Still, the focus of such metaphors remains on the behavior of the individual, not his or her intellectual or emotional status.

9.2.4. Judgment Metaphors

Morality is also described in terms of proprioception: GOOD IS UP/BAD IS DOWN, GOOD IS STRAIGHT/BAD IS CROOKED, GOOD IS BALANCE/BAD IS IMBALANCE. In the Hebrew Bible, a word can be "straight" (ישר, Prov 16:13; Job 6:25) or "crooked" (פתל, עקש, הפך, Prov 8:8; 17:20; 19:1); a person can be "straight up" (ישר, Prov 3:32; Job 8:6; Qoh 7:29) or "bent" (לוז, עוה, Prov 3:32; 12:8); and a path can be "straight" (ישר, Prov 14:2), "level" (פלס, Prov 4:26–27), or "crooked" (לוז, עקש, Prov 14:2; 28:6). Although the property of <evaluation> is itself largely irrelevant to proprioception, some motions are presumably conceptualized as being more efficient means of obtaining a goal than others. These judgment metaphors draw upon this notion, evaluating specific motions as good or bad (<evaluation $_{yes}$>). However, as these metaphors are only realized in complex blends, an extended discussion will have to wait.[54]

---

54. See §10.2 below or my extended discussion in Tilford, "Taste and See," 233–49.

9.3. Summary

Proprioception provides a natural source domain for a variety of cognitive and behavioral metaphors, each of which relies upon the kinesthetic inclinations of the body:

Table 9.2. Metaphorical Mappings: COGNITION IS MOVING

THINKING IS WALKING
 <detection $_{yes}$> $^{projectional/linear}$, <voluntary $_{yes}$>
THINKING IS STANDING
 <detection $_{yes}$> ^{tensional}, <voluntary $_{yes}$>
THINKING IS TURNING
 <detection $_{yes}$> $^{directional\ orientation}$, <voluntary $_{yes}$>
THINKING IS TURNING ONE'S SELF
 <detection $_{yes}$> $^{directional\ orientation}$, <voluntary $_{yes}$>
UNDERSTANDING IS ARRIVING AT A CONCEPT
 <location $_{yes}$>, <detection $_{yes}$> ^{amplitudinal}
LACK OF UNDERSTANDING IS FAR
 <location $_{yes}$>, <detection $_{yes}$> ^{amplitudinal}
TO BE IGNORANT IS TO BE WIDE OPEN
 <detection $_{yes}$> ^{amplitudinal}
ARROGANCE IS BEING HIGH
 <location $_{yes}$>
HUMILITY IS BEING LOW
 <location $_{yes}$>
ARROGANCE IS A BROAD SELF
 <detection $_{yes}$> ^{amplitudinal}
GREED IS A BROAD SELF
 <detection $_{yes}$> ^{amplitudinal}
ACTING IS WALKING
 <detection $_{yes}$> $^{projectional/linear}$, <voluntary $_{yes}$>
ACTING IS TURNING
 <detection $_{yes}$> $^{directional\ orientation}$, <voluntary $_{yes}$>
BEHAVIOR IS A PATH
 <detection $_{yes}$> ^{linear}, <voluntary $_{yes}$>

In each of these metaphors, proprioception's <detection $_{yes}$> property motivates the conceptualization of the abstract domain of cognition. What differentiates these metaphors from one another is the quality of movement that is detected. The THINKING IS WALKING metaphor, for instance, conceptualizes thought via the body's linear quality, while THINKING IS STANDING focuses on the tensional quality of the body's movement, and THINKING IS TURNING focuses on the directional orientation of the body. Yet whatever the quality emphasized, the continuous movement of the kinesthetic body is preserved throughout these mappings. Cognitive metaphors based on proprioception consistently conceptualize cognition as a continual, self-perpetuated process.

10
Complex Metaphors

Like other peoples, biblical sages did not limit their understanding of cognition to primary metaphors. Utilizing the full force of human perceptual experience, these ancient scribes extended, blended, and clustered metaphors together to form new modes of conceptualizing knowledge and prescribe the appropriate means of obtaining it. Such metaphors could draw upon one modality or many, depending on which primary metaphor(s) they were based upon and whether those primary metaphors themselves came from one modal domain or several. Thus the normative pursuit of wisdom in ancient Israel as a whole was neither a one-dimensional nor unimodal experience; rather, it was a complex, multimodal pursuit of those values that Israelites and early Jewish scribes held most dear.[1]

10.1. Metaphorical Extensions

Some metaphors develop new meaning by consciously or preconsciously extending a dominant or dormant element of a conventional metaphor. In the case of wisdom metaphors, such "extensions" extend the base elements of a primary metaphor in order to clarify the means by which knowledge is formed and the roles humans play in its acquisition. Because the primary metaphors upon which metaphorical extensions of wisdom metaphors draw tend to rely upon only one modality, they also tend to focus on one key modality and the mappings associated with it.[2] Yet in the process of

---

1. In order to facilitate analysis, I will limit my discussion here to examples from the book of Proverbs. Similar analyses can be conducted of any wisdom text, although the results would vary according to the particular social context of the text chosen. For additional examples from Proverbs, see Tilford, "Taste and See."

2. This is not to say that all primary metaphors rely on one modality. For instance, as already discussed above, KNOWLEDGE IS A WORD and MORAL QUALITIES ARE WORDS

extending their underlying metaphors, metaphorical extensions transform cognition from a basic biological process into a normative concept by which an individual can evaluate his or her environment and effect change in it.

Take, for instance, the BEHAVIOR IS A PATH metaphor discussed in §9.2.3. This primary metaphor assumes that there are many possible behaviors an individual can routinely choose to engage in over the course of his or her lifetime. One can behave violently (Prov 3:31; 16:29), be greedy (1:19), engage in sexual intercourse (e.g., Prov 30:19, 20), and so on. Such behaviors in themselves are not good or bad. Violent action, for example, is necessary in times of war but can be disruptive among members of the same community. The primary metaphor itself, then, does not evaluate these different paths but leaves it up to individuals to determine the relative value of a behavior and whether they will choose to engage in it (<voluntary $_{yes}$>). Thus Job chooses to behave in a certain way and must subsequently argue that his "paths" are good (Job 13:15; see also 31:37), and the sage must argue that the "paths" of robbers are harmful and should not be followed (Prov 1:15). God himself examines the "paths" of people to determine whether their behavior is beneficial or harmful (Prov 5:21; see also Job 13:27; 14:16; 24:23; 31:4; 33:11; 34:21).

Various passages in Proverbs eliminate this individual evaluation, injecting morality directly into the path metaphor. Some paths are inherently "good"; others are inherently "evil" (GOOD BEHAVIOR IS A PATH; EVIL BEHAVIOR IS A PATH).

> Prov 2:9   Then you will understand righteousness, justice, and uprightness, *every good track* [כל־מעגל־טוב].
>
> Prov 8:13   Fear of the LORD hates evil; pride and arrogance and an *evil path* [דרך רע] and a mouth of perversity I hate.
>
> Prov 16:29   A violent man entices his companion and causes him to walk [והוליכו] on *a path that is not good* [בדרך לא־טוב].

---

each draw upon two modalities, speech and hearing. Complex metaphors based upon these metaphors are also inherently multimodal. However, since most primary metaphors for cognition in sapiential literature focus on a single modal domain, the extensions based on them tend to do the same.

Similarly, some behaviors are deemed "paths of righteousness," while others are considered "paths of wickedness" (RIGHTEOUSNESS IS A PATH; WICKEDNESS IS A PATH):

> Prov 2:20 Therefore, walk in the *way of the good* [בדרך טובים]; keep the *paths of the righteous* [אחרות צדיקים].

> Prov 15:9 An abomination to the LORD is the *path of wickedness* [דרך רשע], but he loves the one who pursues righteousness.

Like the BEHAVIOR IS A PATH metaphor, such expressions presume that people can be identified by the behavior in which they routinely engage.[3] Good people walk on "good paths" (Prov 2:9, 20); evil people walk on "evil paths" (8:13; see also 2:12; 28:10; and the "path that is not good," 16:29). Similarly, righteous people walk on "paths of righteousness (2:20; see also 4:18; 8:20; 12:28); wicked people walk on "paths of wickedness" (15:9; see also 4:14; 12:26).

Paths can also be identified by the rewards they bring. Thus, the BEHAVIOR IS A PATH metaphor also extends to describe some behaviors as "paths of life" and others as "paths of death" (GOOD BEHAVIOR IS A PATH OF LIFE; EVIL BEHAVIOR IS A PATH OF DEATH):

> Prov 2:19 All who go to her do not return [ישובון]; they do not reach [ולא־ישיגו] the *paths of life* [ארחות חיים].

> Prov 14:12 There is a way [דרך] that seems straight to a person, but its end is the *path of death* [דרכי־מות].

The Egyptian sources with which the sages of Proverbs were familiar also frequently conceptualized appropriate behavior as "paths of life." For example, the Instruction of Amenemope proposes to help the student recognize the

---

3. Paths can be described either by the people who walk on them or by the qualities those people possess. For instance, righteous behavior can be described as the "path(s) of the righteous" (ארחות צדיקים, Prov 2:20; see also 4:18) or a "path of righteousness" (ארח־צדקה, 8:20; 12:28). Similarly, wicked behavior can be the "path of the wicked" (e.g., דרך רעים, 4:14; 12:26) or a "path of wickedness" (דרך רשע, 15:9). Although such expressions carry slightly different nuances, I do not ascribe any great conceptual significance to this variation of form.

"way of life" (1.7), and the Instruction of Amennakht describes its teachings as "utterances of the way of life" (1.1).[4] No doubt such examples provided a helpful precedent for the writers of Proverbs. However, in describing certain behaviors as "paths of life," Israelite sages were not simply borrowing an image from the Egyptians. Rather, they nuanced the image based on their own system of beliefs. Most importantly, the extension of BEHAVIOR IS A PATH into a PATH OF LIFE/PATH OF DEATH relies upon a belief that there is a direct correlation between the behavior of an individual and his or her material surfeit. As first articulated by Klaus Koch, this "Tat-Ergehen Zusammenhang" ("acts-consequence connection") presupposes that an individual who performs good deeds will be rewarded with good things, while an individual who acts wickedly will be punished.[5] Later scholars have since demonstrated that the acts-consequence connection is not as rigid, simple, or all-encompassing as Koch assumed, nor does it exclude God's agency, as Koch argued.[6] However, many of the sayings in Proverbs do presuppose that certain actions have positive effects, while others have negative effects.[7] Certain behaviors, for instance, lead to prosperity, health, and long life (Prov 10:16; 11:19; 21:21; 22:4). Others harm the individual, destroy his or her wealth, and ultimately lead to death (10:2; 11:19; 19:16). Because of this conception, certain behaviors are deemed "paths of life" (2:19; see also

---

4. Fox, *Proverbs 1–9*, 130. The translations here follow those of Fox.

5. Klaus Koch, "Is There a Doctrine of Retribution in the Old Testament?," in *Theodicy in the Old Testament*, ed. James Crenshaw (Philadelphia: Fortress, 1983), 57–87. See also the discussion of Koch and the scholars who elaborated on his theory in Peter Hatton, "A Cautionary Tale: The Acts-Consequence 'Construct,'" *JSOT* 35 (2011): 375–84. The translation of Koch's "Tat-Ergehen Zusammenhang" follows that of Hatton.

6. See, for instance, Patrick D. Miller, *Sin and Judgment in the Prophets*, SBLMS 27 (Chico, CA: Scholars, 1982), 121–29; Lennart Boström, *The God of the Sages* (Stockholm: Almqvist & Wiksell, 1990), 90–140; Fox, *Proverbs 1–9*, 91–92; Hatton, "Cautionary Tale," 378–79.

7. This is not to say that *every* passage presumes this connection. As Peter Hatton argues, there are "unresolved tensions" in the book of Proverbs, particularly between human agency and divine retribution (*Contradiction in the Book of Proverbs: The Deep Waters of Counsel* [Aldershot: Ashgate, 2008], 83–116). For instance, when Prov 10:15 states that "the wealth of the rich is a strong fortress" and that "poverty is the destruction of the poor," there is no presumption that material surfeit or scarcity results from one's moral character (92–93). Indeed, Prov 18:10–11 suggests that wealth is negative, a false security enjoyed by those who do not cling to God's ways, that is, the wicked (94–95).

5:6; 10:17; 15:24) and others "paths of death" (14:12; see also 16:25). This latter designation is absent in the Egyptian material,[8] which suggests that a belief in an acts-consequence connection is indeed the primary motivation for the extension in Proverbs here. If good deeds lead to life, evil deeds must lead to death. In other words, because of an underlying belief in the nature of human behavior, the sages developed a polarity in the path metaphors by which to encourage their students to choose a path of life.

As in the primary metaphor, these various paths have a beginning, a middle, and an end, although the focus is on the continual linear trajectory of the movement, that is, the path upon which one walks (<detection $_{yes}$> ^{linear}). Unlike the primary metaphor, however, such expressions simplify the moral choice of the individual. Although there are still many different behaviors one can choose to engage in (righteous deeds, good deeds, wicked deeds, evil deeds, etc.), there are "really only two paths, or types of path, of fatal importance": moral paths and immoral paths.[9] Individuals wishing to be moral choose moral paths; individuals who do not wish to be moral choose immoral paths. Since presumably the student who hears such statements wishes to be moral, the book gives the impression that there is really no choice to be made (<voluntary $_{no}$>). The properly trained student will choose those paths that are inherently good.

Of course, such designations are not unique to wisdom literature. Throughout the Hebrew Bible paths are described as "good" (e.g., 1 Kgs 8:36 // 2 Chr 6:27; Jer 6:16), "evil" (2 Kgs 17:13; Jer 18:11; 26:3; 35:15; 36:7; Jonah 3:8, 10), "righteous" (Ps 1:6; Isa 26:7), "wicked" (Ps 1:6; Jer 12:1), "of life" (Ps 16:11; Jer 21:8), and "of death" (Jer 21:8).[10] This suggests that it was conventional in Israelite and early Jewish society to extend the BEHAVIOR IS A PATH metaphor into such stark moral dichotomies.[11]

---

8. Fox, *Proverbs 1–9*, 130.

9. Ibid., 129. Fox designates all such paths as "paths of life" and "paths of death." The conflation of these different paths, however, is the result of more complex blends (see Tilford, "Taste and See," 246–50), and it is more appropriate to understand the basic distinctions being made as a choice between moral behavior and immoral behavior.

10. These are just six of the types of paths mentioned throughout the Hebrew Bible. See also the "paths of the Lord" (דרך יהוה, Gen 18:19; Judg 2:22; 2 Sam 22:22 // Ps 18:22; Prov 10:29; etc.) and the "paths of justice" (ארח משפט, Prov 2:6; 17:23; Isa 26:8; 40:14), which extend the BEHAVIOR IS A PATH metaphor is a similar fashion.

11. Although some of these path extensions (e.g., in Psalms and Jeremiah) may reflect a relationship between sapiential thought and other generic forms. For the relationship between sapiential literature and the psalms, see, for example, James Cren-

However, the specific behaviors approved or condemned in any given passage depends on the specific morality of the community. Thus pride, arrogance, duplicitous speech, and violence are each "paths" that are condemned in Proverbs (8:13; 15:9; 16:29) because the sapiential community believed that they were behaviors that should be avoided. Righteous, just, and equitable behaviors, on the other hand, are good "paths" (2:9, 20; see also 2:8; 4:14; 8:20; 17:23) because the sapiential community wished its members to engage in them routinely. While there were, of course, certain values that transcended Israelite society as a whole (e.g., sexual morality), the nuances of the path metaphors in Proverbs depended on the specific morality of the scribal community and could subsequently be used to promote the behaviors deemed appropriate for its members.

10.2. Metaphorical Blends

While metaphorical extensions extend a dominant or dormant element of one conventional metaphor, some metaphors develop new meaning by blending the attributes of two or more schemas together. These "input" schemas can be independent experiential domains (e.g., light, treasure) or conventional metaphors (e.g., UNDERSTANDING IS GRASPING or BEHAVIOR IS A PATH). Either way, the input domains chosen must be structurally similar; that is, there must be some observable relationship between the constituent parts of each input space or a blend will not occur. In their work on conceptual blends, Fauconnier and Turner identify fifteen such "vital relations."[12]

---

shaw, "Wisdom Psalms?," *CurBS* 8 (2000): 9–17; J. Kenneth Kuntz, "Reclaiming Biblical Wisdom Psalms: A Response to Crenshaw," *CurBR* 1 (2003): 145–54; William Brown, "Come, O Children ... I Will Teach You the Fear of the Lord (Psalm 34:12): Comparing Psalms and Proverbs," in *Seeking Out the Wisdom of the Ancients: Essays Offered to Honor Michael V. Fox on the Occasionan of His Sixty-Fifth Birthday*, ed. Ronald Troxel, Kelvin Friebel, and Dennis Magary (Winona Lake, IN: Eisenbrauns, 2005), 85–103. For the relationship between sapiential literature and prophetic texts, see Raymond C. Van Leeuwen, "The Sage in Prophetic Literature," in *The Sage in Israel and the Ancient Near East*, ed. John G. Gammie and Leo G. Perdue (Winona Lake, IN: Eisenbrauns, 1990), 295–306.

12. Fauconnier and Turner, *Way We Think*, 92–102.

Change	Space	Representation	Disanalogy	Category
Identity	Cause-Effect	Role	Property	Intentionality
Time	Part-Whole	Analogy	Similarity	Uniqueness

Two input spaces, for instance, may share a similar *time* frame (e.g., one input space occurs on New Year's Day 2000, the other on New Year's Day in 2001) or occur in similar *spaces* (e.g., both input spaces occur in a room). Alternatively, an element in one input space may have the same *identity* as an element in the other (e.g., a baby named Mary in one space and a woman named Mary in another), or an element in one space may *change* into an element in the other (e.g., as a sapling changes into a tree). While not all of these relations need be present, there must be some perceived relationship between the input spaces if a blend between them is to occur. In some cases, conventional metaphors themselves provide the necessary relationship between input spaces. As Grady argues, "primary metaphoric associations stored in memory, which are ultimately based on correlations in experience, provide a means of linking objects in [input spaces] which would otherwise not be mapped onto another."[13] In other words, primary metaphors can serve either as the input space for a blend or as the relation that connects two input spaces.

Take, for example, A RIGHTEOUS PERSON IS A STRAIGHT PERSON and its obverse A WICKED PERSON IS A CROOKED PERSON, two complex metaphors found throughout the book of Proverbs (e.g., 2:21; 3:32; 11:3, 6, 11).

The metaphor A RIGHTEOUS PERSON IS A STRAIGHT PERSON begins as two similarly structured input spaces: a righteous person and a straight person. Each has an agent (a person), an identifying characteristic (moral behavior or physical posture), a key property (good or straight), and a time frame for its condition (permanent or temporary). These structures correspond, but they are not directly related; that is, the person in the righteous person input space is not innately conceptualized as the same person as the one in the straight person input space (there is no relation in their identity). Nor are their identifying characteristics or time frames the same; one deals with permanent behavior, the other with temporary physical status. Instead, the conventional metaphor GOOD IS STRAIGHT provides the necessary relationship to bring the two input spaces together.

---

13. Grady, "Primary Metaphors as Inputs," 1603.

180 COGNITIVE FOUNDATION OF BIBLICAL WISDOM METAPHORS

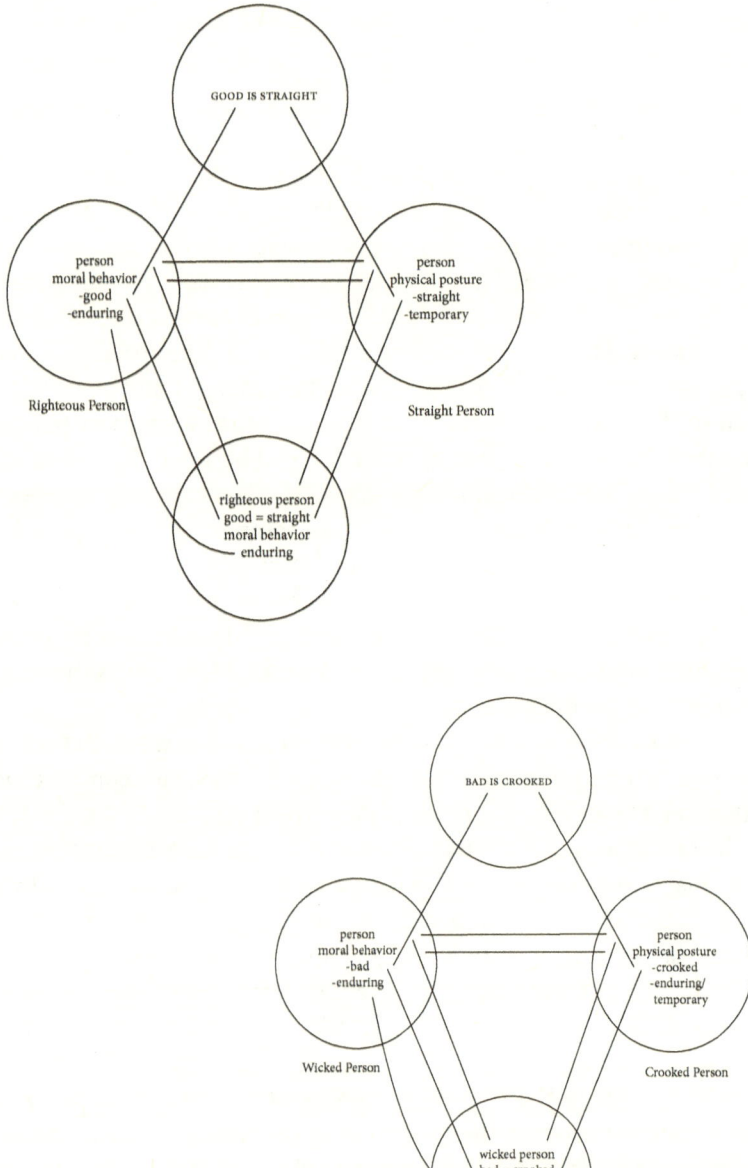

Figure 10.1. A RIGHTEOUS PERSON IS A STRAIGHT PERSON;
A WICKED PERSON IS A CROOKED PERSON

Without it, the two input spaces could not combine. The same can be said of the A WICKED PERSON IS A CROOKED PERSON blend. Two structurally similar but not identical input spaces blend together via the BAD IS CROOKED metaphor.

Metaphors are also constrained in how they project information into the blended space. Relations between input spaces, for instance, tend to "compress" in the blend; that is, they scale down into tighter relationships. As Fauconnier and Turner explain, "one relation may be compressed into a tighter version of itself," as when a lifetime of experiences is compressed into a single event (a time relation).[14] Similarly, "one or more relations may be compressed into another relation." For instance, a cause-effect relation between two entities can compress into a uniqueness relation in the blend as two entities become conceptualized as one.[15] Alternatively, if one input space already contains a tightly integrated scene, it may simply project its structure onto the blended space, where the other input space compresses into it.[16] In the case of perceptually based metaphors, more abstract experiences tend to be described in terms of more concrete experiences (what Yeshayahu Shen and Michal Cohen refer to as a "low to high" constraint). For instance, a speaker is more likely to describe "silence" as "sweet" (audition as ingestion) than to describe "sweetness" as "silent" (ingestion as audition).[17] At any rate, the selection and compression of vital relations is not a "free-for-all." Properties are selectively chosen in an attempt to create

---

14. Fauconnier and Turner, *Way We Think*, 311–12.

15. Ibid., 311. Fauconnier and Turner point, by way of example, to a hypothetical blend in which an "automobile company produces the automobile, but in the blend the company and the automobile are the same thing" (315). The cause-effect relationship between the company in one input space and the automobile in the other becomes a uniqueness relation in the blend.

16. Ibid., 320–21. For other constraints on projections, see 309–25.

17. Yeshayahu Shen and Michal Cohen, "How Come Silence Is Sweet but Sweetness Is Not Silent: A Cognitive Account of Directionality in Poetic Synaesthesia," *Language and Literature* 7 (1998): 128–29. The "low to high" nomenclature is based on the standard Western hierarchy of the senses, which Shen and Cohen use as the basis for their analysis (ranked from high to low: sight, sound, smell, taste, touch; 125). Although, as stated in chapter 3, there is not one universal conception of the perceptual modalities, nor by extension is there a universal hierarchical relationship between them, in as much as a given culture will view some modalities as more accessible than others, maintaining the "low to high" nomenclature can be helpful, with "low" being understood as "more accessible" and "high" being understood as "less accessible."

well-integrated scenes with at least a modicum of "human scale"; that is, they attempt to portray reality with natural and familiar structures that can be easily engaged through concrete experience.[18] This means that, all things being equal, blends will present a scenario with as few participants and as direct intentionality as possible.

Take, again, the example of the righteous person. Based on the GOOD IS STRAIGHT relationship, elements from each input space blend together to form a composite metaphor. Both spaces project their separate identities onto the blend, where they merge into a single individual, the moral person (two identities → one identity). Similarly, both input spaces project their key property onto the blend, where they combine into one: good-straight (two properties → one property). Thus the individual can be identified either by "goodness" (טוב, Prov 13:2; 14:14; 15:3; see also צדיק, "righteousness," 2:20; 3:33; 9:9; תם, "innocence," 10:29; 29:10) or by "straightness" (ישר, 2:7, 21; 3:32; 11:3); the semantic fields are conceptually synonymous. The "straightness" envisioned here is probably a vertical straightness; the person who is straight stands "straight up."[19] The common English translation "upright," then, captures the double nuance of the blend. The one who is "upright" is physically and morally straight. On the other hand, only the RIGHTEOUS PERSON input space projects its time frame onto the blend. Physical straightness is a temporary state. One can temporarily stand up or straighten one's body, but one must also sometimes lie down or bend over; that is, one cannot always stand straight up. On the contrary, morality is an enduring quality, at least in the rhetoric of Proverbs. One is either a moral person or not (Prov 2:21; 10:25, 30; 12:3, 7).[20] It is this enduring conception of morality that dominates the blend. In the final metaphor, the righteous person does not typically alter his or her state but remains

---

18. Fauconnier and Turner, *Way We Think*, 29, 309–12.

19. Although there is no definitive evidence that "straight" here indicates a vertical straightness, rather than a body that is stretched out horizontally, vertical straightness is probably implied when ישר is used to refer to a person. There is no practical advantage for a reclining body to be straight, but standing straight up, with no crookedness to one's body, does have its advantages. One can see further, breath more easily, walk with less difficulty. This physical advantage seems to be the basis for the metaphorical extension of ישר here. Horizontal straightness is reserved for cases in which movement is described as "straight."

20. This position is, at least, the impression that the rhetoric of Proverbs wishes to convey to its reader. As will be discussed in more detail in the conclusion to this study, the moral worldview of Proverbs is more complex than this stark dichotomy suggests.

moral-straight. The desire to present a simple, well-integrated scene thus focuses the blend into a single, enduring time frame.

A similar process occurs with A WICKED PERSON IS A CROOKED PERSON. Based on the BAD IS CROOKED metaphor, elements from each input space blend together to form a new metaphor. Again, both spaces project their separate identities and properties onto the blend, where they become a single person, the immoral person (two identities → one identity), with a single composite quality, wicked-crooked (two properties → one property). Here, however, the time frame operates differently. Although, like straightness, crookedness can be a temporary state (i.e., when one bends down), it can also be a permanent state. A person can be physically deformed such that he or she cannot ever straighten out fully. There exists, then, a similarity between the time frames of the two input spaces that projects onto the blend. The final blend, however, is essentially the same as A RIGHTEOUS PERSON IS A STRAIGHT PERSON. The wicked person cannot alter his or her state; the wicked person remains immoral-crooked.

By focusing on the moral quality of the straight or crooked individual, biblical literature shows a marked contrast to its Egyptian counterparts. In Egyptian wisdom literature, to be "crooked" or "straight" is an intellectual quality: the fool is "crooked" (*gwš*; Instruction of Ani 9.18–19; 10.13–14); the wise person is "straight" (*mty*; Instruction of Ptahhotep 197). By contrast, in the Hebrew Bible to be "straight" or "crooked" is a moral quality: the wicked person is "crooked"; the moral person is "straight."[21] Of course, in both wisdom corpora, the moral and the intellectual dimensions are never completely separate. As Shupak notes, "In the sage's view, the individual is part of the community, and his acts are evaluated in terms of the good or ill they cause others.... The mental state is an inseparable part of a man's character and moral traits."[22] However, the focus of each corpus is different. The biblical metaphor tends to focus more on the moral qualities of the individual in question, while the Egyptian metaphor tends to emphasize one's intellectual character.[23] This demonstrates just how important it is to evaluate the metaphors of each culture in their own right. Even if Israelite and early Jewish sages drew upon the same biological experiences as and were inspired by their Egyptian counterparts when developing these metaphors, they did not simply adopt the metaphors blindly. Rather, they

---

21. Shupak, *Where Can Wisdom Be Found?*, 92–95.
22. Ibid., 197, 214.
23. Ibid., 197.

adapted the metaphors to suit their own cultural climate and the needs of their own community. As Shupak states, "Occasionally Hebrew and Egyptian wisdom words display a close formal similarity but beneath this external resemblance [they] reveal a different content. This may be explained by the differences between ancient Egypt and Israel with respect to religion, physical environment, and way of life, which led to divergent concepts and outlooks."[24] Similar cultural contexts lead to similar metaphors; different cultural specifics lead to different metaphorical nuances.

Through a combination of blends and extensions, metaphors can become increasingly complex. Take, for instance, the idea in Proverbs that wisdom and words more generally are edible objects (WISDOM IS HONEY; GOSSIP IS A DELICACY).

> Prov 24:13–14 My son, eat *honey* [דבש], for it is good [טוב], and *honeycomb* [נפת] is *sweet* [מתוק] upon the palate. Know that wisdom is thus to your נפש; if you find it, then you will have a future, and your hope will not be cut off.

> Prov 18:8 The words of the *gossip* [נרגן] are like *delicacies* [כמת־להמים]. They go down to the *bottom of the belly* [חדרי־בטן].[25]

On the one hand, wisdom is described as a sweet "honey" (דבש) bringing life and healing to the נפש (Prov 24:13–14; see also "pleasant words," אמרי־נעם, as honey in 16:24). Gossip, on the other hand, is described as מתלהמים (Prov 18:8; see also 26:22). The exact meaning of מתלהמים is unclear. Commonly translated "delicacies," מתלהמים (root לחם) is probably related to the Arabic *lahima*, which means "to devour greedily." The *hithpael* participle here, then, would give the impression of "someone wolfing down gossip" as if it were a delicious and savory morsel.[26]

Each of these expressions ultimately derives from a combination of IDEAS ARE FOOD and KNOWLEDGE IS A WORD.

---

24. Ibid., 345.

25. Alternatively to "gossip," "slanderer." As Fox (*Proverbs 10–31*, 640) argues, the verb "seems to mean more broadly 'complain' or 'say bad things about,'" as when the Israelites grumble against God in the desert (Deut 1:27; Ps 106:25). As I read it, the sense here seems to be that of someone who gossips maliciously.

26. Fox, *Proverbs 10–31*, 640–41.

10. COMPLEX METAPHORS

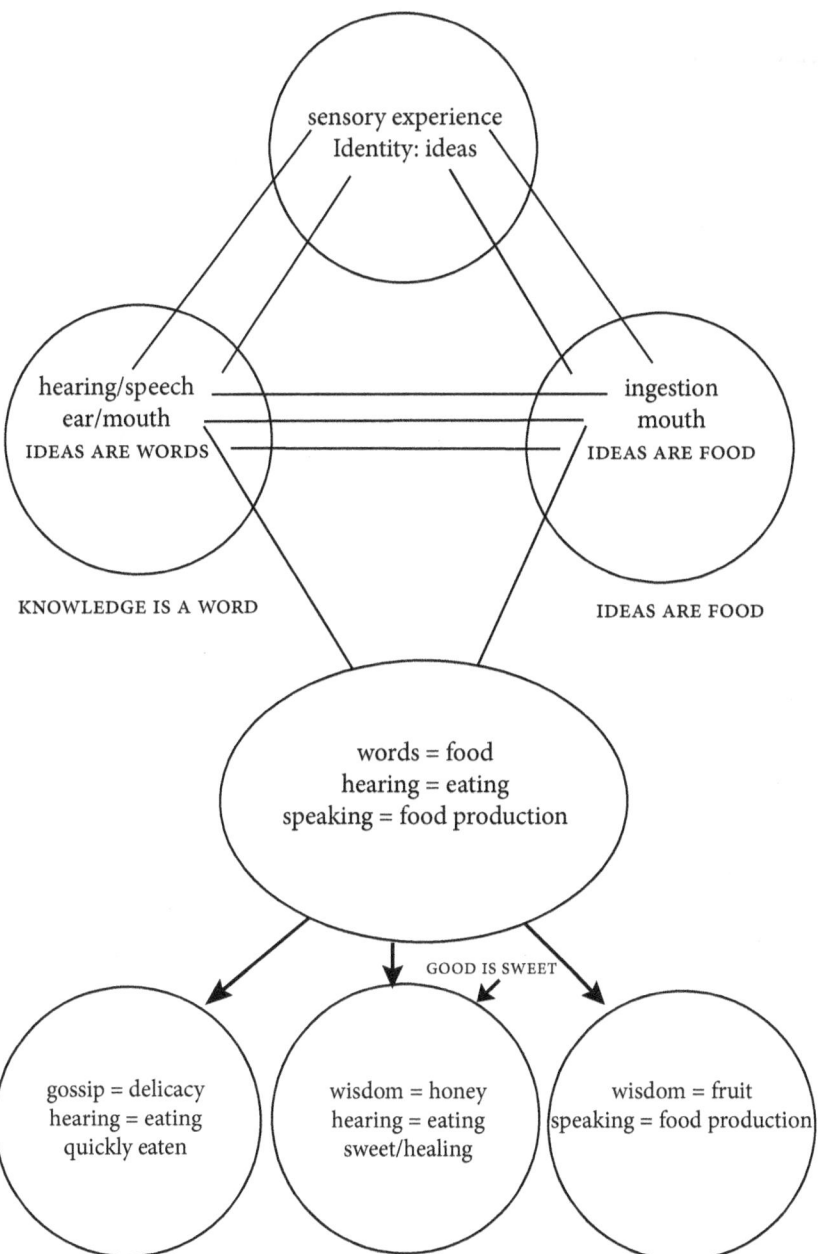

Figure 10.2. WORDS ARE FOOD

Because the subject of these input spaces share a common identity (they are "ideas"), the two input spaces are equated. Words become consumable objects. The processes associated with each also become equated. Since hearing and ingestion are both internal actions (<internal $_{yes}$>), hearing becomes an act of eating (HEARING IS EATING). Due to the "low to high" constraint, hearing takes on the qualities of ingestion; it is a direct acquisition of information through the mouth (<direct $_{yes}$>, <contact $_{yes}$>) that can affect the listener, providing him or her with nourishment and/or knowledge (<effects $_{yes}$> $^{PR \rightarrow P}$). Yet the indirectness of hearing is still present (<direct $_{no}$>). The student may consume the word of the teacher, but he still does not directly experience the information that that word conveys.

Contemporaneous Egyptian texts also describe words as food that could be eaten or produced. "Words," for instance, are said to reside in the "belly" before and after they are spoken. Thus, the Instruction of Amenemope exhorts its student to "make [my words] rest in the casket of your belly" (3.13) and states that "the man whose speech remains in his belly [is better than] him who speaks it to cause harm (22.15-16; see also 3.1-13, 11.10-11; 23.4; Instruction of Ani D 5.2-3; Instruction of Ptahhotep 232-248, 265-269, 399-414; Merikare 144-145; CT 2.176p, 3.57d).[27] These examples suggest that the WORDS ARE FOOD metaphor was a conventional metaphor throughout the ancient Near East. However, as with the path and righteousness metaphors above, the nuances of this metaphor varied depending upon the cultural locale of the individual using it. For instance, the location in which the words resided depended on the cultural setting of the authors. As Shupak notes, the Egyptian phrase "casket of the belly" (*hnw n ẖt*) derives from the Egyptian scribal practice of placing papyrus scrolls in a wooden box. Israelite scribes lacked this practice. Their metaphor therefore envisioned words as residing in the "chamber of the belly" (חדרי־בטן, Prov 18:8; 26:22; see also 20:27, 30), an image that fits more easily with the "chambers" common in Israelite architecture.[28]

---

27. The translation here follows that of Fox, *Proverbs 10–31*, 708. For examples of the metaphor in Egyptian literature, see also Shupak, *Where Can Wisdom Be Found?*, 293–95; Shupak, "The Instruction of Amenemope and Proverbs 22:17–24:22 from the Perspective of Contemporary Research," in Troxel, Friebel, and Magary, *Seeking Out the Wisdom*, 212; Nyord, *Breathing Flesh*, 400, esp. n. 3994.

28. Shupak, "Instruction of Amenemope," 210; see also Shupak, *Where Can Wisdom Be Found?*, 291–93.

More important, there are various types of food available to be eaten (honey, olives, fruit, etc.), some more appealing and beneficial than others. The WORDS ARE FOOD metaphor could thus extend in a variety of ways, and the food item an author chose to describe his words depended upon his cultural setting and the value of the speech that he wished to highlight. Thus in Proverbs gossip is likened to a quickly devoured delicacy in order to highlight the tendency of false information to be quickly and uncritically "consumed" by the listener (Prov 18:8; see also 26:22). Once eaten, this delicacy sits in the "bottom of the belly" (חדרי־בטן); that is, it remains lodged within the listener prejudicing him or her against the gossip's referent. Wise words, on the other hand, are likened to "sweet honey" (דבש + מתוק, Prov 24:13–14). In ancient Israel, honey was a natural sweetening agent; it was found in wild or domestic bee hives and fruit syrups (Exod 3:8; Deut 8:8; 32:13; Judg 14:8) and was used to sweeten the palate (Exod 16:31; 1 Sam 14:27).[29] Fox and Tova Forti both focus on the "pleasant" aspect of this metaphor. Fox, for instance, argues that one of the main points of Prov 24:13–14 is that, "if pursued with love, learning is a joy."[30] While this dimension is present, it is not the only focus of the proverb. As the second half of the proverb makes clear, the value of wisdom is not only that it pleasurable but that it heals the נפש. Throughout the ancient world, honey was thought to have medicinal value; it was used as an anti-inflammatory agent to cure illness of the eyes, ears, mouth, or stomach (e.g., *AMT* 13, 6.6; 21, 4 r. 9; 69, 10.6; *KAR* 194.3; 203 i–iii 54; Vassal-Treaties of Esarhaddon 568–569, 594–598, 643–645; Aristotle, *Hist. an.* 9.624a).[31] By comparing wisdom to honey, then, the proverb highlights both the pleasant and the therapeutic nature of wisdom. Wisdom not only tasted good (it was a pleasant experience), but it healed the נפש, curing it of its ailments (anger, avarice, etc.) by helping the individual discern what behavior was right and what behavior was wrong so that he or she could enjoy a long and productive life. Finally, given that flavor is elsewhere used to describe positive values (see the discussion of GOOD IS SWEET in ch. 7 above), the description of wisdom as sweet here also makes a normative claim about its quality. For the scribal community, wisdom was good to have.

---

29. Tova Forti, "Bee's Honey: From Realia to Metaphor in Biblical Wisdom Literature," *VT* 56 (2006): 327–29.

30. Fox, *Proverbs 10–31*, 748.

31. Forti, "Bee's Honey," 333–34 n. 19. For the uses of honey in ancient Near Eastern medicine, see "Dišpu," *CAD* 3:161–62.

By a similar process, wisdom could also be described as a satisfying "fruit" (WISDOM IS A SATISFYING FRUIT).

> Prov 12:14   From the *fruit* [מפרי] of a *man's mouth* [פי־איש] he will *be satisfied* [ישבע], and the deeds of the hands of a man will be returned to him.

> Prov 13:2   From the *fruit of his mouth* [מפרי פי־איש], a person *eats* good [יאכל טוב], but the desire of the faithless is for violence.

> Prov 18:20   From the *fruit* [מפרי] of a *man's mouth* [פי־איש] his belly will *be satisfied* [תשבע]; [from] the increase of his lips he will *be satisfied* [ישבע].

As in the GOSSIP IS A DELICACY or WISDOM IS HONEY metaphors, the wisdom word here is a food item (a פרי, "fruit") that can be consumed. The one who "eats" (אכל, Prov 13:2) of it is "satisfied" (שבע) with good things (Prov 12:14; 18:20). Here, however, the person who eats the fruit of wisdom is the very same person as the one who produces it from his "mouth" (פה, Prov 12:14; 13:2; 18:20). Shupak suggests that this unusual image arose from an Egyptian court and funerary metaphor in which words were said to *pri* ("go out") from the mouth of an individual.[32] In the Pyramid Texts 218, for instance, "going out" is parallel with speaking: "Geb has spoken, and it has come from the mouth of the Ennead."[33] The Israelite sage, reading this metaphor, either intentionally or unintentionally corrupted the metaphor, understanding that it was פרי (*parî*, "fruit") that came forth from the mouth and subsequently returned to it.[34] Shupak's reconstruction provides a plausible explanation for the literary origin of this phrase, yet it does not explain why the metaphor was successful; that is, it does not explain how the author and his subsequent readers could

---

32. Shupak, *Where Can Wisdom Be Found?*, 322–33. See further Helck, *Inschriften von Zeitgenossen Amenophis' III*, 546, line 9; and Kurt Sethe, ed., *Historisch-Biographische Urkunden*, vols. 13–16 of *Urkunden der 18. Dynastie*, Urkunden des ägyptischen Altertums 4 (Leipzig: Hinrichs, 1909), 1011, line 7.

33. James P. Allen, *The Ancient Egyptian Pyramid Texts*, 2nd ed., WAW 38 (Atlanta: SBL Press, 2015), 37 (= PT 162).

34. Shupak, *Where Can Wisdom Be Found?*, 322–33.

have accepted the new metaphor as a valid way of viewing the wisdom act. Conceptual metaphor theory can.

First, like GOSSIP IS A DELICACY or WISDOM IS A HONEY, wisdom becomes conceptualized as a fruit by naturally extending the WORDS ARE FOOD metaphor. Fruit of various sorts were staples of the Israelite diet: figs, grapes, pomegranates, olives, and so on (see, e.g., Lev 19:10; 25:5; Num 13:20; Deut 8:8; 23:25; 28:40; 1 Sam 25:18; 30:12; 1 Kgs 4:25; Neh 8:15).[35] Although the type of fruit is unspecified here, Proverbs uses the comparison of fruit to highlight the nourishing qualities of wisdom. This extension then blends with the idea that SATISFACTION IS FULLNESS.

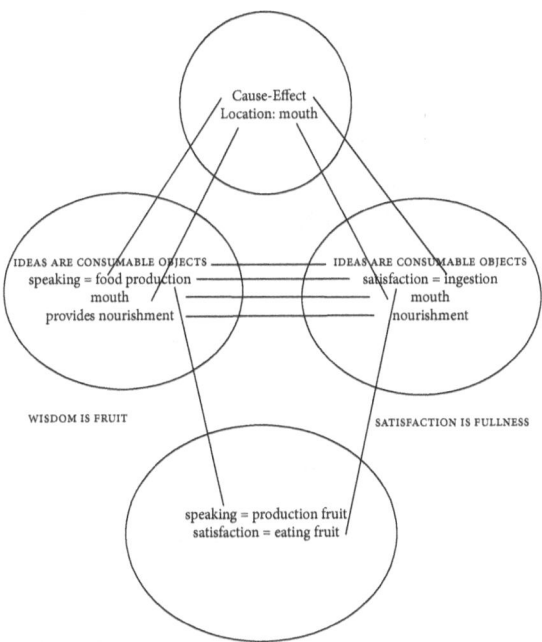

Figure 10.3. WISDOM IS A SATISFYING FRUIT

WISDOM IS A FRUIT and SATISFACTION IS FULLNESS are related to each other through a shared location (the mouth) and through a retributive cause-effect relation. Within the framework of the acts-consequence connection, appropriate speech is thought to have beneficial effects for the

---

35. For a detailed discussion of fruits and other agricultural products in ancient Israel, see Philip King and Lawrence Stager, *Life in Biblical Israel* (Louisville: Westminster John Knox, 2001), 93–107.

speaker.³⁶ The sage speaks, and his words encourage others to behave in a way that is conducive to the community's well-being. The speaker is then rewarded for his speech, perhaps because the behavior of others that he inspires directly benefits him or because God rewards him for his efforts.³⁷ In either case, proper speech ultimately leads to the satisfaction of the speaker's נפש. The WISDOM IS A FRUIT OF THE MOUTH metaphor presupposes this sequence. Because it is an externally oriented process (<internal $_{no}$>), speaking becomes understood as the process by which food is produced and by which the listener is affected (<effects $_{yes}$> $^{OP \rightarrow P}$).³⁸ The wise person produces fruit, which satisfies others. Others then produce fruit of their own, which satisfies the sage. The metaphor, however, compress this sequence into a single event. The one who speaks eats the fruit of his own mouth. By compressing the time frame of this acts-consequence connection, the metaphor increases the immediacy of the speaker's reward and emphasizes the inherent benefit of speaking wisely. Wise speech is itself a satisfying fruit, one that fills the speaker's stomach and provides him or her with good things. The student is thus encouraged to speak wisely, so that he may reap the benefit of his words.

GOSSIP IS A DELICACY and WISDOM IS HONEY both focus on the hearing-eating dimensions of WORDS ARE FOOD. Delicious gossip and sweet wisdom are food products that are consumed directly by the listener (<internal $_{yes}$>, <direct $_{yes}$>, <contact $_{yes}$>) and that affect his or her cognitive state (<effects $_{yes}$> $^{PR \rightarrow P}$), either prejudicing the individual against another or healing the individual's נפש of moral ills. Gossip and wisdom themselves, however, are still indirect words (<direct $_{no}$>); that is, they convey information about an individual or a behavior that the listener otherwise would not have access to. WISDOM IS A SATISFYING FRUIT, on the other hand, focuses on the oral dimensions of WORD IS FOOD (<internal $_{no}$>, <contact $_{yes}$>, <effects $_{yes}$> $^{OP \rightarrow P}$). Although wisdom can still be eaten, the focus of the metaphor is on the sage's mouth. Like a fertile tree that produces fruits of various kinds, the sage produces fruit for the student to eat.

---

36. See the discussion of the acts-consequence connection in §10.1 above.

37. The tension between human agency and divine retribution in the book of Proverbs that Hatton points out (see §10.1 above) makes it difficult to determine the exact mechanisms by which humans were rewarded for their speech.

38. See the analogous metaphor in Prov 15:7, where speaking is an act of "scattering seeds" (זרה).

There are a variety of such metaphors in biblical wisdom literature that create new meaning by blending two or more metaphors together, yet in each case the goal is the same: to rethink the nature of knowledge and prescribe the appropriate means of obtaining it. In doing so, these metaphors transform wisdom from an abstract concept into a more direct, personally relevant, embodied activity that the student can adopt into his daily life.

10.3. Metaphorical Clusters

Whereas metaphorical extensions create new meaning by extending the dominant or dormant elements of one metaphor and metaphorical blends create new meaning by combining two or more input schemas together, some passages develop new meaning by clustering different metaphors together. Each metaphor in the cluster remains distinct, with its own unique and unchanged properties, yet the complete unit forms a cohesive scene by which to describe an object, event, or abstract concept. Consider, for instance, the following example:

Prov 2:20   Therefore, walk in the *way of the good* [בדרך טובים]; keep the *paths of the righteous* [ארחות צדיקים].

The first half of the verse exhorts good behavior (GOOD BEHAVIOR IS A PATH), while the second half promotes righteous behavior (RIGHTEOUSNESS IS A PATH). The two metaphors cluster easily together because they extend the same primary metaphor (BEHAVIOR IS A PATH) and describe similar types of people (the good/the righteous). However, the nuances of each metaphor—the seemingly linear nature of good behavior; the scribal imperative to choose righteousness—remain intact. Neither metaphor is lost or absorbed into the other in the juxtaposition. Rather, the clustering has an emphatic effect; together the metaphors emphasize the need for the student to behave properly. Similarly, when Prov 13:25 juxtaposes two opposing metaphors, neither metaphor is lost.

Prov 13:25   *The righteous eats to the satisfaction of his* נפש [צדיק אכל לשבע נפשו], but *the belly of the wicked is empty* [בטן רשעים תחסר].

Here two analogous metaphors from the ingestive domain stand side by side: SATISFACTION IS FULLNESS and DISSATISFACTION IS EMPTINESS. Each metaphor remains distinct: one metaphor uses ingestion to express a positive state enjoyed by the righteous, the other to describe a negative state suffered by the wicked. Yet by juxtaposing these two ingestive metaphors, the proverb establishes a stark dichotomy between the reward enjoyed by the righteous and the punishment suffered by the wicked. The student would be wise to heed the wisdom of his elders.

A single proverb may contain two or three different metaphors (Prov 14:27; 17:20; 28:18), while an extended pericope may contain well over twenty (Prov 4:10–19).[39] Indeed, the bulk of Proverbs (chs. 10–29) can be described as one long pericope in which the editors of Proverbs clustered one metaphor after another into a series of disjointed and often contradictory proverbial statements. Due to its complexity, the current arrangement of these proverbs has long perplexed modern scholars, who have proposed various literary criteria (e.g., educational principles, paronomasia, catchwords, syntax) to explain how the once-independent proverbs of chapters 10–29 came to be found in the order in which they stand today.[40] While I do not wish to contradict these suggestions, metaphorical clustering can provide another way to explain the structure of these collections, one that respects the *unconscious* cognitive processes that influenced the creative activity of Proverbs' editors. For instance, rather than look for conscious literary connections between Prov 18:20 and 18:21, one can explain the adjacent placement of these verses via their conceptual linkages.

> Prov 18:20   From the *fruit of the mouth a person's stomach is satisfied* [מפרי פי־איש תשבע בטנו]; *the produce of his lips satisfies* [תבואת שפתיו ישבע].

> Prov 18:21   Death and life are in the power[41] of the tongue [לשון], and *those who love it will eat its fruit* [אהביה יאכל פריה].

---

39. For a detailed discussion of the different ways metaphors cluster together, see Kimmel, "Why We Mix Metaphors (And Mix Them Well): Discourse Coherence, Conceptual Metaphor, and Beyond," *Journal of Pragmatics* 42 (2010):97–115 (106–9). Kimmel's categories form the basis for the discussion that follows here.

40. See Knut Heim, *Like Grapes of Gold Set in Silver: An Interpretation of Proverbial Clusters in Proverbs 10:1–22:16* (Berlin: de Gruyter, 2001), 28–68.

41. Literally, "hand." Like elsewhere in the Hebrew Bible, the hand here signifies control over something (CONTROL IS A HAND). In this case, the tongue controls life and death.

10. COMPLEX METAPHORS

Both proverbs conceptualize words as fruits that are produced and consumed by the speaker (WISDOM IS A SATISFYING FRUIT). Drawing upon the acts-consequence connection, they each presume that the effects of eating these fruits will be proportional to the type of speech uttered. Proverbs 18:20 focuses on the positive effects: the one who speaks appropriate words will be satisfied. Proverbs 18:21, on the other hand, explores the positive *and* negative effects of words: appropriate words bring life; inappropriate words produce death; the one who loves the tongue (i.e., fine rhetoric) will therefore either live or die by it. The juxtaposition of the same conceptual metaphor links the two proverbs cognitively, slowing the reader down and forcing him or her to reflect upon the different consequences of speech. Similarly, Prov 25:25 and 25:26 can be explained by their conceptual similarities.

Prov 25:25   *Cool water* [מים קרים] to a thirsty נפש, thus is *good news* [ושמועה טובה] from a distant land.

Prov 25:26   *A muddied spring* [מעין נרפש] or *a polluted fountain* [ומקור משחת] is the righteous person who is shaken before the wicked.

The implications of the two verses are quite different. Proverbs 25:25 draws upon the ingestive properties of water to describe the refreshing quality that a good report has on a person who is anxious to hear it (GOOD NEWS IS COOL WATER). Proverbs 25:26 draws upon agricultural imagery to describe the adverse repercussions that occur when the righteous person capitulates to a wicked person (A RIGHTEOUS PERSON WHO ERRS IS POLLUTED WATER). Although serving different purposes, these two proverbs are grouped together in chapter 25 because each draws upon the same rich image, water. Preconscious conceptual similarities, in other words, encouraged the grouping of certain proverbs, even when their conscious literary connotations were quite distinct.

Metaphors can, of course, cluster together for no apparent reason. Thus a statement comparing a good wife to precious object (A GOOD WIFE IS A GOOD THING, Prov 18:22) immediately follows the WISDOM IS A SATISFYING FRUIT sayings of 18:20–21 without any clear connection. The frequent absence of any observable connection between the proverbs of chapters 10–29 has led some scholars to deny the presence of proverbial groups at all, arguing that the arrangement of the proverbs in the older collections was for the most part random and haphazard[42] or editorial and thus unimportant to the primary meaning of the proverbs.[43] Most scholars, however, have agreed that relationships between proverbs not only exist but that they enhance the meaning of the proverbs.[44] As Knut Heim argues, proverbial clusters are "designed to prepare young Israelites for constructive social interaction in various spheres of private and public life."[45] By reading the collections of Prov 10–29 as a series of metaphorical clusters, one can acknowledge both the conscious and unconscious processes that influenced the editorial activity behind the creation of Proverbs. The editors of Prov 10–29 purposefully bring together discrete and often contradictory material in order to force the student to consider the various ramifications of individual topics and to mold the student's character into one that conforms with the community's most basic moral values. They are able to do so because they choose proverbs that unconsciously fit with the cognitive expectations of the student, because they draw upon the same conceptual metaphor (e.g., Prov 18:20–21) or rich image (e.g., 25:25–26). When Prov 1–9 was collected, the same principles were used. Conscious editorial activity was enhanced by unconscious metaphorical linkages. In the final rendition, wisdom became a complex, dynamic, and multifaceted concept, one that a student eagerly wishes to pursue.

---

42. See, for example, R. B. Y. Scott, "Wise and Foolish, Righteous and Wicked," in *Studies in the Religion of Ancient Israel*, ed. G. W. Anderson, VTSup 23 (Leiden: Brill, 1972), 145–65; McKane, *Proverbs*. For a review of these scholars, see Knut Heim, *Like Grapes of Gold Set in Silver: An Interpretation of Proverbial Clusters in Proverbs 10:1–22:16*, BZAW 273 (Berlin: de Gruyter, 2001), 7–11.

43. See, for example, Claus Westermann, *Forschungsgeschichte zur Weisheitsliteratur 1950–1990*, AzTh 71 (Stuggart: Calwer, 1991), 35–36; Stuart Weeks, *Early Israelite Wisdom*, Oxford Theological Monographs (Oxford: Clarendon, 1994), 20–40. For a review of these scholars, see Heim, *Like Grapes of Gold*, 11–18. As Heim points out, McKane (*Proverbs*, 9) also recognized some coherence in the editorial stage of the proverbs, but his greater focus was on the *randomness* of the proverbial collections.

44. Most notably, see R. Norman Whybray, "Thoughts on the Composition of Proverbs 10–29," in *Priests, Prophets, and Scribes: Essays on the Formation and Heritage of Second Temple Judaism in Honour of Joseph Blenkinsopp*, ed. E. Ulrich et al., JSOTSup 149 (Sheffield: JSOT Press, 1992), 102–14; Leo G. Perdue, *Proverbs*, IBC (Louisville: John Knox, 2000); Heim, *Like Grapes of Gold*, esp. his exegesis of Prov 10–22 on 112–311; Hatton, *Contradiction in the Book of Proverbs*, 46–82. For a discussion of these and other scholars who find intentional linkages between proverbs, see Heim, *Like Grapes of Gold*, 27–66.

45. Heim, *Like Grapes of Gold*, 316.

10. COMPLEX METAPHORS

Just as metaphorical blends and extensions can work together to create more complex metaphors, clusters can turn into blends when the juxtaposition of certain metaphors becomes so conventional that the reader begins to conflate them automatically. Take, for instance, the relationship between wisdom and righteousness in the book of Proverbs. In Prov 10–29, intellectual acumen and moral virtue are two related, yet relatively distinct themes. As Fox states, "within individual sayings, the concept of wisdom is rarely implicated in matters of moral virtue."[46] A person is צדיק (Prov 10:2, 7, 16, 20) or חכם (10:1, 8, 14); one either behaves wickedly (14:2, 5, 11, 14) or acts foolishly (14:3, 6, 7, 8). As Heim states, wise/righteous and fool/wicked are "coreferential" pairs; they refer to the same referent, but they are not synonymous terms.[47] However, as Fox argues, the editors of the older proverbial collections purposefully chose to intersperse wisdom sayings with sayings about righteousness so that the reader would conclude that the two concepts refer to the same thing. "The reader of Proverbs naturally assumes that all the qualities and behaviors ascribed to the righteous are wise, and that the deeds of the wise, when moral factors are at play, are all righteous and honest."[48] To put it in conceptual metaphor terms, the superstructure of the book *clusters* the concepts of righteousness and wisdom together in such a way that the ideas associated with wisdom come to be associated with righteousness and vice versa. Righteous people (Prov 15:6, 8, 9) become wise people (15:5, 7, 10). Wise speech (10:17, 19; 20:5) becomes righteous speech (10:19, 20; 20:7). Although the metaphors used to describe each remain largely distinct, righteousness and wisdom slowly blend in the expectations of the reader.

One sees this clearly in Proverbs' use of path metaphors. In Prov 10–29, righteousness and wickedness are frequently described as "paths" (10:9; 11:5; 12:28; 15:19; 17:23; 22:25); wisdom and folly are not.[49] Yet by juxtaposing proverbs that describe wisdom as proper speech with those

---

46. Fox, *Proverbs 10–31*, 937.
47. Heim, *Like Grapes Set in Silver*, 81.
48. Fox, *Proverbs 10–31*, 937; see also 928–30.
49. Proverbs 23:19 could refer to wisdom as a path. Here, the phrase "make your heart go straight [וְאַשֵּׁר] on *the way* [בְּדָרֶךְ]" is poetically parallel to "hearing [the father] and being wise." Yet that wisdom itself is not described as a way here suggests that "the way" mentioned here is probably conceptualized more generically as the way of the sage (see 23:26), rather than as the specific way of wisdom. Alternatively, following the LXX and Syriac, Fox (*Proverbs 10–31*, 736) repoints בדרך as a construct and suggests reading v. 19b as "go straight [וְאַשֵּׁר] in the way [בְּדֶרֶךְ] of your heart." By

that describe righteousness as a path, the editors of the older collections lead the reader to believe that one who speaks properly walks on the path of righteousness. Take, for example, Prov 10:6–9:

> Prov 10:6   Blessings are on the head of the righteous, but the *mouth of the wicked* [פי רשעים] conceals violence.
>
> Prov 10:7   The memory of the righteous is a blessing, but the name of the wicked will rot.
>
> Prov 10:8   The wise of heart will take commandments [יקח מצות], but the *foolish of lips* [אויל שפתים] *will be thrust down* [ילבט].
>
> Prov 10:9   The one who *walks in integrity* [הולך בתם] will *walk securely* [ילך בטח], but the one *who twists his ways* [מעקש דרכיו] will be known.

Situated within a series of proverbs about righteousness, Prov 10:8 describes the wise as the one who heeds commandments (WISDOM IS A MANIPULABLE WORD) and the fool as one who is destroyed (DESTRUCTION IS FALLING), presumably because the fool fails to heed the commandments.[50] On the one hand, this verse is connected to those around it because they all detail the reward or punishment that people receive for their behavior. The righteous receive blessing (v. 6), a lasting remembrance (v. 7), and prosperity (v. 9); the wicked are forgotten by later generations (v. 7), and their schemes are discovered and thwarted during their lifetimes (v. 9). Although verse 8a does not explicitly state that the wise are rewarded for their actions, the parallel with verse 8b implies as much. Unlike fools, who are destroyed (v. 8b), the wise are rewarded. By grouping verse 8 with these other verses, the editors draw out this implication, making it explicit. Like the righteous, the wise are rewarded. On the other hand, the juxtaposition of these verses serves to equate the wise person with the righteous person (and fools with the wicked). Having encountered several verses about the righteous and wicked, the reader of this section would assume that the cat-

---

such reading, the implication would be that the student should follow the desires of his heart. In either case, a specific path of wisdom is not envisioned here.

50. For more on these metaphors, see Tilford, "Taste and See," 218–20, 250–51.

egories mentioned in verse 8 are the same as those mentioned in the verses around it. The righteous person is wise; the fool is wicked. While wisdom itself is not described as a path, it becomes a quality possessed by those who walk on the path of righteousness. Clusters like this can be found scattered throughout Prov 10–29 (see, e.g., 11:19-23; 13:14-16; 14:2-3), such that by the end the reader of the older collections assumes that righteousness and wisdom are synonymous.

Because the two concepts are so closely related, wisdom and righteousness eventually blend together. Metaphors associated with one become associated with the other. A few verses in Prov 10–29, for instance, use the language of wisdom metaphors to describe righteousness or the language of righteous metaphors to describe wisdom.

> Prov 10:17   The one who keeps discipline is [on] the *path of life* [ארח לחיים], but the one who forsakes rebuke *goes astray* [מתעה].

> Prov 11:30   The *fruit of righteousness* [פרי־צדיק] is a *tree of life* [עץ חיים]; the one who acquires [לקח] נפשות is wise.[51]

Proverbs 10:17 describes wisdom as a path of life, a description typically reserved for the righteous (see also 21:16). Proverbs 11:30, on the other hand, describes righteousness as a tree of life, a description often reserved for the wise speaker. In each case the metaphor itself remains intact, but the referent changes. Thus in Prov 10:17, the properties of RIGHTEOUSNESS IS A PATH OF LIFE do not change; the path of life remains a positive evaluation of certain behavior that the student will presumably follow without question (<evaluation $_{yes}$>, <voluntary $_{no}$>). Yet it is wisdom, not righteousness, that brings one to this path. Similarly, in

---

51. The second half of the verse is hard to decipher. It could be read that the wise man "captivates souls"; that is, he wins their hearts by his words or behaviors (so Fox, *Proverbs 10–31*, 545). Alternatively, it could mean that the wise man "saves souls"; that is, he keeps them from danger (so Riyqam); the term לקח here could also mean to "teach," in which case the wise man "teaches souls" (so Ramaq). See Fox, *Proverbs 10–31*, 545. It could also mean to "kill," as when one "takes a life" (so Crawford Toy, *A Critical and Exegetical Commentary on the Book of Proverbs*, ICC [Edinburgh: T&T Clark, 1899], 238; William McKane, *Proverbs: A New Approach*, OTL [Philadelphia: Westminster, 1970], 432). In this last reading, חכם is typically emended to חכס ("violence"). In any case, Prov 11:30b is a separate metaphor from 11:30a.

Prov 11:30 the fruit of the speaker remains a life-giving food, yet it is the righteous who produce this fruit, not the wise. Righteousness and wisdom become interchangeable.

In Prov 1–9 the blend of these two concepts is complete. Righteousness is consistently portrayed as a quality of the wise, and wisdom is a quality of the righteous. Wisdom enables the individual to "understand righteousness, justice, and uprightness, every good track" (Prov 2:9) and to avoid the "way of evil, those who speak crookedly, who forsake the paths of straightness, to walk in the ways of darkness, who rejoice at doing evil, who delight in the crookedness of evil, whose paths are crooked and whose tracks are bent" (2:12–15) (see also 1:8–19; 3:1–4, 21–26; 4:10–19; 6:20–24). Similarly, the prologue to the book specifically states that its contents have been recorded so that one might "gain instruction in wise dealing, righteousness, justice, and equity" (1:3). Wisdom is even referred to as a "path of life" (6:23; see RIGHTEOUSNESS IS A PATH OF LIFE). The clustering of moral virtue and wisdom leads the reader to presume that, whichever concept is being discussed at the moment, both are involved.

10.4. SUMMARY

As the preceding analysis demonstrates, the book of Proverbs draws upon a variety of conceptual metaphors from diverse perceptual domains in order to encourage the student to engage wisdom and embody it in his daily affairs. Some of these metaphors are relatively straightforward extensions of a primary metaphor (e.g., BEHAVIOR IS A PATH → GOOD BEHAVIOR IS A PATH; EVIL BEHAVIOR IS A PATH OF DEATH). Others are complex blends derived from different metaphors or rich images (e.g., IDEAS ARE FOOD and KNOWLEDGE IS A WORD → WORDS ARE FOOD) or clusters of distinct metaphors (e.g., SATISFACTION IS FULLNESS and DISSATISFACTION IS EMPTINESS). Yet by whatever mechanisms these complex metaphors formed, the book of Proverbs uses them to present a more dynamic, multimodal depiction of wisdom. Wisdom becomes a concept that is experienced simultaneously by the ear, mouth, eye, hand, foot, and entire body. It is one to be sought and desired above all else.

Conclusions

Metaphors are deeply embedded within the conceptual worldviews of their authors and audiences. They structure how individuals understand their environment, how cultures communicate their core values, and how authors convey specific messages to their audiences. Primary metaphors, for instance, derive from common sensory activities and structure the way that individuals understand their most basic abstract experiences. Thus the abstract experience of cognition is frequently described as an act of seeing, ideas are understood as objects that can be physically manipulated, and emotions are portrayed as flavors that can be tasted. Because they rely upon such common experiences, primary metaphors are fairly universal; that is, they are found cross-culturally and are realized in similar fashions around the world. However, their specific nuances vary depending on the underlying social conceptualizations of the perceptual modalities upon which they draw.

Although biblical authors did not produce cogent theories about human perception, the preceding analysis has suggested that they operated according to the following typology.

Table 11.1. Distribution of Prototypical Properties in the Hebrew Bible

Properties	vision	audition	speech	tactiliy	ingestion	breathing	propr.
PR → OP							
<contact>	yes?	no	no	yes	yes	no	
<closeness>	no	no	no	yes	yes	no	
<internal>	no	yes	no	no	yes	yes/no	
<limits>				???[a]			
<location>	yes	yes		???[a]		no	yes

Properties	vision	audition	speech	tactiliy	ingestion	breathing	propr.
PR → P							
<detection>	yes	yes		yes	yes	yes	yes
<identification>	yes	yes		yes	yes	yes	yes
<voluntary>	yes/no	no	yes	yes/no	yes	no	yes
<directness>	yes	no	no	yes	yes	no	
<effects>	yes	yes	yes	yes	yes	yes	yes[b]
<cor. hyp.>	yes/no	yes/no		yes/no		yes/no	
<subjectivity>	no	no	yes	yes	yes	yes	yes
OP → P							
<effects>	yes	no	yes	yes	yes	yes	yes[b]
<evaluation>	yes	yes		yes	yes	yes	
<briefness>	yes	no	no	yes	yes	no	no

a. Although these properties are applicable to tactility, the values of these properties in ancient Israel remain unclear. See §6.1 above.

b. As noted in §9.1 above, in proprioception, the perceiver and the object perceived are the same, so there is no real need to distinguish between the two. However, in order to facilitate comparison with the other modalities, I have preserved the distinction on this chart here.

Given the common biological foundations of perception and the fact that modern Western societies are contiguous with biblical culture, at least in terms of their religious-philosophical heritage, it is unsurprising that the two systems contain many similar conceptions of the perceptual modalities. There are, however, significant differences. Most notably, biblical authors focused more on the affective nature of perception than individuals in the modern West do. Although modalities still affect the modern individual (more so than perhaps Ibarretxe-Antuñano recognizes), this dimension of perception remains in the background of Western thought. We do not typically think of how smell, hearing, or touch affects us. In biblical thought, however, this dimension was foregrounded. Biblical authors recognized the affective nature of perception and took special precautions to ensure that each modality was properly utilized. Instructions were given as to what one could look at, whom one could listen to, how one should speak, what one could touch, and what one could eat.

CONCLUSIONS

The preceding discussion has also suggested distinctions between the modalities based on how they detect objects or operate in the environment.

Table 11.2. Biblical Modes of Detection

vision	hearing	speech	touch	ingestion	breathing	proprioception
direct	indirect	indirect	direct	direct	indirect	—
simultaneity	sequence	sequence	simultaneity through sequence	composite simultaneity through sequence	delayed simultaneity	dynamic continuity

In biblical wisdom literature, each modality provides a distinct mode of engaging the world. Hearing, for instance, is an indirect, sequential experience, while sight is a direct, instantaneous one. Admittedly, since biblical authors did not reflect on the operation of the modalities, these distinctions are largely based on comparisons with ancient Greek and modern Western theories of perception. They may not, therefore, accurately reflect the full complexity of biblical understandings of perception. However, in as much as the biblical data conforms to these theories (and the data frequently seem to do so), these distinctions can help differentiate between the modalities and how they operated in Israelite and early Jewish societies.

Because they offer distinct modes of engaging the world, the modalities generate distinctive sets of metaphors, each of which provides a unique way of conceptualizing the cognitive experience. Proverbs, Job, and Qoheleth include the following conceptual metaphors for cognition.

Vision
    CONSIDERING IS SEEING
    UNDERSTANDING IS SEEING
    CONCLUDING IS SEEING
    TEACHING IS SHOWING
    SATISFACTION IS A GOOD EYE
    DISSATISFACTION IS A BAD EYE
    ENJOYING IS SEEING
    JUDGING IS SEEING

Hearing/Speech
- THINKING IS SPEAKING
- THINKING IS SPEAKING TO ONE'S SELF
- CONCLUDING IS SPEAKING
- CONCLUDING IS SPEAKING TO ONE'S SELF
- KNOWLEDGE IS A WORD
- PAYING ATTENTION IS HEARING
- UNDERSTANDING IS HEARING
- OBEYING IS HEARING
- MORAL QUALITIES ARE WORDS

Touch
- THINKING IS MANIPULATING OBJECTS
- THINKING IS TRANSFERRING AN OBJECT TO ONE'S SELF
- THINKING IS MANIPULATING ONE'S SELF
- UNDERSTANDING IS GRASPING
- ACQUIRING KNOWLEDGE IS ACQUIRING OBJECTS
- HAVING KNOWLEDGE IS POSSESSING HEART
- TEACHING IS TRANSFERRING AN OBJECT TO ANOTHER
- INSTRUCTION IS A LASHING
- BEING AFRAID IS BEING SEIZED
- PERSISTENCE IS GRASPING
- ANGER/SORROW IS HEAVY
- FEAR IS A SOFT HEART
- STUBBORNNESS IS A HARD HEART/NECK

Ingestion
- DESIRE IS HUNGER/THIRST
- DESIRE IS A HUNGRY/THIRSTY SELF
- SATISFACTION IS FULLNESS
- DISSATISFACTION IS EMPTINESS
- SATISFACTION IS A FULL
- DISSATISFACTION IS AN EMPTY SELF
- ENJOYMENT IS SWEET/DISTRESS IS BITTER
- DISTRESS IS A BITTER SELF
- ENJOYMENT IS TO EAT GOOD
- JUDGING IS TASTING
- GOOD IS SWEET/BAD IS BITTER
- MORAL IDENTITY IS FOOD EATEN

Breathing
- KNOWLEDGE IS BREATH
- IGNORANCE IS BREATH
- PATIENCE IS A LONG BREATH
- IMPATIENCE IS A SHORT BREATH
- HUMILITY IS A LOW BREATH
- PRIDE IS A HIGH BREATH
- ANGER IS A HOT NOSE
- CALM IS A COOL BREATH
- TO BE DISLIKED IS TO STINK

Proprioception
- THINKING IS WALKING
- THINKING IS STANDING
- THINKING IS TURNING
- THINKING IS TURNING ONE'S SELF
- UNDERSTANDING IS ARRIVING AT A LOCATION
- LACK OF UNDERSTANDING IS FAR
- ARROGANCE IS BEING HIGH
- HUMILITY IS BEING LOW
- ARROGANCE IS A BROAD SELF
- GREED IS A BROAD SELF
- ACTING IS WALKING
- ACTING IS TURNING
- BEHAVIOR IS A PATH

While the overarching metaphors that govern these metaphors are relatively universal (e.g., COGNITION IS SEEING, COGNITION IS HEARING, COGNITION IS MOVING), these specific iterations reflect the distinct culturally nuanced properties of the modalities from which they are drawn. CONSIDERING IS SEEING maps vision's ability to directly, simultaneously, and voluntarily detect objects in the environment onto the abstract domain of cognition (<detection $_{yes}$> [simultaneity], <voluntary $_{yes}$>, <directness $_{yes}$>, <subjectivity $_{no}$>). THINKING IS SPEAKING, however, focuses on speech's indirect, subjective, and voluntary nature (<internal $_{no}$>, <voluntary $_{yes}$>, <directness $_{no}$>, <subjective $_{yes}$>). Because these metaphors' properties vary, their distribution across the semantic domains of cognition varies. Vision, for instance, serves as a source domain for various types of cognition: knowledge, emotion, and judgment. Ingestion, on the other hand, is primarily used as a source domain for emotional and judgmental experience, and touch is a source domain for intellectual and emotional experience. Moreover, metaphors within the same perceptual field vary, depending upon which properties are emphasized. ENJOYING IS SEEING focuses on the <effect $_{yes}$> [PR → P] property of vision, while JUDGING IS SEEING focuses on the <evaluation $_{yes}$> property. However, because they draw on the same perceptual experience, metaphors within a given perception field tend to portray similar conceptions of cognition. Visual metaphors routinely portray cognition as a direct, immediate experience, while oral/auditory metaphors describe it as an indirect, sequential experience. Tactile metaphors depict cognition as a direct, manipulable experience; ingestive and breathing metaphors portray cognition as a subjective, personal experience; and kinesthetic metaphors render it as a continual, self-perpetuated process.

The distribution of these metaphors across texts varies, depending upon how an author conceptualizes the origin of human knowledge. As scholars have long recognized, biblical sapiential literature contains three distinct positions on the origin of human knowledge.[1] One position holds that knowledge resides in the elders of the community and can only be transmitted to successive generations verbally. Another position argues that each person is capable of comprehending the world and thus prioritizes human experience as a means to human understanding. A third position, marginal in early sapiential literature, suggests that knowledge is a divine attribute and must be revealed to humanity by God.

Which position an author subscribes to largely influences the metaphors he chooses to utilize in any given passage. If knowledge is thought to be a direct experience, the direct metaphors of sight, touch, ingestion, and kinesthesia prevail; if indirect, the indirect metaphors of hearing and speaking take precedence. In the few cases where divine revelation is reflected upon, the metaphors are mixed, with the divine experiencing knowledge directly and humanity indirectly. Most of the book of Qoheleth, for instance, values human experience as the most effective means of acquiring knowledge. It therefore favors direct metaphors of cognition, especially visual metaphors. Thus the Teacher routinely "sees" the occupa-

---

1. For the enumeration of these three positions, sans the conceptual metaphors, see, for example, Collins, *Jewish Wisdom in the Hellenistic Age*, 2–14; Alex Jassen, *Mediating the Divine: Prophecy and Revelation in the Dead Sea Scrolls and Second Temple Judaism*, STDJ 68 (Leiden: Brill, 2007), 241–45; Shupak, *Where Can Wisdom Be Found?*, 241–42.

tions of humankind (Qoh 3:10; 8:16, CONSIDERING IS SEEING); he "sees" that human toil is from God (3:22, JUDGING IS SEEING) and "sees" good in his work (5:17, ENJOYMENT IS SEEING). He also "seizes" folly (2:3; UNDERSTANDING IS GRASPING), "gives" knowledge to his self (7:2; 9:1, THINKING IS TRANSFERRING AN OBJECT TO ONE'S SELF), and "tastes" how "bitter" a woman can be (7:26, MORAL EVALUATIONS ARE FLAVORS). Each of these metaphors conveys an impression of knowledge as something that can be directly experienced.

Conversely, the book of Job contains a variety of positions. Eliphaz, for instance, frequently presents his knowledge as that which he has obtained through direct experience (Job 4:8; 5:3, 27; 15:17). Similarly, Job responds that he has "seen" all that his friends have told him (13:1) and describes his emotional distress as the "bitterness" of the נפש (3:20; 7:11; 9:18; 10:1; 27:2). In such passages, direct metaphors dominate (e.g., UNDERSTANDING IS SEEING, CONCLUDING IS SEEING, DISTRESS IS BITTER). Many passages in Job, however, portray knowledge as the verbal transference of information. Thus Elihu defers to the words of his elders (32:6–7, 11–12), and Job is implored to "ask" for wisdom from the generations past (8:8–10). Indeed, the greater part of the book is constructed as a verbal dialogue between different individuals, which assumes that verbal persuasion is as effective a means of acquiring knowledge as direct experience, if not more so. Because of this cultural bias, various passages in Job favor indirect metaphors. The dialogues, for instance, contain frequent exhortations for Job or his friends to *pay attention* (שמע, קשב, e.g., 13:6, 17; 33:31, PAYING ATTENTION IS HEARING) and *understand* (שמע, e.g., 5:27, UNDERSTANDING IS HEARING) the words being spoken. In such passages, the individual is not commanded to experience knowledge for himself but to accept the knowledge given by his community.

Finally, various passages in Job present human knowledge as the product of divine revelation (Job 4:12–21; 12:12–13; 15:2–16; 28:1–28; 32:8; 33:13–18; 38:1–30; 42:2–6).[2] In them, God experiences knowledge directly, while humans must rely on God to inform or inspire them. Thus humans

---

2. Jassen, *Mediating the Divine*, 243 n. 7. Job 38:1–30 does not actually say that knowledge is revealed to humanity, but it reflects on the limitations of human knowledge and thus fits with this list. The only other passages in this early sapiential literature that seem to depict knowledge as divine revelation are Prov 16:1–2 and perhaps Prov 2:6 (see the discussion of WISDOM IS A DIVINE WORD in Tilford, "Taste and See," 203–4).

can "turn back" from God's spirit (שוב, 15:13, ACTING IS TURNING); they can "drink" iniquity (שתה, 15:16, MORAL IDENTITY IS FOOD EATEN) and refuse to attend to God's knowledge; however, they cannot "see" the gates of death (ראה, 38:17, UNDERSTANDING IS SEEING) or "walk about" the deep (התהלך, 38:16, UNDERSTANDING IS ARRIVING AT A LOCATION). Even Abaddon and Death can only "hear a rumor" of understanding (באזנ־ינו שמענו שמעה, 28:22, UNDERSTANDING IS HEARING). Only God can directly *judge* the stars (לא־זכו בעיניו, 15:15, JUDGING IS SEEING), "see" (חקר, ראה, נבט) everything under heaven (28:23–24, 27, UNDERSTANDING IS SEEING), and "open the ears of humanity" (יגלה אזן אנשים) to that knowledge (33:16, PAYING ATTENTION IS HEARING).

Like Job, Proverbs also contains various positions on the origin of knowledge. Although on the surface the book seems to privilege audition, many passages in Proverbs value direct experience. The clearest examples of this are Prov 6:6, which directs the student to "see" the ways of the ant, and 24:32, which describes the sage's visual observation and consideration of the fool's vineyard (CONSIDERING IS SEEING). These direct visual experiences, though rare, are not accidental. Passages that focus on the kinesthetic or tactile dimensions of cognition similarly support the need for human experience in knowledge acquisition. Thus, the sage "goes" to the ant (6:6, THINKING IS WALKING), "turns" his heart to understanding (2:2, THINKING IS TURNING ONE'S SELF), and "seizes" abstract concepts (e.g., 1:3, UNDERSTANDING IS GRASPING). Individuals "run" toward evil (1:16, ACTING IS WALKING), ingest moralities (e.g., 4:17; 15:14; 31:27, MORAL IDENTITY IS FOOD EATEN), and "walk" on specific "paths" (e.g., 1:15, BEHAVIOR IS A PATH). According to these passages, knowledge is not simply something that is passively heard; it is actively grasped, ingested, and continually engaged throughout one's life. Of course, in the final rendition of Proverbs, all of this is subsumed under the rubric of transmitted knowledge. The student knows that he is to seek knowledge or to walk toward righteousness only because the sage has instructed him to do so. The book of Proverbs, then, reframes the direct experience of the student as an indirect experience. Knowledge becomes that which is accessible only through the sages, the elders of the community. Thus in the superstructure of Proverbs, indirect metaphors dominate. The student is to "pay attention" (e.g., 7:24, PAYING ATTENTION IS HEARING) and *obey* the words of the teacher (e.g., 5:7–8, OBEYING IS HEARING).

These distribution patterns, of course, are not absolute. For instance, although Qoheleth favors direct metaphors, the text does not hesitate to draw upon indirect metaphors to describe the cognitive experience. Thus the Teacher "speaks" *in* and *to* his לב (e.g., Qoh 1:16; 2:1, THINKING IS SPEAKING TO ONE'S SELF) and *concludes* that all is vanity (e.g., 2:15, CONCLUDING IS SPEAKING TO ONE'S SELF). Such passages imply that indirect experience is not completely without its worth for the author of Qoheleth. This slippage stems from the inherent complexity of biblical thought. Biblical authors did not conceptualize thought *only* in terms of sound or *primarily* in terms of vision. Rather, they used a variety of metaphors to describe the abstract domain of cognition, a diversity that mimics the diversity of human experience itself. Like other humans, biblical authors routinely engaged the world through a variety of modalities: they saw their environment, spoke to others, touched and ingested objects, and moved through space. Except in cases of extreme disability, no one modality was experienced to the exclusion of others. Sight, hearing/speech, touch, ingestion, breathing, and movement were habitually repeated, such that each formed lasting impressions in the neural pathways of the brain that structured subsequent abstract experiences, in this case, the experience of cognition. The diversity of expression found in biblical cognitive metaphors is therefore neither haphazard nor accidental but reflects the biological predisposition of the human condition.

It is this inherent multimodal diversity of cognition that enabled biblical authors to extend, blend, and cluster primary metaphors together and transform routine cognitive activities into the normative and praiseworthy pursuit of wisdom. Wisdom and its associated concept of righteousness become a "path of life" (e.g., Prov 2:19; 4:12; GOOD BEHAVIOR IS A PATH OF LIFE), straight posture (e.g., 2:21; 3:32; A RIGHTEOUS PERSON IS A STRAIGHT PERSON), and sweet honey (e.g., 24:13–14; WISDOM IS HONEY). Like the primary metaphors upon which they build, such complex metaphors provided the means by which the sages could enact the educational program of the scribal community.

Take, for instance, the book of Proverbs. On the surface, the book of Proverbs seems to present a rather stark moral dichotomy: one is righteous or not; one is wise or not. However, the moral worldview of Proverbs is more complicated than it at first appears.[3] As Anne Stewart has argued,

---

3. As Anne Stewart notes in "A Honeyed Cup: Poetry, Pedagogy, and Ethos in the Book of Proverbs" (PhD diss., Emory University, 2014), the "pervasiveness of binary character oppositions in the book [of Proverbs] has led many scholars to presume that its moral psychology is similarly binary and simple." She points, for instance, to the

the book of Proverbs presumes that an individual's character is a malleable entity, that one is not born righteous or wicked but that virtue is a trait that must be "cultivated" continually and that vice is a trait that must be ardently avoided lest it corrupt the individual's moral character.[4] By such a reading, the many descriptions of righteousness and wickedness throughout the book are designed to educate students not merely on how to recognize goodness and wickedness in others but also on how to cultivate positive morality in themselves. Proverbs presumes, in other words, what Stewart calls an "educated moral selfhood," a belief that "one's moral selfhood must be disciplined into being."[5]

The multimodality of wisdom metaphors provides the sages one means by which to accomplish this moral education.[6] Some passages, for instance, encourage the student to pursue wisdom (and thus behave morally) by using complex perceptual metaphors to make it a more accessible concept. Righteousness is an abstract concept. Walking, on the other hand, was a common experience for the scribal student. By portraying righteousness as a path, Prov 2:20 could make the abstract experience of wisdom more familiar and commonplace. Other passages encourage the student to pursue wisdom by making it more physically appealing. There is nothing inherently desirable about obtaining the abstract concept of

---

work of Crenshaw and John Barton, each of whom adopts the rhetoric of Proverbs when they insist that the worldview of the sages inherently identifies individuals as either righteous or wicked. Stewart and Hatton (*Contradiction in the Book of Proverbs*), however, have both argued that the book of Proverbs is more complex than it first appears. Hatton, for instance, has revealed many contradictions in the belief system of Proverbs, including tensions between human and divine agency, the qualities leading to reward and punishment, and the value of speech and silence. Similarly, Stewart's attention to the poetry of Proverbs has revealed a complex moral psychology revolving around the need to discipline the student's moral character. Together, Hatton's and Stewart's observations suggest that the worldview of Proverbs is anything but simple.

4. Stewart, "Honeyed Cup."
5. Ibid.
6. Stewart (ibid.) identifies four main "models" that the sages use to shape the moral character of the student: rebuke, motivation, desire, and imagination. According to her, the use of metaphors facilitates each of these models of formation, as do other poetic devices such as imagery, wordplay, and the use of various voices. Stewart indicates that the way in which the book talks about character and uses poetic form is part of the didactic mode itself. Here I focus only on the functions of the complex metaphors in Proverbs.

wisdom, yet there is something appealing about eating honey. By blending IDEAS ARE FOOD with KNOWLEDGE IS A WORD and the rich image of fruit, Prov 12:14 could transform wisdom into a quality that the student wishes to obtain. The student no longer obeys his teacher out of simple obedience but ardently desires to obtain wisdom and behave morally out of his own self-interest. By presenting wisdom as a perceptual pursuit, the sages could mold the student's entire character and shape it into one that conformed to the expectations of the scribal community. The multimodality of wisdom metaphors transformed cognition from a set of fairly straightforward propositions into a complex, all-encompassing engagement with the human corporeal experience.

Wisdom metaphors, in other words, were not simply literary devices. They were conceptual systems that drew upon embodied experiences to structure the worldview of ancient sapiential communities and enable those communities to communicate their core values to future generations. Realizing this has important implications for the study of Israelite and early Jewish literature. First, a conceptual analysis of biblical metaphor often reveals more about the nuances of specific passages and the connections between them than more traditional literary approaches. Literarily, Prov 4:4 and 24:13–14 have little to do with one another.

> Prov 4:4: [My father] taught me and said to me, "Let your heart *grasp* [יתמך] my words; *keep* [שמר] my commandments and live."

> Prov 24:13–14 My son, eat *honey* [דבש], for it is good [טוב], and *honeycomb* [נפת] is *sweet* [מתוק] upon the palate. Know that wisdom is thus to your נפש; if you find it, then you will have a future, and your hope will not be cut off.

One proverb describes wisdom as a word that can be physically grasped or stored within the heart (Prov 4:4), while the other describes wisdom as a honey that can be eaten (24:13–14). Yet conceptually each passage uses tactile or ingestive experience to describe wisdom and thus envisions wisdom as a direct experience that the student willingly undertakes. Recognizing the shared perceptual foundations of these passages enables scholars to appreciate the nuances of each passage and the differences between their conceptions of wisdom. Although both view wisdom as a direct experience, Prov 4:4 motivates the student to acquire wisdom by promising longevity; Prov 24:13–14 motivates him by providing him immediate healing. Conceptually the two are linked, even if literarily they have little in common.

As Pierre van Hecke notes, however, the primary goal of the conceptual metaphor approach is descriptive rather than hermeneutical: "the theory answers the question how it is possible that we understand metaphors and does not deal directly with the question how an obscure metaphor should be understood."[7] Studying the conceptual framework of a book such as Proverbs may reveal novel readings, but that is not its primary goal. Rather, examining the conceptual framework of metaphor helps scholars understand how Israelites and early Jews *thought*. Israelites and early Jews were not more concrete or simplistic thinkers than people in the modern West. Like us, ancient authors understood the world around them by physically interacting with their environment, and they used such interactions to understand more abstract experiences. They simply had different cultural assumptions about their perceptual experiences and thus used different metaphors to describe God, humanity, and the world. A conceptual analysis of biblical literature can reveal those cultural differences, while respecting the universal cognitive processes by which all people attribute meaning to their experiences.

Finally, a conceptual approach to biblical metaphor can help scholars understand how biblical traditions as a whole developed. When an author describes God as a father or wisdom as a lover, he or she is using metaphor to express a more fundamental belief about human-divine relations. Metaphor, in other words, is a common vehicle by which biblical authors transmit deeper religious convictions. However, metaphors are not static entities. They are intimately connected to embodied experiences and thus continue to develop subconsciously and be manipulated consciously within the conceptual system of the people who use them. Primary metaphors develop into imaginative metaphors; imaginative metaphors develop into even more complex imaginative metaphors. Neither sits passively on a page waiting for an author to come along and borrow them. Rather, they grow and develop organically within the living conceptual systems of the people who use them. The same can be said of biblical traditions more generally. Biblical traditions do not sit idly on a page wait-

---

7. Pierre van Hecke, "Conceptual Blending: A Recent Approach to Metaphor; Illustrated with the Pastoral Metaphor in Hos 4, 16," in *Metaphor in the Hebrew Bible*, ed. Pierre van Hecke (Leuven: Leuven University Press, 2005), 229.

ing for a later author to interpret them. Rather, they continue to develop and operate on a prelinguistic level to structure the conceptual systems of the people who transmit them. A conceptual approach to biblical metaphor can attune scholars to these organic developments and help them appreciate the deeper conceptual commitments such traditions represent.

Taste and see. Hear and grasp. Stand and walk. Whatever the exact modalities drawn upon, such phrases reflect the same basic process. Embodied experiences become the foundation for abstract experiences, and as long as people walk upon paths, hear words spoken, and manipulate objects around them, perceptual experience will continue to structure their understanding of the environment and shape their abstract religious imaginations.

Bibliography

Aaron, David. *Biblical Ambiguities: Metaphor, Semantics, and Divine Imagery.* BRLJ 4. Leiden: Brill, 2001.
Abusch, Tzvi. "Ghost and God: Some Observations on a Babylonian Understanding of Human Nature." Pages 363–83 in *Self, Soul, and Body in Religious Experience.* Edited by Albert Baumgarten, Jan Assman, and Guy Stroumsa. SHR 78. Leiden: Brill, 1998.
Ackerman, Diane. *A Natural History of the Senses.* New York: Vintage Books, 1990.
Ahrens, Kathleen. "Conceptual Metaphors of the 'Self.'" *HPKU Papers in Applied Language Studies* 12 (2008): 47–67.
Albright, William. "The Goddess of Life and Wisdom." *AJSL* 36 (1919–1920): 258–94.
Allen, James P. *The Ancient Egyptian Pyramid Texts.* 2nd ed. WAW 38. Atlanta: SBL Press, 2015.
Alter, Robert. *The Art of Biblical Poetry.* Rev. ed. New York: Basic Books, 2011.
Annas, Julia. *Hellenistic Philosophy of the Mind.* Berkeley: University of California Press, 1992.
Asher-Greve, Julia. "The Essential Body: Mesopotamian Conceptions of the Gendered Body." *Gender and History* 9 (1997): 432–61.
Avrahami, Yael. *The Senses of Scripture: Sensory Perception in the Hebrew Bible.* LHBOTS 545. T&T Clark, 2011.
Bal, Mieke. "Metaphors He Lives By." *Semeia* 61 (1993): 185–207.
Barr, James. *The Semantics of Biblical Language.* London: Oxford University Press, 1961.
Boman, Thorleif. *Hebrew Thought Compared to the Greek.* Translated by Jules Moreau. The Library of History and Doctrine. Philadelphia: Westminster, 1961.
Boström, Lennart. *The God of the Sages.* Stockholm: Almqvist & Wiksell, 1990.

Boyarin, Daniel. *Carnal Israel: Reading Sex in Talmudic Culture*. New Historicism 25. Berkeley: University of California Press, 1993.

Breslin, Paul, and Liquan Huang. "Human Taste: Peripheral Anatomy, Taste Transduction, and Coding." Pages 152–90 in *Taste and Smell: An Update*. Edited by Thomas Hummel and Antje Welge-Lüssen. Advances in Oto-Rhino-Laryngology 63. Basel: Karger, 2006.

Brotzman, Ellis. "Man and the Meaning of נֶפֶשׁ." *BSac* 145 (1988): 400–409.

Brown, William. "Come, O Children … I Will Teach You the Fear of the Lord (Psalm 34:12): Comparing Psalms and Proverbs." Pages 85–103 in *Seeking Out the Wisdom of the Ancients: Essays Offered to Honor Michael V. Fox on the Occasionan of His Sixty-Fifth Birthday*. Edited by Ronald Troxel, Kelvin Friebel, and Dennis Magary. Winona Lake, IN: Eisenbrauns, 2005.

Caballero, Rosario, and Iraide Ibarretxe-Antuñano. "Ways of Perceiving, Moving, and Thinking: Re-vindicating Culture in Conceptual Metaphor Research." In "Conceptual Metaphor Theory: Thirty Years After." Special Issue. *Cognitive Semiotics* 5 (2013): 268–90.

Camp, Claudia. "The Female Sage in Biblical Literature." Pages 185–203 in *The Sage in Israel and the Ancient Near East*. Edited by John G. Gammie and Leo G. Perdue. Winona Lake, IN: Eisenbrauns, 1990.

———. "Metaphor in Feminist Biblical Interpretation: Theoretical Perspectives." *Semeia* 61 (1993): 3–36.

Carasik, Michael. "Theologies of the Mind in Biblical Israel." PhD diss., Brandies University, 1996.

———. *Theologies of the Mind in Biblical Israel*. StBibLit 85. New York: Lang, 2006.

Chidester, David. *Word and Light: Seeing, Hearing, and Religious Discourse*. Urbana: University of Illinois Press, 1992.

Classen, Constance. "Fingerprints: Writing about Touch." Pages 1–9 in *The Book of Touch*. Edited by Constance Classen. Oxford: Berg, 2005.

———. "Foundations for an Anthropology of the Senses." *International Social Science Journal* 153 (1997): 401–12.

Collins, John J. *Jewish Wisdom in the Hellenistic Age*. OTL. Louisville: Westminster John Knox, 1997.

Crenshaw, James. "Wisdom Psalms?" *CurBS* 8 (2000): 9–17.

Dell, Katharine. "Scribes, Sages, and Seers in the First Temple." Pages 125–44 in *Scribes, Sages, and Seers: The Sage in the Eastern Mediterranean World*. Edited by Leo G. Perdue. FRLANT 219. Göttingen: Vandenhoeck & Ruprecht, 2008.

Eilberg-Schwartz, Howard. "The Problem of the Body for the People of the Book." *Journal of the History of Sexuality* 2 (1991): 1–24.

———. *The Savage in Judaism: An Anthropology of Israelite Religion and Ancient Judaism*. Bloomington: Indiana University Press, 1990.

Elliott, John. "The Evil Eye in the First Testament: The Ecology and Culture of a Pervasive Belief." Pages 147–59 in *The Bible and the Politics of Exegesis: Essays in Honor of Norman K. Gottwald on His Sixty-Fifth Birthday*. Edited by David Jobling, Peggy L. Day, and Gerald T. Shepperd. Cleveland: Pilgrim, 1991.

———. *Introduction, Mesopotamia, and Egypt*. Vol. 1 of *Beware the Evil Eye: The Evil Eye in the Bible and the Ancient World*. Eugene, OR: Cascade, 2015.

Evans, Nicholas, and David Wilkins. "In the Mind's Ear: The Semantic Extensions of Perception Verbs in Australian Languages." *Language* 76 (2000): 546–92.

Farnell, Brenda. *Dynamic Embodiment for Social Theory: "I Move Therefore I Am."* New York: Routledge, 2012.

Fauconnier, Gilles, and Mark Turner. *The Way We Think: Conceptual Blending and the Mind's Hidden Complexities*. New York: Basic Books, 2002.

Ford, James Nathan. "Ninety-Nine by the Evil Eye and One from Natural Causes: KTU^2 1.96 in Its Near Eastern Context." *UF* 30 (1998): 201–78.

Fortescue, Michael. "Thoughts about Thought." *Cognitive Linguistics* 12 (2001): 15–45.

Forti, Tova. "Bee's Honey: From Realia to Metaphor in Biblical Wisdom Literature." *VT* 56 (2006): 327–41.

Fox, Michael V. "Frame-Narrative and Composition in the Book of Qohelet." *HUCA* 48 (1977): 83–106.

———. "Ideas of Wisdom in Proverbs 1–9." *JBL* 116 (1997): 613–33.

———. *Proverbs 1–9: A New Translation with Introduction and Commentary*. AB 18A. New York: Doubleday, 2000.

———. *Proverbs 10–31: A New Introduction and Commentary*. AYB 18B. New Haven: Yale University Press, 2009.

———. "Qohelet's Epistemology." *HUCA* 58 (1987): 137–55.

———. "Words for Wisdom." *ZAH* 6 (1993): 149–69.

Frankenberg, Wilhelm, and Carl Siegfried. *Die Sprüche, Prediger und Hoheslied*. HKAT 2/3. Göttingen: Vandenhoeck & Ruprecht, 1898.

Gapenne, Olivier. "Kinesthesia and the Construction of Perceptual Objects." Pages 183–218 in *Enaction: Toward a New Paradigm for Cog-*

nitive Science. Edited by John Robert Stewart, Olivier Gapenne, and Ezequiel A. Di Paolo. Cambridge: MIT Press, 2010.

Gillmayr-Bucher, Susanne. "Body Images in the Psalms." *JSOT* 28 (2004): 301–26.

Goering, Gregory Schmidt. "Sapiential Synesthesia: The Conceptual Blending of Light and Word in Ben Sira's Wisdom Instruction." Pages 121–44 in *Cognitive Linguistic Explorations in Biblical Texts*. Edited by Bonnie Howe and Joel B. Green. Berlin: de Gruyter, 2014.

Golka, Friedemann W. *The Leopard's Spots: Biblical and African Wisdom in Proverbs.* Edinburgh: T&T Clark, 1993.

Grady, Joseph. "Foundations of Meaning: Primary Metaphors and Primary Scenes." PhD diss., University of California, Berkeley, 1997.

———. "Primary Metaphors as Inputs to Conceptual Integration." *Journal of Pragmatics* 37 (2005): 1595–1614.

Grady, Joseph, Todd Oakley, and Seana Coulson. "Blending and Metaphor." Pages 101–24 in *Metaphor in Cognitive Linguistics*. Edited by Raymond W. Gibbs Jr. and Gerard J. Steen. Amsterdam: Benjamins, 1999.

Green, Deborah. *The Aroma of Righteousness: Scent and Seduction in Rabbinic Life and Literature.* University Park: Pennsylvania State University Press, 2011.

———. "Soothing Odors: The Transformation of Scent in Ancient Israelite and Ancient Jewish Literature." PhD diss., University of Chicago, 2003.

Habel, Norman C. *The Book of Job: A Commentary.* OTL. Philadelphia: Westminster, 1985.

Harvey, Susan Ashbrook. *Scenting Salvation: Ancient Christianity and the Olfactory Imagination.* Berkeley: University of California Press, 2006.

Hatton, Peter. "A Cautionary Tale: The Acts-Consequence 'Construct.'" *JSOT* 35 (2011): 375–84.

———. *Contradiction in the Book of Proverbs: The Deep Waters of Counsel.* Aldershot: Ashgate, 2008.

Hatwell, Yvette. "Introduction: Touch and Cognition." Pages 1–14 in *Touching for Knowing: Cognitive Psychology of Haptic Manual Perception.* Edited by Yvette Hatwell. Amsterdam: Benjamins, 2003.

Hecke, Pierre van. "Conceptual Blending: A Recent Approach to Metaphor; Illustrated with the Pastoral Metaphor in Hos 4, 16." Pages 215–31 in *Metaphor in the Hebrew Bible.* Edited by Pierre van Hecke. Leuven: Leuven University Press, 2005.

Heim, Knut. *Like Grapes of Gold Set in Silver: An Interpretation of Proverbial Clusters in Proverbs 10:1–22:16*. BZAW 273. Berlin: de Gruyter, 2001.
Helck, Wolfgang, ed. *Inschriften von Zeitgenossen Amenophis' III*. Vol. 21 of *Urkunden der 18. Dynastie*. Urkunden des ægyptischen Altertums 4. Berlin: Akademie, 1958.
Hermission, Hans-Jürgen. *Studien zur israelitischen Spruchweisheit*. WMANT 28. Neukirchen-Vluyn: Neukirchener Verlag, 1968.
Hoffman, Yair. *A Blemished Perfection: The Book of Job in Context*. JSOTSup 213. Sheffield: Sheffield Academic, 1996.
Howe, Bonnie. *Because You Bear This Name: Conceptual Metaphor and the Moral Meaning of 1 Peter*. BibInt 81. Leiden: Brill, 2006.
Howe, Bonnie, and Joel B. Green, eds. *Cognitive Linguistic Explorations in Biblical Studies*. Berlin: de Grutyer, 2014.
Howes, David. "Sensory Anthropology." Pages 161–91 in *The Varieties of Sensory Experience: A Sourcebook in the Anthropology of the Senses*. Edited by David Howes. Toronto: University of Toronto Press, 1991.
Ibarretxe-Antuñano, Iraide. "Mind as Body." *Miscelánea* 25 (2002): 93–119.
———. "Polysemy and Metaphor in Perception Verbs: A Cross-Linguistic Study." PhD diss., University of Edinburgh, 1999.
———. "Vision Metaphors for the Intellect: Are They Really Cross-Linguistic?" *Atlantis* 30 (2008): 15–33.
Jacobsen, Thorkild. *The Treasures of Darkness: A History of Mesopotamian Religion*. New Haven: Yale University Press, 1976.
Jassen, Alex. *Mediating the Divine: Prophecy and Revelation in the Dead Sea Scrolls and Second Temple Judaism*. STDJ 68. Leiden: Brill, 2007.
Jindo, Job. *Biblical Metaphor Reconsidered: A Cognitive Approach to Poetic Prophecy in Jeremiah 1–24*. HSM 64. Winona Lake, IN: Eisenbrauns, 2010.
Johnson, Mark. *The Body in the Mind*. Chicago: University of Chicago Press, 1987.
———. *The Meaning of the Body: Aesthetics of Human Understanding*. Chicago: University of Chicago Press, 2007.
———. "Mind Incarnate: From Dewey to Damasio." *Daedalus* 135 (2006): 46–54.
Johnston, Philip. *Shades of Sheol: Death and Afterlife in the Old Testament*. Downers Grove, IL: InterVarsity Press, 2002.
Jonas, Hans. "The Nobility of Sight: A Study in the Phenomenology of

the Senses." Pages 135–56 in *The Phenomenon of Life: Toward a Philosophical Biology*. New York: Harper & Row, 1966.

Kimmel, Michael. "Why We Mix Metaphors (And Mix Them Well): Discourse Coherence, Conceptual Metaphor, and Beyond." *Journal of Pragmatics* 42 (2010): 97–115.

King, Philip, and Lawrence Stager. *Life in Biblical Israel*. Louisville: Westminster John Knox, 2001.

Klatzky, Roberta, and Susan Lederman. "The Haptic Identification of Everyday Life Objects." Pages 105–22 in *Touching for Knowing: Cognitive Psychology of Haptic Manual Perception*. Edited by Yvette Hatwell. Amsterdam: Benjamins, 2003.

Koch, Klaus. "Is There a Doctrine of Retribution in the Old Testament?" Pages 57–87 in *Theodicy in the Old Testament*. Edited by James Crenshaw. Philadelphia: Fortress, 1983.

Korsmeyer, Carolyn. *Making Sense of Taste: Food and Philosophy*. Ithaca, NY: Cornell University Press, 1999.

Kuntz, J. Kenneth. "Reclaiming Biblical Wisdom Psalms: A Response to Crenshaw." *CurBR* 1 (2003): 145–54.

Labahn, Antje, ed. *Conceptual Metaphors in Poetic Texts*. PHSC 18. Piscataway, NJ: Gorgias, 2013.

Lakoff, George. "The Contemporary Theory of Metaphor." Pages 202–51 in *Metaphor and Thought*. Edited by Andrew Ortony. Cambridge: Cambridge University Press, 1993.

Lakoff, George, and Mark Johnson. *Metaphors We Live By*. Chicago: University of Chicago Press, 1980.

———. *Philosophy in the Flesh: The Embodied Mind and Its Challenge to Western Thought*. New York: Basic Books, 1999.

Lakoff, George, and Mark Turner. *More Than Cool Reason: A Field Guide to Poetic Metaphor*. Chicago: University of Chicago Press, 1989.

Lambert, Wilfred. "The Babylonian Theodicy." Pages 63–91 in *Babylonian Wisdom Literature*. Winona Lake, IN: Eisenbrauns, 1996.

Landy, Francis. "On Metaphor, Play, and Nonsense." *Semeia* 61 (1993): 219–37.

Lang, Bernhard. *Wisdom and the Book of Proverbs: A Hebrew Goddess Redefined*. New York: Pilgrim, 1986.

Langacker, Ronald. *Foundations of Cognitive Grammar*. 2 vols. Stanford, CA: Stanford University Press, 1987.

Lemaire, André. *Les écoles et la formation de la Bible dans l'ancien Israel*. OBO 39. Göttingen: Vandenhoeck & Ruprecht, 1981.

———. "The Sage in School and Temple." Pages 165–81 in *The Sage in Israel and the Ancient Near East*. Edited by John G. Gammie and Leo G. Perdue. Winona Lake, IN: Eisenbrauns, 1990.

Lorenz, Hendrick. "Plato on the Soul." Pages 243–66 in *The Oxford Handbook of Plato*. Edited by Gail Fine. New York: Oxford University Press, 2008.

Mack, Burton. "Wisdom Myth and Myth-ology." *Int* 24 (1970): 46–60.

Malul, Meir. *Knowledge, Control, and Sex: Studies in Biblical Thought, Culture, and Worldview*. Tel Aviv: Archaeological Center Publications, 2002.

Mandler, Jean. "How to Build a Baby II: Conceptual Primitives." *Psychological Review* 99 (1992): 587–604.

Martin, Dale. *The Corinthian Body*. New Haven: Yale University Press, 1995.

McKane, William. *Proverbs: A New Approach*. OTL. Philadelphia: Westminster, 1970.

McVittie, Fred. "The Role of Conceptual Metaphor within Knowledge Paradigms." PhD diss., Manchester Metropolitan University, 2009.

Miller, Patrick D. *Sin and Judgment in the Prophets*. SBLMS 27. Chico, CA: Scholars Press, 1982.

Mueller, Enio. "The Semantics of Biblical Hebrew: Some Remarks from a Cognitive Perspective." http://tinyurl.com/SBL2634a.

Muffs, Yochanan. *Studies in the Aramaic Legal Papyri from Elephantine*. Leiden: Brill, 1969.

Newsom, Carol. "The Book of Job as Polyphonic Text." *JSOT* 97 (2002): 87–108.

Nyord, Rune. *Breathing Flesh: Conceptions of the Body in the Ancient Egyptian Coffin Texts*. CNI Publications 37. Copenhagen: Museum Tusculanum Press, 2009.

Ong, Walter. "The Shifting Sensorium." Pages 25–30 in *The Varieties of Sensory Experience: A Sourcebook in the Anthropology of the Senses*. Edited by David Howes. Toronto: University of Toronto Press, 1991.

Palache, Juda Lion. *Semantic Notes on the Hebrew Lexicon*. Leiden: Brill, 1959.

Pedersen, Johannes. *Israel: Its Life and Culture*. Translated by A. Møller and A. I. Fausbell. 2 vols. London: Oxford University Press, 1926–1947.

Perdue, Leo G. *Proverbs*. IBC. Louisville: John Knox, 2000.

———. "Scribes, Sages, and Seers in Israel and the Ancient Near East: An Introduction." Pages 1–34 in *Scribes, Sages, and Seers: The Sage in the*

Eastern Mediterranean World. Edited by Leo G. Perdue. FRLANT 219. Göttingen: Vandenhoeck & Ruprecht, 2008.

———. *The Sword and the Stylus: An Introduction to Wisdom in the Age of Empires*. Grand Rapids: Eerdmans, 2008.

Ringgren, Helmer. *Word and Wisdom: Studies in the Hypostatization of Divine Qualities and Functions in the Ancient Near East*. Lund: Ohlssons Boktryckeri, 1947.

Ritchie, Ian. "Fusion of the Faculties: A Study of the Language of the Senses in Hausaland." Pages 192–202 in *The Varieties of Sensory Experience: A Sourcebook in the Anthropology of the Senses*. Edited by David Howes. Toronto: University of Toronto Press, 1991.

Robinson, William E. W. *Metaphor, Morality, and the Spirit in Romans 8:1–17*. ECL 20. Atlanta: SBL Press, 2016.

Ross, Allen P. "Studies in the Life of Jacob, Pt 2: Jacob at the Jabbok, Israel at Peniel." *BSac* 142 (1985): 338–54.

Savran, George W. "Seeing Is Believing: On the Relative Priority of Visual and Verbal Perception of the Divine." *BibInt* 17 (2009): 320–61.

Schmid, Konrad. "The Authors of Job and Their Historical and Social Setting." Pages 145–53 in *Scribes, Sages, and Seers: The Sage in the Eastern Mediterranean World*. Edited by Leo G. Perdue. FRLANT 219. Göttingen: Vandenhoeck & Ruprecht, 2008.

Schroer, Silvia, and Thomas Stabli. *Body Symbolism in the Bible*. Translated by Linda M. Maloney. Collegeville, MN: Liturgical Press, 2001.

Scott, R. B. Y. "Wise and Foolish, Righteous and Wicked." Pages 145–65 in *Studies in the Religion of Ancient Israel*. Edited by G. W. Anderson. VTSup 23. Leiden: Brill, 1972.

Seow, C. L. *Ecclesiastes: A New Translation with Introduction and Commentary*. AB 18C. New York: Doubleday, 1997.

———. "The Social World of Ecclesiastes." Pages 189–217 in *Scribes, Sages, and Seers: The Sage in the Eastern Mediterranean World*. Edited by Leo G. Perdue. FRLANT 219. Göttingen: Vandenhoeck & Ruprecht, 2008.

Sethe, Kurt, ed. *Historisch-Biographische Urkunden*. Vols. 13–16 of *Urkunden der 18. Dynastie*. Urkunden des ægyptischen Altertums 4. Leipzig: Hinrichs, 1909.

Sheets-Johnstone, Maxine *The Primacy of Movement*. Advances in Consciousness Research 14. Amsterdam: Benjamins, 1999.

Shen, Yeshayahu, and Michal Cohen. "How Come Silence Is Sweet but

Sweetness Is Not Silent: A Cognitive Account of Directionality in Poetic Synaesthesia." *Language and Literature* 7 (1998): 123–40.

Shupak, Nili. "The Instruction of Amenemope and Proverbs 22:17–24:22 from the Perspective of Contemporary Research." Pages 203–20 in *Seeking Out the Wisdom of the Ancients: Essays Offered to Michael V. Fox on the Occasion of His Sixty-Fifth Birthday.* Edited by Ronald L. Troxel, Kelvin G. Friebel, and Dennis R. Magary. Winona Lake, IN: Eisenbrauns, 2005.

———. *Where Can Wisdom Be Found? The Sage's Language in the Bible and in Ancient Egyptian Literature.* OBO 130. Göttingen: Vandenhoeck & Ruprecht, 1993.

Sinha, Chris. "The Cost of Renovating the Property: A Reply to Marina Rakova." *Cognitive Linguistics* 13 (2002): 271–76.

Smith, A. D. "Taste, Temperatures, and Pains." Pages 341–54 in *The Senses: Classical and Contemporary Philosophical Perspectives.* Edited by Fiona Macpherson. New York: Oxford University Press, 2011.

Sorabji, Richard. "Aristotle on Demarcating the Five Senses." Pages 64–82 in *The Senses: Classical and Contemporary Philosophical Perspectives.* Edited by Fiona Macpherson. New York: Oxford University Press, 2011.

Stewart, Anne. "A Honeyed Cup: Poetry, Pedagogy, and Ethos in the Book of Proverbs." PhD diss., Emory University, 2014.

Sweetser, Eve. *From Etymology to Pragmatics: Metaphorical and Cultural Aspects of Semantic Structure.* Cambridge: Cambridge University Press, 1990.

Synnott, Anthony. "Puzzling over the Senses: From Plato to Marx." Pages 61–76 in *The Varieties of Sensory Experience: A Sourcebook in the Anthropology of the Senses.* Edited by David Howes. Toronto: University of Toronto Press, 1991.

Szlos, Mary B. "Body Parts as Metaphor and the Value of a Cognitive Approach: A Study of the Female Figures in Proverbs via Metaphor." Pages 185–95 in *Metaphor in the Hebrew Bible.* Edited by Pierre Hecke. BETL 187. Leuven: Leuven University Press, 2005.

———. "Metaphor in Proverbs 31:10–31: A Cognitive Approach." PhD diss., Union Theological Seminary, 2001.

Tappenden, Frederick S. *Resurrection in Paul: Cognition, Metaphor, and Transformation.* ECL 19. Atlanta: SBL Press, 2016.

Thomsen, Marie-Louis. "The Evil Eye in Mesopotamia." *JNES* 51 (1992): 19–32.

Tilford, Nicole L. "The Affective Eye: Re-examining a Biblical Idiom." *BibInt* 23 (2015): 207–21.

———. "Taste and See: Perceptual Metaphors in Israelite and Early Jewish Sapiential Epistemology." PhD diss., Emory University, 2014.

———. "When People Have Gods: Sensory Mimicry and Divine Agency in the Book of Job." *HeBAI* 5 (2016): 42–58.

Toy, Crawford. *A Critical and Exegetical Commentary on the Book of Proverbs*. ICC. Edinburgh: T&T Clark, 1899.

Ulmer, Rivka. *The Evil Eye in the Bible and Rabbinic Literature*. Hoboken, NJ: Ktav, 1994.

Van Leeuwen, Raymond C. "The Sage in Prophetic Literature." Pages 295–306 in *The Sage in Israel and the Ancient Near East*. Edited by John G. Gammie and Leo G. Perdue. Winona Lake, IN: Eisenbrauns, 1990.

Vignemont, Frédérique de. "Bodily Awareness." In *The Standford Encylopedia of Philosophy*. Edited by Edward Zalta. http://tinyurl.com/SBL2634b.

Viljoen, Francois. "A Contextual Reading of Matthew 6:22–23: 'Your Eye Is the Lamp of Your Body.'" *HvTSt* 65.1 (2009): art. 152. doi: 10.4102/hts.v65i1.152.

Wallace, Anthony. "Culture and Cognition." Pages 67–74 in *Language, Culture and Cogntion: Anthropological Perspectives*. Edited by Ronald W. Casson. New York: Macmillan, 1981.

Wazana, Nili. "A Case of the Evil Eye: Qohelet 4:4–8." *JBL* 126 (2007): 685–702.

Weeks, Stuart. *Early Israelite Wisdom*. Oxford Theological Monographs. Oxford: Clarendon, 1994.

Wenham, Gordon. *Genesis 16–50*. WBC 2. Dallas: Word, 1994.

Westermann, Claus. *Forschungsgeschichte zur Weisheitsliteratur 1950–1990*. AzTh 71. Stuggart: Calwer, 1991.

———. *Roots of Wisdom: The Oldest Proverbs of Israel and Other Peoples*. Translated by J. D. Charles. Louisville: Westminster John Knox, 1994.

Whybray, R. Norman. *The Intellectual Tradition in the Old Testament*. BZAW 135. Berlin: de Gruyter, 1974.

———. "Thoughts on the Composition of Proverbs 10–29." Pages 102–14 in *Priests, Prophets, and Scribes: Essays on the Formation and Heritage of Second Temple Judaism in Honour of Joseph Blenkinsopp*. Edited by E. Ulrich, J. W. Wright, R. P. Carroll, and P. R. Davies. JSOTSup 149. Sheffield: JSOT Press, 1992.

Wierzbicka, Anna. *Semantics, Culture, and Cognition: Universal Human Concepts in Culture-Specific Configurations.* New York: Oxford University Press, 1992.

Wieseltier, Leon. "Jewish Bodies, Jewish Minds." *JQR* 95 (2005): 435–42.

Wolde, Ellen van, ed. *Job 28: Cognition in Context.* BibInt 64. Leiden: Brill, 2003.

———. *Reframing Biblical Studies: When Language and Text Meet Culture, Cognition, and Context.* Winona Lake, IN: Eisenbrauns, 2009.

Yu, Ning. "Chinese Metaphors of Thinking." *Cognitive Linguistics* 14 (2003): 141–65.

Ancient Sources Index

Hebrew Bible

Genesis
1:2	140
1:4	65
1:10	65
1:12	65
1:18	65
1:21	65
1:25	65
2:7	138
2:9	86
2:16–17	98, 122
2:17	86
3:1–22	122
3:3	98
3:5	86
3:6	120–21
3:8	70
3:10	70
3:22	86, 92, 118
4:2	25
4:3	70
4:23	97
5:22	162
6:3	139
6:5	65
6:21	97
7:2	98
7:15	139
7:22	138
8:3	155
8:5	155
8:9	97
8:21	139
9:4	10
9:14	57
9:21	120, 122
9:23	154
11:7	86, 121
11:8	121
11:29	97
11:31	97
12:1–3	70
12:5	97
12:7	57
12:9	155
12:17	97
13	153
13:10	55
13:14	55–56, 153
13:17	153
14:7	160
14:14	72
15:2	155
16:3	97
16:4	54
16:13	54
17:1	57
18:1	57, 154
18:2	56–57, 152, 155
18:4	97
18:6	155
18:7	155
18:8	97, 150
18:19	177
18:20–33	71
18:21	72
19:1	152, 154
19:2	153

Genesis (cont.)
19:4 150
19:16 97–98, 155
19:20 154
19:27 150
19:28 55
20:8 70
21:14 97, 154
21:16 58, 154
21:17 72
21:18 98
21:19 57
22:4 154
22:10 97
22:11 72
22:13 94, 97
22:15 72
23:10 70
23:11 55
23:13 70
23:16 70
23:18 53
24:17 155
24:18 121
24:22 97
24:30 72
24:33–54 122
24:44 121
24:46 121
24:52 152
24:54 117, 120
24:58 152
24:64 57
24:65 54, 97
24:67 97
25:26 92
25:34 121, 155
25:35 117
26:1 154
26:30 117, 120
27 95
27:1 52
27:11–12 95
27:20 155
27:21–30 96
27:22 73
27:23 95
27:25 117
27:27 96, 138–39
28:10 154
28:11 92, 152
28:18 92
29:1 150, 154
29:10–11 54
29:13 72
30:27–43 25
30:37 97
31:34 95, 152
31:35 152
31:37 95
31:44 97
32:22–32 154
32:23–33 93–94
32:26 92
32:30 54
32:31 93
32:32 152
32:33 122
33:14 152, 155
34:2 97
34:2–3 54
34:13 72
34:40 146
35:18 10
36:6 154
37:15 154
37:18 154
38:15 57, 160
38:18 94
39:7 54
39:13 94
39:19 72
41:17 150
41:38 145–46
42:20 72
42:23 86
43:30 155
43:34 122
44:3 55
44:16 71

44:18	70	14:30–31	55
45:2	72	15:14	111
45:12	71	15:15	111
47:19	55	15:23	118
48:14	100	15:25	118
48:17	92	16:31	120, 187
50:4	71	17:12	152
50:21	73	19:5	87
		19:12	93, 98
Exodus		19:13	71, 92–93, 98
2:4	154	21:12	97
2:15	150	21:18	97, 152
3:1	25	21:20	97
3:7	86, 97	21:25	97
3:8	153, 187	21:28	122
3:16	57	28:28	100
4:4	94, 98	29:33	122
4:12	71	29:37	98
4:21	111	30:1	138
4:24–25	94	30:25	138
4:25	92	30:29	98
5:21	146	30:35	118
6:3	60	31:3	145–46
7:9	93	32:9	113
7:13	111, 113	32:17	72
7:14	113	32:27	159
7:15	93	33:3	113
7:19	160	33:5	113
7:20	55	34:9	113
7:21	140	34:28	117, 122
7:22	111, 113	35:31	145–46
8:1	160		
8:2	160	Leviticus	
8:11	113	5:2	98
8:14	140	5:2–4	98–99
8:15	111	5:3	98
8:28	113	6:14	138
9:10	93	6:18	98
9:16	159	7:19	98
9:29	154	7:21	91
10:13	140	10:17	122
10:23	55	11	122
12:9	122	11:2–24	122
12:39	155	11:24	93, 150
13:17	154	11:27	93

Leviticus (cont.)		19:11	83
11:30	93	19:13	10
11:40–43	122	20:17	160
12:4	93	20:19	150
15:7	93	21:9	54
15:21–23	93	21:22	160
15:22–23	98	21:32	153
15:26–27	98	22:23	160
17:11	10	22:24	153
17:14	10	22:26	153–54
19:10	189	23:13	54
19:28	10	24:16	85
21–22	25	33:7	160
21:1	10		
21:11	10	Deuteronomy	
21:18	152	1:24	153
22:3–6	98	1:27	184
22:4	10	1:34	73
22:8	122	1:38	111
25:5	189	2:6	117
26:31	138–39	2:27	154
26:37	155	2:28	150
		3:10	155
Numbers		3:21	55
4:16	138	4:3	55
5:2	10	4:6	85
5:18–19	118	4:12	39, 73
5:23–24	118	5:1	70
6:3	119	6:4–7	73
6:6	10	8:3	122
6:11	10	8:8	187, 189
7:89	72	8:10	122
9:6–7	10	8:12	122
9:10	10	9:2	85
11:1	70	9:9	122
11:16	132	9:18	122
13:1–14:10	56	11:15	122
13:20	189	14:3–21	122
13:26–14:23	73	15:9	53
13:30	57	19:12	132
13:32–33	57	21:2–4	132
14:6–9	57	21:11	54
15:39	157	22:15–18	132
16:19	57	23:25	189
18	25	25:3	97

25:11	98	8:13	160
27:21–30	94	9:11	118
28:29	94–95	11:29	145–46
28:34	54	13:4	119
28:40	189	13:7	119
28:49	86	13:14	119
28:54	53	13:25	145
28:56	53	14:6	145–46
29:3	8, 85	14:8	187
31:13	85	14:9	145
32:13	187	15:19	120
34:7	52	16:3	97
		16:21	97
Joshua		16:26–30	97
1:3	150, 153	18:10	153
2:1	153	18:25	71
2:8	150	19:17	153
2:11	73	20:6	97
3:13	150		
3:17	155	Ruth	
4:3	155	2:9	122
5:1	73	2:13	73
5:13	57	2:14	120
6:3–4	154	3:7	122
6:5	71, 154	4:2–11	132
6:7	154	4:4	70
6:14–15	154		
6:20	154	1 Samuel	
6:25	153	1:10–18	78
7:2	153	1:16	73, 78
8:18	160	2:28	138
10:1–2	73	3:2	52, 150
13:16	155	3:4–18	70
23:14	8	3:5	152
		3:6	152
Judges		3:10	71
1:6	97	3:18	71
2:20	87	4:6	72
2:22	177	5:2	154
3:26	155	6:9	92
4:21	98	6:12	154
5:27	152	9:15	70
6:21	93	9:27	159
7:5	120	10:6	146
7:5–6	152	10:10	146

1 Samuel (cont.)		13:5–6	118
12:17	60	13:19	155
13:3–4	72	14:1–24	28
13:4	146	14:17	86
14:24	117	15:5	92
14:27	52, 118, 187	15:12	26
14:28	122	15:16–17	150
14:29	52	15:18	150
14:38	60	16:2	122
14:43	94	16:21	146
15:27	98	17:29	122
16:7	55	18:9	92, 98
16:11	25	18:14	94
16:14	146	19:27	152
16:23	146	19:35	121
17:40	95	19:36	86, 88
18:9	54	20:14–22	26
18:10	146	20:16–22	28
19:9	146	20:19	154
20:2	70	21:12	153
20:12	70	22:16	140
20:13	70	22:22	177
21:13	132	23:12	154
21:14–16	57	24:13	60
22:15	71		
23:22	60	1 Kings	
23:23	60	1:41–45	72
24:12	60	1:50	94
25:17	60	2:28	94
25:18	189	3:9	83, 86, 88
25:36	71	4:20	122
27:12	146	4:25	189
28:20	122	4:29	163
28:22	122	6:2	153
30:12	122, 189	6:7	72
		8:36	177
2 Samuel		8:66	130
1:11	98	10:7	57
2:21	154	12:8	27
5:24	72	12:10	27
6:6–7	99	14:6	72
9:13	152	14:12	150
10:6	146	16:9	122
11:2–4	54	17:6	120
11:13	122	17:21–22	10

18:17–40	73	1 Chronicles	
18:42	153	11:14	154
19:5	93	14:15	72
19:6	118	24:6	26
19:7	93		
19:7–8	122	2 Chronicles	
20:7	60	2:55	26
20:16	122	6:27	177
20:22	60	6:40	70
20:37	97	17:7–9	27
22:23	138	20:17	159
22:35	97	24:11	25
22:37	153	28:15	152, 155
		34:10–11	25
2 Kings			
1:13	152	Ezra	
2:9–15	54	3:12–13	72
3:1–27	25	3:13	72
4:34–35	154	4:8	26
4:35	57		
4:40	121	Nehemiah	
5:7	60	2:2	8
6:1	153	2:12	152
6:1–2	27	5:2	122
6:17	57	8:2	86
6:20	57	8:15	189
10:1	27	9:20	118
10:5–6	27	12:37	154
12:1–13:13	25		
12:10	25	Esther	
13:21	151	1:10	130
15:5	97	5:2	94
17:13	177		
18:17–36	72	Job	
18:18–19:7	25	1:1	165–66, 169
18:26	26	1:1–23	30
18:28	72	1:5	75–76, 78–79
19:16	70	1:6	166
22:3–11	25–26	1:7	153
22:3–20	26	1:8	83, 104–5
22:5–6	25	1:11	97
24:14	25	1:14–19	72
24:16	25	1:22	114
25:6	88	2:2	153
25:19	26	2:3	104, 111, 166

Job (cont.)

Reference	Pages
2:5	97
2:9	111
2:12	55, 57
3:1–31:40	30
3:18–19	87
3:20	129, 131, 205
4:4	152
4:8	63, 114, 205
4:9	145
4:12	70
4:12–21	205
4:16	57
5:3	205
5:5	125, 127–28
5:9	63
5:13	99
5:14	99
5:27	63, 85, 205
6:2–3	112
6:6	118
6:7	91, 127
6:10	97
6:19	63
6:25	169
6:30	120, 131
7:4	75–76, 78, 129, 151
7:7	52, 63–64, 139
7:8	52
7:9	54
7:11	78, 87, 130, 143, 205
7:13	76, 78
7:17	104
8:2	141–42
8:6	169
8:8	63
8:8–10	205
9:5	145
9:10	63
9:11	57
9:13	145
9:16	83
9:18	129, 205
9:25	64
9:27	76, 78
9:33	114
10:1	130, 205
10:4	52
10:18	52
11:4	65
11:7	63
12:10	139
12:11	119–20
12:12–13	205
12:13	48
12:20	132
12:24	106
12:25	99
13:1	52, 63, 205
13:6	83, 205
13:7	72, 88–89
13:15	166–67, 174
13:17	83–84, 205
13:27	174
14:1	129
14:16	54, 174
14:22	97
15:1	73
15:2	141–42
15:2–16	205
15:12	106
15:13	206
15:15	64–65, 206
15:16	133, 206
15:17	63, 205
15:23	73
16:3	141–42
16:6	73, 87
16:9	145
17:4	100
17:5	113
17:7	52
18:4	144
18:9	92
18:20	111
19:11	145
19:15	65
19:17	140
19:21	97
19:25–26	57

19:27	52	28:22	86, 206
19:29	144	28:23–24	206
20:9	52	28:28	165
20:18–19	125	29:8	152
20:20	125, 127	29:11	52
20:22	127	29:18	76
20:23	145	29:21	48
20:28	145	30:20	151
21:2	83	31:4	174
21:4	143	31:4–5	167
21:6	111	31:5	164–65
21:17	145	31:6	114
21:20	52	31:21	63
21:23–25	129, 131	31:24	76
22:12	55	31:37	174
22:14	55	32–37	31
22:29	76, 79, 163	32:1	65
23:2	76	32:1–37:24	30
23:5	86	32:2	144
23:8	154	32:3	144
23:8–9	57	32:5	63, 144
23:10	167	32:6	81
23:13	127–28	32:6–7	205
23:16	112	32:7	75–76
23:33	77	32:8	145–46, 205
24:2	77	32:10	80–82
24:11	63	32:11	81–82
24:15	52, 55, 76	32:11–12	205
24:23	174	32:13	76
24:24	163	32:17	81
25:5	65	32:18	142
26:14	71, 85, 166–67	32:20	73, 87
27:2	129, 131, 205	33:11	174
27:4	72, 77, 89	33:13–18	205
27:5	165–66	33:14	57
27:6	111	33:20	125
27:12	63	33:16	84, 206
27:14	127	33:17	165–66
27:19	57	33:31	83, 205
28	31	34:3	119–20
28:1–28	30, 205	34:21	52, 174
28:10	51	34:27	100
28:11	55	34:29	57
28:12	48, 161–62	34:32	63
28:20	48, 162	34:33	81–82

Job (cont.)			
34:35	100	5:2	86
35:5	55	6:2	128
35:15	145	7:6	9
36:10	84, 165	12:4	71
36:12	85	13:4	52
36:13	144	16:9	9
36:15	84	16:10	9
36:18	144	16:11	177
36:21	165–66	17:6	70
36:25	55	18:16	140
36:26	63	18:22	177
36:33	145	19:11	118
37:2	77	22:15	9
37:14	83, 85, 158, 160–61	22:15–16	9
37:21	55	26:12	150, 155
38:1–30	205	30:4	9
38:1–42:17	30	30:13	9
38:2	48	31:8	60
38:4	48	33:6	138, 140
38:11	76	34:1	132
38:15–17	55	34:9	39, 123
38:16	161, 206	38:9	8
38:17	206	38:11	52
38:22	161–62	42:3	124
38:39	125	45:6	95
39:25	139	48:7	111
39:29	52	49:16	9
40:11–12	54	52:4	95
41:5	161–62	55:22	95
41:10	52	57:5	95
41:12	52	57:9	9
41:13	10	63:2	124, 127–28
41:22	95	66:6	150
42:1–6	39	69:2	10
42:2–6	205	69:4	120
42:3	48	69:21	119
42:5	52, 57, 70	69:22	121
42:7	145	69:24	52
42:7–17	30	74:9	60
		78:3	85
		78:30	118
Psalms		81:6	86
1:6	177	89:49	9
3:6	152	101:5	163
4:9	152	105:18	10

106:25	184	3:5	48, 162
107:4	154	3:7	65, 165–66
107:7	154	3:11	110
108:2	9	3:11–12	109
115:6	138	3:13	48, 106
115:7	92	3:19	48
119:32	163	3:21–26	198
119:53	111	3:22	10
119:66	131	3:24	129
119:103	120	3:31	169, 174
119:131	125	3:32	169, 179, 207
120:4	95	3:33	182
121:1	57	3:35	163
122:2	150, 152	4:1	49, 85–86
135:17	138	4:2	106
137:1	151–52	4:4	49, 209
138:6	60	4:5	49, 106
		4:7	106
Proverbs		4:8	163
1–9	29–30, 194, 198	4:10	49, 83, 87
1:2	81	4:10–19	192, 198
1:2–7	30	4:11	49
1:3	105, 108, 198, 206	4:11–12	49
1:5	100, 102, 106, 108	4:12	207
1:6	165	4:13	49
1:8	83, 87	4:14	175, 178
1:8–19	198	4:17	133–34, 206
1:15	167, 169, 174, 206	4:18	39, 175
1:16	206	4:20	49, 70, 84
1:19	174	4:21	49
1:20–33	24	4:23	49
1:23	81–82, 141	4:25	49, 52, 56
2:2	48, 84, 160–61, 206	4:26–27	49, 169
2:6	48, 108, 177, 205	5:1	48, 70, 82, 84
2:8	178	5:3	95, 113, 133
2:9	174–76, 178, 198	5:4	95, 132–33
2:10	48, 129	5:6	177
2:12	89, 175	5:7	83
2:12–15	198	5:7–8	86–87, 206
2:16	113	5:12	76
2:19	175, 207	5:13	27, 70, 83–84, 87
2:20	175, 178, 182, 191, 208	5:21	166–67, 174
2:21	179, 182, 207	5:27	85
3:1–4	198	6:6	63, 157, 166–67, 206
3:4	64–65	6:8	167

Proverbs (cont.)

Ref	Page	Ref	Page
6:17	163	10:21	107
6:20–24	198	10:25	182
6:23	198	10:26	55
6:24	113	10:29	177, 182
6:30	127	10:30	182
6:32	107	11:3	179
7	62	11:5	195
7:5	113	11:6	179
7:6–27	55–56	11:11	163, 179
7:7	107	11:12	107
7:8	56	11:13	71, 164
7:17	139	11:14	100
7:21	113, 166	11:19	164, 176
7:24	83–84, 87, 206	11:19–23	197
8:1	48	11:22	132
8:6	88–89	11:30	197–98
8:7	77	12:3	182
8:8	169	12:5	100, 102
8:13	174–75, 178	12:8	169
8:20	175, 178	12:11	29, 107, 127–28, 164–65
8:32	83	12:14	188, 209
9:4	107	12:15	48, 65
9:9	106, 108, 182	12:25	88
9:10	48	12:26	175
9:15	154	12:28	175, 195
9:16	107	13:1	86
9:17	129, 134	13:2	182, 188
10–29	29–30, 192–97	13:4	126, 128
10:1	195	13:4–5	128
10:2	176, 195	13:5	146
10:3	124–28	13:14–16	197
10:5	29	13:19	129
10:6	196	13:24	109–10
10:6–9	196	13:25	126–28, 191
10:7	182, 195–96	14:2	169, 195
10:8	195–97	14:2–3	197
10:9	195–96	14:3	145
10:13	107	14:5	195
10:14	195	14:6	195
10:15	176	14:7	195
10:16	176, 195	14:8	195
10:17	177, 195, 197	14:10	129, 131
10:19	71, 74, 195	14:11	195
10:20	195	14:12	175, 177
		14:14	182, 195

14:16	165	18:20–21	193–94
14:27	192	18:21	192–93
14:29	143	18:22	193
14:34	163	19:1	169
15:1	88, 143–44	19:2	128
15:3	182	19:8	107
15:5	195	19:16	176
15:6	195	19:20	48
15:7	190, 195	19:27	81
15:8	195	19:28	134
15:9	164, 176, 178, 195	20:5	195
15:10	195	20:7	195
15:14	133–34, 206	20:9	76
15:15	130	20:12	52
15:17	29	20:13	127
15:19	175, 195	20:14	72
15:23	88	20:17	134
15:24	177	20:18	48
15:28	76, 78–79	20:19	164–65
15:30	64, 87–88	20:22	76
15:31	83, 87	20:27	186
15:32	106	20:30	109, 186
15:33	110	21:2	65, 114
16:1–2	205	21:4	163
16:2	114	21:10	127–28
16:6	165	21:11	105
16:13	89, 169	21:13	84
16:16	106	21:14	144
16:18	142	21:16	197
16:21	106	21:21	164, 176
16:23	106	21:25	127
16:24	184	22:4	176
16:25	177	22:12	52
16:26	127	22:15	110
16:29	169, 174–75, 178	22:17	70, 84, 104
17:1	118	22:24	144
17:4	83, 87	22:25	195
17:16	106	23:1–5	29
17:20	169, 192	23:3	134
17:23	177–78, 195	23:6	134
17:27	144	23:6–8	53
17:28	100	23:12	81
18:8	184, 186–87	23:13	110
18:10–11	176	23:13–14	97
18:20	188, 192–93	23:16	88–89

Proverbs (cont.)

23:19	195	28:22	53
23:26	195	28:23	113
23:29	78	28:24	72, 76
23:33	52, 76, 78–79, 88–89	28:25	163
23:35	78, 97–98	29:1	113
24:2	79, 89	29:5	113
24:12	114	29:8	144
24:13	118	29:10	182
24:13–14	184, 187, 207, 209–10	29:13	52
24:18	52, 65	29:15	109
24:29	76	29:19	109
24:30–34	62	29:22	144
24:32	63, 104, 206	29:23	143
25	193	30	29
25:6–7	29	30:2–3	48
25:7–8	51	30:8	134
25:13	95, 127	30:9	76
25:16	127	30:12	65
25:21	122	30:13	163
25:25	118, 193	30:19	167, 174
25:25–26	194	30:20	76, 174
25:26	193	30:29	167
26:3	109	30:32	100, 163
26:5	65	30:33	144
26:6	134	31	29, 131, 134
26:12	65	31:1–9	29
26:16	65, 132	31:6	129, 131
26:19	72	31:10–31	30
26:22	184, 186–87	31:18	131
26:28	113	31:27	133–34, 206
27:3	95, 112	32:16	100
27:4	144	*Qoheleth*	
27:7	118, 127	1–2	79
27:9	132–33, 138–39	1:1	32–33
27:10	63	1:2–12:8	32
27:17–24:22	29	1:8	52, 63
27:23	104	1:10	61, 161
27:27	134	1:11	161
28:6	169	1:12	33
28:10	175	1:13	104, 157–58
28:11	65	1:14	59–60, 141
28:14	112	1:16	76–79, 83, 106, 207
28:18	192	1:17	104, 141
28:19	164	1:18	106

2:1	76–79, 83, 157–58, 207	5:11	129–30
2:2	76, 80	5:12	59
2:2–3	32	5:16	141
2:3	65, 105, 157–58, 205	5:17	64–65, 205
2:5	32	5:17–18	32, 64
2:7	161	5:17–29	32
2:9	161	5:18	64
2:10	63, 88	6:1	59
2:10–11	32	6:2	125, 127–28
2:11	64, 141, 159	6:2–3	128
2:12	59–60, 159, 161	6:3	76, 79, 125, 127–28
2:13	61, 65	6:5	60
2:15	76–77, 80, 207	6:6	64
2:16	161	6:9	141
2:17	141	7:2	103, 205
2:18	161	7:6	132
2:24	61, 64–65	7:8	143
2:24–26	32	7:10	76
2:25	123	7:14	61
2:26	108, 141	7:15	59
3:7	71	7:17–18	105
3:10	59–60, 205	7:23	76
3:11	108	7:23–24	162
3:12	60	7:25	157–59, 161
3:13	64	7:26	133, 205
3:14	60	7:27	32
3:16	59–60	7:29	169
3:17	76, 80	8:5	88
3:18	62, 76, 78, 80	8:9	60, 104
3:22	32, 64–65, 161, 205	8:10	59
4:1	59–60, 160	8:11	32
4:3	59	8:14	76, 79
4:4	59–61, 141	8:15	59, 104
4:6	141	8:16	205
4:7	160	8:16–17	59–60
4:8	63	8:17	60, 76, 78
4:14	32, 61	9:1	103, 105, 205
4:15	59, 151	9:7	130
4:16	141	9:9	64
5:1	71, 73	9:11	61, 159–61
5:3	71	9:16	76, 79
5:7	59	10:4	144
5:9	125, 127–28	10:5	59, 65
5:9–10	127	10:5–6	59
5:10	47, 55	10:17	122

Qoheleth (cont.)
10:19	122	11:4	138
11:7	52, 59, 64, 129	13:8	111
11:9	63, 157	21:3	111
12:1	76, 79	26:7	177
12:3	154	26:8	177
12:7	139	26:19	9
12:9	33	28:7–13	27
12:9–14	32	29:8	122
12:11	33	29:15	60
12:11–12	33	33:13	86
12:12	33	33:19	86
		35:5	57, 70
		36:3–37:7	26
Song of Songs		36:11	26
1:3	142	40:3	154
1:3–4	139	40:4	155
2:1	142	40:14	177
2:9	159	40:21	85
2:12	57	40:28	85
2:12–13	142	40:30	152
2:13	138	41:3	150
3:6	142	41:22	85
3:8	105	41:26	85
4:1	54	42:7	57
4:3	54	42:14	125
4:6	142	44:12	122
4:10	142	47:1	150
4:10–11	139	48:6–8	86
4:14	142	48:8	70
4:16	139, 142	49:20	153
5:1	142	50:4	86
5:5	142	50:5	70
5:13	142	52:15	86
6:7	54	57:6	95
7:8	142		
7:9	139	Jeremiah	
		1:9	93
Isaiah		1:16	88
1:6	95	2:19	60
5:28	95	2:23	60
6:7	93, 98	4:10	10
6:9	86	4:12	88
6:10	86	5:1	60
8:16	27	5:3	97
10:24	97	5:15	86

6:16	159, 177	35:7	159
6:18	86	37:10	151–52
11:3	87	46:9	154
11:6	87		
12:1	177	Daniel	
12:3	60	10:3	118
15:9	10	10:6	52
18:11	177	11:10	159
21:8	177	12:2	9
26:3	177	12:8	86
31:9	154		
35:15	177	Hosea	3
36	26	4:11	107
36:4–18	26		
36:7	177	Amos	
36:10	26	2:6–8	73
36:12	26	4:3	154
36:10–21	26		
36:20–21	26	Jonah	
39:5	88	2:6	10
42:1–22	73	3:7	117
48:19	159	3:8	177
52:9	88	3:10	177
52:25	26		
		Micah	
Lamentations		3:1	86
3:56	70		
5:13	152	Nahum	
5:17	52	1:12–15	73
		2:6	47
Ezekiel		3:7	54
1:7	153		
1:23	153	Habukkuk	
2:1	152	2:1	152, 159
2:2	150	3:16	88
2:8	119		
3:2–3	119	Haggai	
3:3	120	2:13	10
3:6	86		
3:10	74	Zechariah	
3:24	151	7:14	159
23:14–17	54	9:8	159
26:16	150	11:17	52
27:29	105	12:1	10
30:25	160	12:1–13:13	25

Zechariah (cont.)
    14:12   151

Ancient Near Eastern Texts

Assyrian Medical Texts
    13, 6.6   187
    21, 4 r. 9   187
    69, 10.6   187

Atrahasis
    1.192–226   7

Babylonian Theodicy
    26   82
    265   82
    287–288   62

Biography of Amenhetep
    4.1817.8–17   82

Bologna
    1094 3   109

Book of the Dead   114

Coffin Texts
    2.176p   186
    3.300f–g   54
    3.57d   186
    4.325c   54
    6.175g–j   54
    7.60h   54
    7.97q   54
    7.142b   54

Dialogue between a Man and His God
    35–45   108

Instruction by a Man for His Son
    1.2   82
    1.3   157

Instruction of Amenemope
    1.7   176
    3.1–13   186
    3.9–10   103
    3.12   165
    3.13   186
    7.14   124
    11.10–11   186
    15.9   124
    18.8   124
    22.15–16   186
    23.4   186
    27.13–15   102
    29   53

Instruction of Amenhetep   62–63

Instruction of Amennakht
    1.1   176
    4   157
    8   123
    9   159

Instruction of Ani   156
    5.2–3   186
    8.6–7   124
    9.18–19   183
    10.3–4   82
    10.13–14   183

Instructions of Kagemni
    1.2–3   166
    1.9   124
    2.5   157

Instruction of Khakheperre-seneb   62–63

Instruction of Merikare
    144–145   186

Instruction of Ptahhotep   62–63
    42   102
    50   164
    151   157
    197   183
    227–297   124
    232–248   186

ANCIENT SOURCES INDEX

265–269	186
399–414	186
550–556	82
608–611	102

Instruction of Sehetep-ib-Ra
7, 6	157

Papyrus Anastasi
3.3, 13	109
3.4, 3	80
4.2, 4	106
4.4, 11	123
4.8, 7	109
5.8, 5–6	109
5.8, 7–8	109
5.17, 3	159
5.23, 5–6	156
5.23, 6	80

Papyrus Chester Beatty
4, pl. 18, verso 2, 13	103
4, pl. 19, verso 4, 6	156

Papyrus Insinger
9.6	109
11.1–2	109

Papyrus Lansing
3, 5	159
13b, 9	123

Papyrus Sallier
1.4, 5–6	123

Prophecies of Neferti
7	102

Pyramid Texts
218	188

Story of Sinuhe
B 30	82

Vassal-Treaties of Esarhaddon
568–569	187
594–598	187
643–645	187

Early Jewish Writings

1 Enoch	162

4QInstruction	33

Ben Sira
	33
6:5	48
38:6	48
38:24	28
38:31–34	29
38:34	28
39:1–8	28
51:23	27

Philo, *De Abrahamo*
84	102
150	52
157	52

Philo, *De agricultura*
69	102

Philo, *Legum allegoriae*
3.80	102

Philo, *De sacrificiis Abelis et Caini*
105	102

Testament of Job
18:3	52

Wisdom of Solomon	33

Greco-Roman Literature

Aristotle, *De anima*
422b17–423b15	
429a	23

Aristotle, *Ethica nicomachea*
    1176   23

Aristotle, *Historia animalium*
    9.624a   187

Aristotle, *Metaphysica*
    980a   23

Galen, *De placitis Hippocratis et Platonis*
    287–288   8

Plato, *Phaedo*   4
    79c   5
    80b   5

Plato, *Phaedrus*
    246b–249d   8

Plato, *Respublica*
    434e–444d   8

Plato, *Timaeus*   8
    35a   8
    69c–71a   8

Modern Authors Index

Aaron, David 3, 23, 213
Abusch, Tzvi 7, 213
Ackerman, Diane 138, 213
Ahrens, Kathleen 77, 213
Albright, William 2, 213
Alter, Robert 1, 213
Annas, Julia 8, 213
Asher-Greve, Julia 82, 213
Avrahami, Yael 44, 47, 50–53, 55, 63, 65, 69–70, 83–85, 87, 89, 105, 110, 113, 117, 123, 130, 134, 138, 151, 153, 156, 213
Bal, Mieke 3, 213
Barr, James 101, 213
Boman, Thorleif 51, 69, 101, 213
Boström, Lennart 176, 213
Boyarin, Daniel 6, 214
Breslin, Paul 120, 214
Brotzman, Ellis 9–10, 214
Brown, William 178, 214
Caballero, Rosario 36, 46, 214
Camp, Claudia 2, 28, 214
Carasik, Michael 51, 55, 60, 63, 70, 74–78, 83, 85–87, 91, 214
Chidester, David 52, 55, 70, 91, 214
Classen, Constance 44, 91, 107–8, 214
Cohen, Michal 181, 220
Collins, John 33–34, 204, 214
Coulson, Seana 20, 216
Crenshaw, James 176, 208, 214
Dell, Katharine 28, 30, 214
Eilberg-Schwartz, Howard 6, 215
Elliott, John 53, 215
Evans, Nicholas 37, 215
Farnell, Brenda 151, 215
Fauconnier, Gilles 3, 15, 178, 181–82, 215
Ford, James Nathan 53, 215
Fortescue, Michael 48, 215
Forti, Tova 187, 215
Fox, Michael 27, 29–30, 32, 47–49, 62–63, 88, 124–25, 132, 134, 157, 160, 163, 167–68, 176–77, 184, 186–87, 195, 197, 215
Gapenne, Olivier 150, 153, 155, 215
Gillmayr-Bucher, Susanne 9–10, 216
Golka, Friedemann 27, 29, 216
Grady, Joseph 14, 16–17, 20–21, 23, 36, 50, 58, 144, 179, 216
Green, Deborah 91, 137–38, 216
Green, Joel B. 3, 217
Habel, Norman 31, 75, 107, 112, 114, 125, 161, 167, 216
Harvey, Susan Ashbrook 91, 216
Hatton, Peter 176, 190, 194, 208, 216
Hatwell, Yvette 95–96, 216
Heim, Knut 192, 194–95, 217
Hermission, Hans-Jürgen 29, 217
Hoffman, Yair 31, 217
Howe, Bonnie 3, 217
Howes, David 22, 217
Huang, Liquan 120, 214
Ibarretxe-Antuñano, Iraide 36–47, 56–57, 66, 71, 86, 94, 96, 98, 120, 122, 151, 200, 214, 217
Jacobsen, Thorkild 7, 217
Jassen, Alex 204–5, 217
Jindo, Job 2–3, 217
Johnson, Mark 2–3, 5–7, 10–20, 24, 35–36, 77, 154, 167–68, 217–218

-245-

Johnston, Philip 9, 217
Jonas, Hans 41, 55–56, 70, 92, 95–96, 120, 217
Kimmel, Michael 192, 218
King, Philip 189, 218
Klatzky, Roberta 94–96, 218
Koch, Klaus 176, 218
Korsmeyer, Carolyn 118–21, 218
Kuntz, J. Kenneth 178, 218
Labahn, Antje 3, 218
Lakoff, George 2–3, 5, 7, 11–15, 17–20, 24, 35–36, 45, 77, 103, 154, 167–68, 218
Lambert, Wilfred 62, 82, 218
Landy, Francis 3, 20, 218
Lang, Bernhard 2, 29, 218
Langacker, Ronald 3–4, 15, 218
Lederman, Susan 94–96, 218
Lemaire, André 27, 218
Lorenz, Hendrick 5, 8, 219
Mack, Burton 2, 219
Malul, Meir 38, 53–54, 69, 85–86, 100, 106, 117, 130, 150, 153, 158–59, 219
Mandler, Jean 23, 219
Martin, Dale 8, 219
McKane, William 194, 197, 219
McVittie, Fred 36, 219
Miller, Patrick D. 176, 219
Mueller, Enio 101, 219
Muffs, Yochanan 130, 219
Newsom, Carol 31, 113, 219
Nyord, Rune 54, 186, 219
Oakley, Todd 20, 216
Ong, Walter 22, 219
Palache, Juda Lion 100, 219
Pedersen, Johannes 101, 219
Perdue, Leo G. 26–32, 194, 219
Ringgren, Helmer 2, 160, 220
Ritchie, Ian 44, 220
Robinson, William E. W. 3, 220
Ross, Allen P. 93, 220
Savran, George W. 91, 220
Schmid, Konrad 31, 220
Schmidt Goering, Gregory 55, 70, 216
Schroer, Silvia 8, 53, 220
Scott, R. B. Y. 194, 220
Seow, Choon-Leong 32, 59, 61, 80, 126–27, 157–59, 220
Sheets-Johnstone, Maxine 149–53, 155, 220
Shen, Yeshayahu 181, 220
Shupak, Nili 63, 80, 82, 84, 88, 100, 102–3, 106, 109, 123–25, 157, 159, 161, 164–66, 183–84, 186, 188, 204, 221
Siegfried, C. G. 32, 215
Sinha, Chris 24, 221
Smith, A. D. 91, 221
Sorabji, Richard 92–93, 221
Stabli, Thomas 8, 53, 220
Stager, Lawrence 189, 218
Stewart, Anne 207–8, 221
Sweetser, Eve 16, 35–37, 41, 56, 66, 84, 97, 111, 221
Synnott, Anthony 22, 221
Szlos, Mary B. 2, 133–34, 221
Tappenden, Frederick S. 3, 221
Thomsen, Marie-Louis 53, 221
Tilford, Nicole L. 53, 110, 113, 137, 145, 166, 168–69, 173, 177, 196, 205, 222
Toy, Crawford 197, 222
Turner, Mark 3, 15, 19, 103, 178, 181–82, 215, 218
Ulmer, Rivka 53, 222
Van Hecke, Pierre 210, 216
Van Leeuwen, Raymond C. 178, 222
Van Wolde, Ellen 3, 223
Vignemont, Frédérique de 154, 222
Viljoen, Francois 52–53, 222
Wallace, Anthony 12, 23, 222
Wazana, Nili 53, 222
Weeks, Stuart 194, 222
Wenham, Gordon 93, 222
Westermann, Claus 29, 194, 222
Whybray, Norman 27, 194, 222
Wierzbicka, Anna 22, 223
Wieseltier, Leon 6, 223
Wilkins, David 37, 215
Yu, Ning 36, 223

www.ingramcontent.com/pod-product-compliance
Lightning Source LLC
Chambersburg PA
CBHW021701230426
43668CB00008B/690